PHILOSOPHY
OF
LIBERATION

To the peoples of
Nicaragua,
El Salvador,
and Guatemala

Enrique Dussel

PHILOSOPHY

OF

LIBERATION

Translated from the Spanish by
Aquilina Martinez
and
Christine Morkovsky

ORBIS BOOKS

Maryknoll, New York 10545

First published as *Filosofía de la liberación*, copyright © 1980 by the Universidad
Santo Tomás, Centro de Enseñanza Desescolarizada, Cra. 9a, No. 51-23, Bogotá,
Colombia

English translation copyright © 1985 Orbis Books, Maryknoll, NY 10545
Manufactured in the United States of America

Manuscript Editor: William E. Jerman

Library of Congress Cataloging in Publication Data

Dussel, Enrique D.
  Philosophy of liberation.

  Translation of: Filosofía de la liberación.
  Includes index.
  1. Liberty. I. Title.
JC585.D87313   1985   323.44   85-5103
ISBN 0-88344-405-4 (pbk.)

"There is no peace;
they even tear up the flowers."
—my daughter Susana,
age 9

CONTENTS

Chapter 5
FROM SCIENCE TO
PHILOSOPHY OF LIBERATION

Appendix
PHILOSOPHY AND PRAXIS

PREFACE

What follows is addressed to neophytes in philosophy of liberation. It does not claim to be an exhaustive exposition. It is a discourse that proceeds by elaborating one thesis after another, using its own categories and its own method. It is a provisional theoretical philosophical framework.

Except in the Appendix, this work has few footnotes and no bibliography. Writing in the sorrow of exile (in Mexico), I did not have access to my personal library (in Argentina). My memory had to take its place.

Written from the periphery, for persons and peoples of the periphery, this book nonetheless also addresses readers in the center of the present world system. It is like the alienated child who protests against the overbearing father; the child is becoming an adult. Philosophy, the exclusive patrimony of, first, the Mediterranean world and then of Europe, now finds an origination that allows it to be authentically worldwide for the first time in the course of human history.

It is my hope that the theoretical philosophical framework that I am proposing—an ensemble of theses calculated to foster a certain type of thinking—will spark a worldwide philosophical dialogue. It sets out, of course, from the periphery but, for the most part, it uses the language of the center. It could not do otherwise. The slave, in revolt, uses the master's language; the woman, when she frees herself from the dominative male, uses macho language.

Philosophy of liberation is postmodern, popular (of the people, with the people), profeminine philosophy. It is philosophy expressed by ("pressed out from") the youth of the world, the oppressed of the earth, the condemned of world history.

1

HISTORY

The following introductory chapter serves simply as an example of how one essential phase of a philosophy of liberation can be developed. A philosophy of liberation must always begin by presenting the historico-ideological genesis of what it attempts to think through, giving priority to its spatial, worldly setting.

1.1   GEOPOLITICS AND PHILOSOPHY

1.1.1   *Status Questionis*

1.1.1.1   From Heraclitus to Karl von Clausewitz and Henry Kissinger, "war is the origin of everything," if by "everything" one understands the order or system that world dominators control by their power and armies. We are at war—a cold war for those who wage it, a hot war for those who suffer it, a peaceful coexistence for those who manufacture arms, a bloody existence for those obliged to buy and use them.

Space as a battlefield, as a geography studied to destroy an enemy, as a territory with fixed frontiers, is very different from the abstract idealization of empty space of Newton's physics or the existential space of phenomenology. Abstract spaces are naive, nonconflictual unrealities. The space of a world within the ontological horizon is the space of a world center, of the organic, self-conscious state that brooks no contradictions—because it is an imperialist state. I am not speaking of the space of the claustrophobic or the agoraphobic. I am speaking of political space, which includes all existentially real spaces within the parameters of an economic system in which power is exercised in tandem with military control.

Unnoticed, philosophy was born in this political space. In more creative periods, it was born in peripheral spaces. But little by little it gravitated toward the center in its classic periods, in the great ontologies, until it degenerated into the "bad conscience" of moral—or rather, moralistic—times.

1.1.1.2   I am trying, then, to take space, geopolitical space, seriously. To be born at the North Pole or in Chiapas is not the same thing as to be born in New York City.

DIAGRAM 1

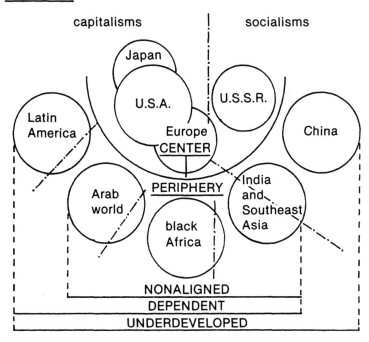

1.1.2   Oppression of the Colonial and Neocolonial Periphery

1.1.2.1   The claim that philosophy of liberation is postmodern is grounded in the following thesis: modern European philosophy, even before the *ego cogito* but certainly from then on, situated all men and all cultures—and with them their women and children—within its own boundaries as manipulable tools, instruments. Ontology understood them as interpretable beings, as known ideas, as mediations or internal possibilities within the horizon of the comprehension of Being.

Spatially central, the *ego cogito* constituted the periphery and asked itself, along with Fernández de Oviedo, "Are the Amerindians human beings?" that is, Are they Europeans, and therefore rational animals? The theoretical response was of little importance. We are still suffering from the practical response. The Amerindians were suited to forced labor; if not irrational, then at least they were brutish, wild, underdeveloped, uncultured—because they did not have the culture of the center.

1.1.2.2 That ontology did not come from nowhere. It arose from a previous experience of domination over other persons, of cultural oppression over other worlds. Before the *ego cogito* there is an *ego conquiro*; "I conquer" is the practical foundation of "I think." The center has imposed itself on the periphery for more than five centuries. But for how much longer? Will the geopolitical preponderance of the center come to an end? Can we glimpse a process of liberation growing from the peoples of the periphery?

1.1.3 Geopolitical Space and the History of Philosophy

1.1.3.1 Philosophy, when it is really philosophy and not sophistry or ideology, does not ponder philosophy. It does not ponder philosophical texts, except as a pedagogical propaedeutic to provide itself with interpretive categories. Philosophy ponders the nonphilosophical; the reality. But because it involves reflection on its own reality, it sets out from what already is, from its own world, its own system, its own space. The philosophy that has emerged from a periphery has always done so in response to a need to situate itself with regard to a center—in total exteriority.

1.1.3.2 Pre-Socratic thought appeared not in Greece but in Turkey and southern Italy, from a political periphery (they were dominated), from an economic periphery (they were colonies), and from a geopolitical periphery (they were threatened by the armies of the center). Medieval thought emerged from the frontiers of the empire; the Greek fathers were peripheral, as were the Latin fathers. Even in the Carolingian renaissance, renewal came from the peripheral Ireland. From peripheral France arose a Descartes, and Kant burst in from distant Königsberg.

Distant thinkers, those who had a perspective of the center from the periphery, those who had to define themselves in the presence of an already established image of the human person and in the presence of uncivilized fellow humans, the newcomers, the ones who hope because they are always outside, these are the ones who have a clear mind for pondering reality. They have nothing to hide. How could they hide domination if they undergo it? How would their philosophy be an ideological ontology if their praxis is one of liberation from the center they are opposing? Philosophical intelligence is never so truthful, clean, and precise as when it starts from oppression and does not have to defend any privileges, because it has none.

1.1.4   The Center, Classic Ontology, and the System

1.1.4.1   Critical thought that arises from the periphery— including the social periphery, the oppressed classes, the *lumpen* —always ends by directing itself toward the center. It is its death as critical philosophy; it is its birth as an ontology and ideology. Thought that takes refuge in the center ends by thinking it to be the only reality. Outside its frontiers is nonbeing, nothing, barbarity, non-sense. Being* is the very foundation of the system, the totality of the sense of a culture, the macho world of the man of the center.

1.1.4.2   For Aristotle, the great philosopher of the classical period, reared to accept slavery and pursue self-centeredness, the Greek was human. The European barbarians were not human, because they were unskilled; nor were Asians human, because they lacked strength and character; slaves were not human either; women were halfway human and children were only potentially human. The human being par excellence is the free man of the *polis* of Hellas. For Thomas Aquinas the feudal lord exercised his

---

*I differentiate between Being (Latin, *esse;* German, *Sein*) and being(s) (Latin, *ens, entia;* German, *das Seiende*).

jus dominativum over the servant of his fiefdom, and the man did the same over the woman (Eve, even though she had sinned, could not transmit original sin, because the mother only supplies the matter, but the man gives Being to the child). For Hegel the state that bears the Spirit is the "dominator of the world," before which all other states are "devoid of rights *(rechtlos)*." For this reason Europe appointed itself "the missionary of civilization" to the world.

1.1.4.3   Ontology, the thinking that expresses Being—the Being of the reigning and central system—is the ideology of ideologies, the foundation of the ideologies of the empires, of the center. Classic philosophy of all ages is the theoretical consummation of the practical oppression of peripheries.

1.1.4.4   Thus philosophy of domination, at the center of the ideological hegemony of the dominant classes, plays an essential role in European history. Nonetheless, one could trace throughout all that history a critical thinking that is in some way a philosophy of liberation insofar as it articulates the ideological formation of dominated classes.

1.1.5   Greek Philosophy

1.1.5.1   Parmenides, from the periphery of Magna Graecia, proclaimed the radical beginning of philosophy as ontology: "Being is; non-Being is not." What is Being if not the foundation of the world, the horizon that encompasses the totality within which we live, the frontier that our armies control? Being coincides with the world; it is like the light *(phos)* that illumines an area but is not itself seen. Being is not seen; what it illuminates is seen—things *(onta)*, tools, instruments *(pragmata)*.

Being is that which is Greek, the light of Greek culture. Being extends as far as the frontiers of Hellenism. Over the horizon is non-Being, uncivilization, Europe and Asia. This sense of ontology is found in the political thought of Plato, Aristotle, Epicurus, and the Stoics.

1.1.5.2   From the poor colonist who like Heraclitus experienced Being as the *logos* that walls the city (defending it from barbarians), to the Alexandrine or Roman cosmopolitan who confused the city with the cosmos, the Greco-Roman city was divinized and identified with nature itself. Thus did ontology end up affirming that Being, the divine, the political, and the eternal are "one and the same thing." Power, domination, and the center are identical, above the colonies with other cultures, above slaves of other skin colors. The center is; the periphery is not. Where Being reigns, there reign and control the armies of Caesar, the emperor. Being is; beings are what are seen and controlled.

1.1.5.3   Classic Greco-Roman philosophies, with some exceptions, in fact articulated the interests of the dominant proslavery classes and justified their domination from the horizon of Being itself. It is easy to understand Aristotle's "The slave is a slave by nature" or the inclination of Stoics and Epicureans to extend deliverance to all the citizens of the empire, so as to ensure a "good conscience" in all its members, on the one hand, and to sanctify the empire, finite manifestation of the gods of cosmopolitanism, on the other.

1.1.6   Mediterranean Thought between Ancient and Modern Times

1.1.6.1   The peripheral humans of this transition were the poor Bedouin of the Arabian desert, not the Indo-Europeans who, crossing the Eurasian steppes with their horses, one day invaded Greece, Rome, and India. The Bedouin and shepherds of the desert did not experience Being as light but as proximity, face-to-face encounter with a brother or sister of the same ethnos or a stranger to whom hospitality was offered. One day the Bedouin comprised the kingdoms of Akkad, Assyria, and Babylonia; they will depart in exile to Egypt. They will be liberated with Moses. They will be the origin of the vision of the world that Maimonides will be able to define centuries later as "the philosophy of creation," a theoretical metaphysics that justifies the practico-political revolution of slaves and the oppressed (3.4.4).

1.1.6.2   From the periphery, the Being that strikes the ear of the attentive listener as freedom will also triumph in its classic epochs: in Constantinople after the fourth century, in Rome after the sixth century, in Baghdad after the ninth century, in Córdoba after the tenth century, in Paris after the thirteenth century. The Semitic world (Christian, Muslim, and Jewish) will also have its ontology, its expressed fundamental ideology. After having begun by stating "Blessed are the poor," and after having understood that Abel never built his city as Augustine prescribed in the *City of God*, they ended by again identifying Being with the ruling system, the earthly city (of the medievals or of the caliphs) with the city of God. Creation—which permitted the understanding of things, profits, systems, and kingdoms as contingent and possible (not necessary) and therefore changeable (3.4.5.2)—came to justify the medieval Mediterranean system: God wanted things *this way*. The ideologizing of the subversive and political metaphysics of creation was the beginning of its end, of its fossilization, of the modern centro-European revolution.

1.1.6.3   In the same way methodical Semitic-Christian thought, first articulated by the nomadic and austere tribes of the desert, ended by justifying the dominating class, the world of medieval feudalism. Critics of the mode of feudal production and the structure of prescribed tribute were not lacking, but they frequently ended up in the hands of the Holy Office, the Inquisition.

1.1.7   Modern European Philosophy

1.1.7.1   The modern age began when the Mediterranean millennium crumbled. For Cretans and Phoenicians as well as Arabs and Venetians, the Mediterranean was the central sea (*medi-terra*), the center of world history. Nevertheless, Germano-Latin Europe enclosed by the Turko-Arabic world (which extended, after the fall of Constantinople, from Andalusia in southern Spain to the gates of Vienna) could not expand into the wider world. The medieval Crusades were the first European expansionist attempts, but the Arabs were sufficiently powerful to return the frontiers to their former positions. Beginning with the fourteenth century, the Portuguese and then the Spanish began to control the North Atlantic (which from the end of the fifteenth century until today will be the center of history). Spain and Portugal opened Europe to the west; Russia will do it to the east. In the sixteenth century Spain discovered the Pacific to the west and Russia did the same to the east. Now the Arab world is enclosed and loses the centrality it had exercised for almost a thousand years. Later Spain and Portugal will give way to the British empire. Now Europe is the center. From the experience of this centrality gained by the sword and by power, Europe begins to consider itself the archetypal foundational "I."

1.1.7.2   From the "I conquer" applied to the Aztec and Inca world and all America, from the "I enslave" applied to Africans sold for the gold and silver acquired at the cost of the death of Amerindians working in the depths of the earth, from the "I vanquish" of the wars of India and China to the shameful "opium war"—from this "I" appears the Cartesian *ego cogito*. This *ego* will be the unique substance, divine in Spinoza. In Hegel the *ich denke* of Kant will recover perfect divinity in the *absolutes Wissen*, absolute knowledge, which is the very act of totality as such: God on earth. If faith, the perfect cult of absolute religion in Hegel's *Philosophy of Religion*, is the certitude that the representation of the understanding is the absolute Idea, such certitude is that which world dominators have: they are the manifestation on earth of the divinity. The empires of the center—England and France as colonial powers, Nazi Germany, and later the United States with its Central Intelligence Agency (CIA)—thus once more possess an ontology that justifies them, a subtle ideology that gives them a "good conscience."

What is Nietzsche if not an apology for the human conqueror and warrior? What are phenomenology and existentialism if not the description of an "I" or a *Dasein* from which opens a world, always one's own? What are all the critical schools, or even those that launch themselves in search of a utopia, but the affirmation of the center as the future possibility of "the same"? What is structuralism but the affirmation of totality—though not leading to a politico-economic resolution in real liberation?

1.1.7.3   "God is dead"—that is to say, Europe is dead because it deified itself. At least the fetish has died for us and with it the United States as its quantitative extension. The death of the fetish is important, for just as "all criticism begins with the critique of (fetishist) religion," so liberation is possible only when one has the courage to be atheistic vis-à-vis an empire of the center, thus incurring the risk of suffering from its power, its economic boycotts, its armies, and its agents who are experts at corruption, violence, and assassination.

1.1.7.4 *Homo homini lupus* is the real—that is, political—
definition of the *ego cogito* and of modern and contemporary
European philosophy. It is the ontological expression of the
ideology of the bourgeois class, triumphant in the British revolution, which will dominate the capitalist world. Philosophy again
becomes the center of the ideological hegemony of the dominating class.

1.2 PHILOSOPHY OF LIBERATION OF THE PERIPHERY

1.2.1 Critique of the Conquest

1.2.1.1 Philosophy of liberation is recent. Nevertheless, its
antecedents are older than modern European philosophy. Barto-
lomé de Las Casas (1484–1566) wrote that "they have used two
ways to extirpate these pitiable nations from the face of the
earth," referring to the two ways Europeans used to dominate the
periphery. "One is by unjust, cruel, bloody, and tyrannical
wars"—that is, the Europeans assassinated the inhabitants of the
periphery. "The other way is that after they have assassinated all
those, such as adult males, who can yearn for freedom—usually
they do not leave any survivors of war except children and
women—they then oppress survivors with the most violent, horrible, and hateful slavery." They assassinated the Amerindians; if
they left any alive, they debased them, oppressing them with
servitude. They spared women, to live in concubinage (sexual
domination) and children, to be educated in European culture
(pedagogical domination). And thus in the name of the "new
god" (gold, silver, money, pounds sterling, or the dollar) there
have been immolated to the god of nascent mercantilism, the god
of economic imperialism, and the contemporary imperialism of
the multinational corporations, millions more human beings of
the periphery than those the Aztecs immolated to their god
Huitzilopochtli—to the horror of civilized, religious-minded Europeans!
1.2.1.2 The philosophy that knows how to ponder this
reality, the de facto world reality, not from the perspective of the
center of political, economic, or military power but from beyond

the frontiers of that world, from the periphery—this philosophy will not be ideological. Its reality is the whole earth; for it the "wretched of the earth" (who are not nonbeing) are also real.

1.2.2   Colonial Mercantile Philosophy

1.2.2.1   I call colonial philosophy that which was exported to Latin America, Africa, and Asia beginning with the sixteenth century (the universities of Mexico and Lima were founded in 1552 with the same academic ranking as those of Alcalá and Salamanca), and especially the spirit of pure imitation or repetition in the periphery of the philosophy prevailing in the imperialist center.

1.2.2.2   Latin American colonial philosophy was cultivated in the Hispanic periphery. Spain, like no other metropolitan power (through the influence of the Renaissance and the Iberian "Golden Age"), founded in its American colonies more than thirty centers of higher studies that granted licentiates and doctorates in philosophy (the majority with a view to ecclesiastical studies). The most famous faculties of philosophy were those of Mexico and Lima. Their professors published their works in Louvain, Leipzig, Venice, and other prestigious publishing centers of Europe, as in the case of the *Logica mexicana* by Antonio Rubio (1548–1615), which was used as a textbook in the University of Alcalá (one of its ten editions was the 1605 edition of Cologne). The Peruvian Juan Espinoza Medrano (1632–1688) published in Cuzco his famous *Cursus philosophicus* in 1688. The faculties in Bogotá, Guatemala City, Quito, Santiago de Chile, Córdoba del Tucumán, and others, can also be named. Nevertheless, all this was, although partly creative, a reflection of the neoscholasticism of Spain.

In the eighteenth century, the Baroque Jesuit educational program, with its *reducciones*—settlements of Amerindians converted to Christianity (the most famous were in Paraguay)—made important advances in philosophy, physics, mathematics, and politics. However, it never went beyond imitation, and it was doubly ideological: repeating in the periphery (and concealing the domination suffered there) an ideological process initiated in Europe.

1.2.2.3   The colonial mercantile stage in the Portuguese and first English colonies did not envision the foundation of philosophical centers in the periphery. Colonial elites were formed in Coimbra and London. This was the beginning of a cultural domination that would be perfected later on.

1.2.3   Colonial Mercantile Emancipation

1.2.3.1   Two centuries ago, in 1776 to be exact, the process of emancipation from colonial mercantilism began. In New England a group of valiant colonists arose against the British homeland and began a war of national emancipation. This process will continue in Luso-Hispanic America from 1810 to 1898—from the emancipation of Argentina and Peru to that of Mexico, and thence to the Caribbean. Puerto Rico, from being a Spanish colony, becomes an *estado libre asociado* (a "free associated state," a contradiction in terms) of the United States, which a half-century before had annexed Texas, New Mexico, and California, lopping them off from Mexico.

From Washington to Hidalgo, Bolívar and San Martín ignited the thought of emancipation, which did not become an explicit philosophy. Bentham sights it at the end of the eighteenth century, and Hegel describes it in his *Philosophy of Right* in 1821: "England understood that emancipating the colonies was more useful than keeping them dependent." The English empire had learned that it cost less to withdraw its bureaucracy and armies from its colonies. The emancipator heroes did not fathom the full impact of their deeds. The liberation of which the philosophy of liberation speaks was still an unsuspected future horizon. From them, nevertheless, present-day philosophers can imbibe a deep yearning for freedom.

1.2.4   Imperialist Recolonization

1.2.4.1   As soon as the first crisis of the industrial revolution could be overcome in England and France, principally around 1850—that is, when sufficient accumulation of capital was in place—the imperialist center began a second colonial age (in the second half of the nineteenth century). Now the Arab world, black Africa, India, Southeast Asia, and China are to undergo the impetuous onslaught of what will quickly become monopolistic economic imperialism.

1.2.4.2   Colonial elites were now systematically trained in the imperialist center. Oxford, Cambridge, and Paris were transformed into theaters of "reeducation," of brainwashing, until well into the twentieth century. The colonial oligarchies were brown, black, or yellow, and they aped the philosophy they had learned abroad. True puppets, they repeated in the periphery what their eminent professors of the great metropolitan universities had propounded. In Cairo, Dakkar, Saigon, and Peking—as in Buenos Aires and Lima—they taught their pupils the *ego cogito* in which they themselves remained constituted as an idea or thought, entities at the disposal of the "will to power," impotent, dominated wills, castrated teachers who castrated their pupils.

1.2.4.3   These colonized philosophers had forgotten their past. The Arab world did not return to its own splendid philosophy dating back to the ninth century. India was ashamed of its sages and so was China, though both nations had produced treasures of thought for more than three millennia. The past did not withstand the attack of modern imperialist metropolitan thinking, at least in its most progressive, modernizing, and developmentalist forms.

1.2.4.4   Modern European philosophers ponder the reality that confronts them; they interpret the periphery from the center. But the colonial philosophers of the periphery gaze at a vision foreign to them, one that is not their own. From the center they see themselves as nonbeing, nothingness; and they teach their pupils, who are something (although illiterate in the alphabets imposed on them), that really they are nothing, that they are like nothings walking through history. When they have finished their studies they, like their colonial teachers, disappear from the map—geopolitically and philosophically, they do not exist. This pathetic ideology given the name of philosophy is the one still taught in the majority of philosophy schools of the periphery by the majority of its professors.

1.2.5 Neocolonial Imperialist Emancipation

1.2.5.1   With the coming of World War II a new world power emerged. The United States took the lead in reapportioning the world at Yalta (1945). The colonies of the British empire and what remained of French and other European colonies were redistributed. The heroes of neocolonial emancipation worked in an ambiguous political sphere. Mahatma Gandhi in India, Abdel Nasser in Egypt, and Patrice Lumumba in the Congo dream of emancipation but are not aware that their nations will pass from the hands of England, France, or Belgium into the hands of the United States.

As in the first stage of colonization (1.2.2.), philosophy has rich material to apply itself to. Freedom is a distant utopia, not a foreseeable prospect. Nevertheless, a substantive, explicit philosophy of national anticolonial emancipation has never been elaborated. There have been only manifestos, pamphlets, and political works (which implicitly include a philosophy but are not philosophy in the strict sense). The thinking reflected in them was the most polished of peripheral thinking in the modern world. Its thinkers situated themselves in an appropriate hermeneutical space, in the correct perspective. But it was not yet philosophy, even though the work of Frantz Fanon was already a beginning.

1.2.5.2   The new imperialism is the fruit of the third industrial revolution. (If the first was mechanistic and the second monopolistic, the third is the international effort of the transnationals, which structure their neocolonies from within.)

The transnationals do not occupy territories with armies or create bureaucracies. They are owners, directly or indirectly, of the key enterprises—production of raw materials, process industries, and services—of the periphery. Furthermore, the new imperialism exercises political control over its neocolonies and their armies. One utterly new feature is that the empire pursues a policy of cultivating desires, needs (4.3.3). This empowers it, through mass media advertising, to dominate peripheral peoples and their own national oligarchies. An ideological imperialism (4.2.7 and 5.7) is also at work here.

1.2.5.3   Progressivist philosophy of the center, when sim-

ply repeated in the periphery, becomes an obscurantist ideology. I
am not thinking only of phenomenology or existentialism, or of
functionalism or critical theory, of science that becomes scientism, but also of a Marxism that does not redefine its principles
from the viewpoint of dependency (5.9.1.2–5). Ontology and
nonradical criticism (such as that which thinks science cannot be
ideology, because of its presuppositions or its real but unac-
knowledged goal) are thus the last ideological underpinnings of
imperialist ideology (3.3.6).

1.2.6   Philosophy of Liberation

1.2.6.1   What is at stake is neocolonial liberation from the
last and most advanced degree of imperialism, North American
imperialism, the imperialism that weighs down part of Asia and
almost all of Africa and Latin America. Only China and Vietnam
in Asia, Cuba and Nicaragua in Latin America, and Mozam-
bique, Angola, and Ethiopia in Africa have a certain modicum of
freedom, certainly much more than other peripheral nations.
Clearly they must know how to use the geopolitical division
established in Yalta, must know how to rely on the politico-
military power that controls the sphere outside the "partitioned"
world, within whose frontiers they have achieved relative freedom. Thus China relies on the United States to safeguard its
freedom from the nearby U.S.S.R., and Cuba relies on Russia to
safeguard its freedom from the nearby United States. Far be it
from me to trivialize the content of their politico-economic models. I want only to point out a geopolitical factor that peripheral
nations can never forget or they will be lost. The cat can make a
mistake; it is only toying with its prey. But the mouse cannot
make a mistake; it will be its death. If the mouse lives, it is because
it is smarter than the cat.
1.2.6.2   Against the classic ontology of the center, from
Hegel to Marcuse—to name the most brilliant from Europe and
North America—a philosophy of liberation is rising from the
periphery, from the oppressed, from the shadow that the light of
Being has not been able to illumine. Our thought sets out from
non-Being, nothingness, otherness, exteriority, the mystery of
no-sense. It is, then, a "barbarian" philosophy.

1.2.6.3   Philosophy of liberation tries to formulate a metaphysics (2.4.9.2)—not an ontology (2.4.9.1)—demanded by revolutionary praxis (3.1.7–8) and technologico-design poiesis (4.3) against the background of peripheral social formations. To do this it is necessary to deprive Being of its alleged eternal and divine foundation; to negate fetishist religion in order to expose ontology as the ideology of ideologies; to unmask functionalisms—whether structuralist, logico-scientific, or mathematical (claiming that reason cannot criticize the whole dialectically, they affirm it the more they analytically criticize or operationalize its parts); and to delineate the sense of liberation praxis. Post-Hegelian critics of the European left have explained it to some extent. Only the praxis of oppressed peoples of the periphery, of the woman violated by masculine ideology, of the subjugated child, can fully reveal it to us (5.9).

2

FROM PHENOMENOLOGY
TO LIBERATION

Phenomenology, as its name implies, concerns itself with what appears and how it appears from the horizon of the world, the system, Being. Epiphany, on the other hand, is the revelation of the oppressed, the poor—never a mere appearance or a mere phenomenon, but always maintaining a metaphysical exteriority. Those who reveal themselves transcend the system and continually question the given. Epiphany is the beginning of real liberation.

2.1   PROXIMITY

2.1.1   *Status Questionis*

2.1.1.1   The Greek or Indo-European and modern European experience exalted the person-to-nature relationship (nature as *physis* or *natura*) because it understood Being as light or cognition (*cogito*). In both cases the world and politics were defined in terms of the seen, the dominated, the controlled.

2.1.1.2   If, on the contrary, we give a privileged place to spatiality (proximity or farness, center or periphery) and to the political (dominator and dominated; 3.1) and to person-to-person relationship, which was the original Semitic experience of reality as freedom, we shall be able to begin a philosophical discourse from another origin.

2.1.1.3   It is a matter, then, of beginning with somebody who is encountered beyond the world of ontology or Being, anterior to the world and its horizon. From proximity—beyond physical closeness, anterior to the truth of Being—we come to the "light of day" when we appear, when our mother gives us birth. To give birth (maternal act) is to appear (filial act).

2.1.2   Approaching the Other

2.1.2.1   I am not speaking here about going toward a table, a chair, or a thing—to approach something, to get close to it so as to take it, buy it, sell it, or use it. Nearness to things I shall denominate *proxemic*.* I am speaking here of approaching a person, of shortening the distance between someone who can accept or reject us, shake our hand or injure us, kiss or kill us. To approach in justice is always a risk because it is to shorten the distance toward a distinct freedom.

2.1.2.2   To draw near is to arise from beyond the origin of the world. It is an "archaic" act (if *arche* is the origin anterior to all other origins). It is anteriority anterior to all other anteriority. If the system or the world is anterior to the things that dwell in it, if responsibility for the world of the other is anterior to responsibility for one's own world, then to approach the immediacy of proximity is the anteriority of all other anteriority.

2.1.2.3   To move closer toward proximity is anterior to signifier and signified. It is to go in search of the origin of the signified-signifier relationship, the very origin of signification. It is to advance oneself; it is to present oneself anterior to presence; it is a signification signifying itself; it is to advance as the origin of semiotics (4.2.6).

2.1.2.4   To shorten the distance is praxis. It is acting toward the other as other; it is an action that is directed toward proximity. Praxis is this and nothing more: an approach to proximity. To direct oneself to things involves physical closeness, the proxemic. But touching or feeling something is very different from caressing or kissing someone. Comprehension of Being, neuter, is very dif-

---

*Abraham Moles (*Sociodynamique de la culture*, Moutan, 1971) has used this term, as I use it here, in the sense of "physical, existential closeness."

ferent from embracing in love the desirous reality of another person.

2.1.2.5   To approach is to advance toward the originating origin, toward the very archeology of metaphysical discourse (which is philosophical but still more historical and political).

2.1.3   Originating Proximity

2.1.3.1   A person is not born in nature. A person is not born from hostile elements, nor from stars or plants. A person is born from the maternal uterus and welcomed by maternal arms. One person is born from another and is given security by her. If we' were viviparous, one could say that the experience of physical closeness, the person-to-nature experience, would be the primal experience. The fish must defend itself alone in the infinite hostile waters that surround it. A person, on the other hand, is born from someone, not from something; the newborn is fed by someone, not by something.

2.1.3.2   The first proximity, the immediacy before all other immediacy, is nursing. Mouth and nipple form a proximity that feeds, warms, and protects. The hands of the child that touch the mother do not yet play or work. The little feet have not walked or gone deeply into farness. The mouth that sucks has not yet launched speeches, insults, or benedictions; it has not bitten someone it hates or kissed a beloved. Nursing is the immediacy anterior to all farness, to all culture, to all work (4.3); it is proximity anterior to economics (4.4); it is already the sexual (3.2), the pedagogical (3.3), and the political (3.1). The proximity of nursing is nevertheless eschatological: it projects itself into the future as does the ancestral past; it calls like an end *and* a beginning. And it is unique no matter how often repeated.

2.1.4   Historical Proximity

2.1.4.1   The mother-child immediacy is lived within a culture-people framework. Birth is always within a symbolic totality, which nurtures the newborn in the signs of its history. A person is born into and grows up in a family, or other social group, and in a society in a historical epoch within which one's world of sense will unfold. Before the world, then, there was already proximity, the face-to-face that welcomed us with a cordial smile or harmed us with the rigidness, harshness, or violence of traditional rules—the ethos of the people.

2.1.4.2   Anterior to the world is the people; anterior to Being is the reality of the other; anterior to all other anteriority is the responsibility for the weak one, the one who as yet is not—a responsibility of those who procreate new persons (parents) or new systems (heroes and liberating teachers).

2.1.4.3   Whether in the face-to-face of the child-mother relationship in nursing, or the sex-to-sex of the man-woman relationship in love, or the shoulder-to-shoulder of colleagues in an assembly where the fate of a country is decided, or the word-hearing of the teacher-pupil relationship in the apprenticeship of living, proximity is the word that best expresses the essence of persons, their first (archeological) and last (eschatological) fulness, an experience whose remembrance mobilizes persons in their inmost recesses and their most ambitious, most magnanimous undertakings.

2.1.5   Proximity, Timeless Synchrony

2.1.5.1   In face-to-face relationship, in the historical immediacy par excellence, reciprocity is risked. A handshake, a gentle caress, a hard struggle, comradely collaboration, friendly dialogue, a passionate kiss—all are the originative reciprocity of proximity. There is no distance yet; the anterior farness has not been shortened; one lives the absolute instant where time is only a distant context.

2.1.5.2   Economic, technological, semiotic history is diachronic. Time passes while one waits for future proximity, inspired by the remembrance of past proximity. But in the immediacy of proximity itself, time becomes synchronic: my time is your time, our time; our time is your time, the time of fellowship in justice and festival. The synchrony of those who live proximity becomes timeless. In the instant of proximity, distinct and separate times converge and dissolve in the joy of being together. The timelessness of the instant of proximity is, nevertheless, the point of reference for history; it is where ages and epochs begin and end.

2.1.5.3   The timelessness of proximity overcomes abstract temporality and opens the door that had been closed to spatiality. The nonspatiality of proximity will also originate the feeling of distance and farness. Proximity, the nonspatial timelessness of the instant, is anterior to all thematization by consciousness and to all economic activity.

2.1.5.4   Nonspatial timelessness is a saying without the said; it is the concreteness of someone who advances without needing the significant universal. Proximity is the root of praxis and the point of departure for all responsibility for the other. Only those who have lived proximity in justice and joy accept responsibility for the poor, desire for them the proximity of equals.

2.1.6   From Archeological to Eschatological Proximity

2.1.6.1   The "happy" proximities—the erotic proximity of the kiss and coitus, the political proximity of collegiality, the pedagogy of nursing—are essentially equivocal. The kiss of lovers can be auto-erotic totalization, a hedonistic utilization of the other. The assembly of colleagues can close itself off as a group of dominating sectarians and assassinators. Nursing itself can be experienced by a mother in compensation for the absence of orgasm with a castrating, macho husband. Proximity becomes equivocal.

2.1.6.2   Metaphysical proximity materializes unequivocally, truly, before the face of the oppressed, the poor, the one who—outside all systems—cries out for justice, arouses a desire for freedom, and appeals to responsibility. Proximity is unmistakable where it is established with the one who needs help because of weakness, misery, and need.

2.1.6.3   The first, or archeological, proximity anticipates the last, or eschatological, proximity, situated beyond all aspiration, like the always unfulfilled desire or the realized infinite. It is a desire for proximity without farness, without economics, without contradictions, without war. It is the utopia that keeps us in suspense.

2.1.6.4   Both the first and the final proximity are always a festival. A festival indicates a metaphysical category of fulfilled proximity, like joy, if joy is understood as the realization of the real, the satisfaction due to confluence of desire with the desired.

2.1.6.5   Proximity is a festival: a political celebration of colleagues, companions, and fellow citizens who express their joy in demonstrations after elections won for the people or for the fall of a dominating enemy, or the banquet of a labor union that has succeeded in a strike. It is the pedagogical festival of rebellious youth and their university reform in Córdoba, Argentina, in 1918, or the celebration of the young in their dances and music where they express their distinctiveness, originality, creativity. It is the sexual celebration in solitude and darkness of the caress, the kiss, the rhythm of orgasm. It is the festival, banquet, liturgy, and *diakonia* of the community in jubilation, the originative and final reference.

2.1.6.6   Proximity is security and warmth, the immediacy of flesh or of wine; it forgets afflictions and absorbs with pleasure what one deserves. Proximity is a feast—of liberation, not of exploitation, injustice, or desecration. It is a feast of those who are equal, free, and just, of those who yearn for an order of proximity without counterrevolutions or relapses.

2.1.6.7   Archeologically timeless and eschatologically utopian, proximity is the most essential reality of a person, the beginning of the philosophical discourse of liberation, and metaphysics in its strict sense—real, reflective, and carefully thought out.

2.2   TOTALITY

2.2.1   *Status Questionis*

2.2.1.1   Proximity, the face-to-face of person with person, always leaves room for farness. The baby is put in the cradle; the lover must leave for work; the teacher and pupil must part to pursue their future lives; citizens leave the political assembly to take up again their work in the political economy; even worship points to service. The detour into farness makes future proximity possible.

2.2.1.2   When they leave proximity, persons do of course approach beings, things, objects. Sense-things,* beings, confront

---

*I use the expression "sense-thing" (*cosa-sentido*) as in Xavier Zubiri's *On Essence* (Washington, D.C.: Catholic University Press, 1981).

us in an almost indefinite multiplicity. Nevertheless, they are moments that are never isolated; they are always within a system, part of a totality that includes, embraces, and unifies them organically. There is not one being (*ens;* pl., *entia*) here and another there, fortuitously. They have a place in an order; they have a function in a whole; they are placed-with, put together (*sys-tema* in Greek, "system"). The level of beings is the proxemic or ontic; the level of Being *(esse)* is that of totality—whether worldly, natural, economic, artistic, and the like—the ontological. Interpretive, evaluative, productive intelligence concerns itself with beings (4.1-4); dialectical intelligence concerns itself with totality (*esse*) (2.2.5); historical, analectical (5.3), or liberating intelligence, or practico-poietic intelligence (5.5), concern themselves with exteriority (2.4).

2.2.2   World, Totality

2.2.2.1   Sense-things, beings, do not surround us chaotically. They form part of a world. When we speak of world, we refer to the daily horizon within which we live—the world of my home, my neighborhood, my country, my working class. World is thus an instrumental totality of sense. It is not merely an external aggregate of beings but the totality of the beings that are meaningful to me. It is not a question of the cosmos as a totality of real things (2.2.3.1) but of a totality of things with sense. The world, we can say, slowly unfolds from the moment of our conception. It is not the first experience, as ontology believes. Proximity is first, anteriority anterior to any world. But proximity immediately gives way to farness. From that moment the world begins to be populated with beings, the first stimuli of cold, heat, hunger—and moving shadows, which surround the one who has just seen the light of day. But very soon the other—mother, father, brother, sister—begins to give meaning to each stimulus and slowly, one after the other, they begin to establish the first circle, the world of a day-old child. It is already a world, and yet how narrow its horizon!

2.2.2.2   Every world is a totality. Totality indicates the horizon of horizons. It is not strange that a Kant or a Wittgenstein could say that the world can be neither an object nor a fact. It is evidently the horizon within which all beings (which can be objects or facts) find their meaning. The world is the fundamental totality; it is the totality of totalities. This notion frightens mathematical analysts, for they are accustomed to formalize beings. Totality corresponds to dialetical reason (2.2.8 and 5.2) and not to ontic understanding or to analytic or synthetic reason. From now on, when I refer to totality without further qualification, I am speaking of the world.

2.2.3   World, Cosmos

2.2.3.1   I shall use the word "cosmos," of Greek origin, to designate the totality of real things, whether or not any human being knows them—the totality of heavenly bodies, life, and reality insofar as they are something constituted "of themselves," by their own essence (3.4.6 and 4.1.2.1).

2.2.3.2   On the other hand, "world," *mundus* in Latin, designates the totality of sense included in one's fundamental horizon (2.2.5). World is the totality of beings (real, possible, or imaginary) that exist because of their relationship to humankind; they are not only real "of themselves." The wood of the table is "of itself," from within itself; it is a substantive reality. The table, on the other hand, is a moment of the world. Without a world there is no table; there is only wood. Without humankind there is no world, only a cosmos. Evidently there was a cosmos before humankind, for the human species emerged only a few million years ago (4.1.5), but only with the appearance of humankind in the cosmos did the world appear as a cosmic reality. The world is thus the system of all systems that have humankind as their foundation. Economic, political, sociological, mathematical, psychological, and other systems are only subsystems of a system of systems: the world.

2.2.3.3   This does not mean that the world is a part of the cosmos but that some real things in the cosmos have in the world the function of sense-things. There are, nevertheless, beings that are not cosmic but only worldly (all imaginary beings, for example). This is why we say *there are* things in the cosmos (in reality), or that beings *are* (*sein*) in the world.

2.2.3.4   Idealism considers the world to be the only reality;

naive realism or equally naive materialism consider the cosmos as the only reality. Against idealism, I claim the cosmos is a partially real anteriority; against realism, I claim the world is a real constitutive (4.1.5.2) of human nature, and thus even imaginary beings have a meaning (4.1.2.1).

2.2.4   World, Time, Space

2.2.4.1   The everyday world, the obvious one that we live in each day, is a totality in time and space. As a temporal totality, it is a retention of the past, a launching site for the fundamental undertakings projected into the future, and the stage on which we live out the present possibilities that depend on that future. As a spatial totality, the world always situates the "I," the person, the subject, as its center; from this center beings are organized spatially from the closest ones with the most meaning to the ones furthest away with the least meaning—peripheral beings.

2.2.4.2   European philosophy has given almost exclusive preponderance to temporality. No wonder it has now given a privileged place to the fundamentality of the future in its emphasis on *Entwurf* (*proyecto**) and the *Prinziphoffnung* ("hope principle"). This philosophy must be understood well, and its snares must be discovered. If persons actually are what they are because of their ontological *proyecto*, because of what they try to achieve as individuals or as groups, nevertheless the *proyecto* is the fundamental possibility of "the same." What you "already" are is what, in short, is attempted. The *proyecto,* no matter how utopian its desired future, is only the actualization of what is in potentiality in the present world. To give prominence to future temporality is to give a privileged place to what we are already.

2.2.4.3   The world, on the other hand, in spatiality or the totality of beings in a certain proximity or farness (from the other in the first proximity), gives a privileged place to the past as the

---

*The Spanish word *proyecto* is retained in this translation because the English word "project" does not do justice to the author's meaning. He uses it in the Heideggerian sense *(Entwurf):* "self-projection into the future." German philosophy emphasizes its influence on our present self; we are what we are because of what we strive (actively hope) to become or achieve.—Ed.

"place" where "I" was born. The "where-I-was-born" is the predetermination of all other determinations. To be born among pygmies in Africa or in a Fifth Avenue neighborhood in New York City is the same thing—as far as being born is concerned. But it is to be born into another world; it is to be born spatially into a world that predetermines—radically, though not absolutely—the orientation of one's future *proyecto*. The one born among the pygmies will strive to become a great hunter of animals; the one born in New York will strive to become a great entrepreneur (a hunter of persons).

2.2.4.4   To say "world" is to enunciate a *proyecto* that is temporally future. It is also to affirm a past within a spatiality that, because it is human, signifies the center of the world. But that world can impinge on other worlds. This is why philosophy of liberation will fix its attention on the past of the world and on spatiality to detect the origin (archeology) of dependence, weakness, suffering, apparent incapacity, and backwardness.

2.2.5   Foundation, Identity, and Difference

2.2.5.1   What functionalists (who observe and explain only parts) or those who claim that only what is mathematically formalized is scientific (the ontic level) generally do not understand is that beings form part of a totality—the everyday world, the point of departure and foundation of every other partial system. It is said that the everyday world is the foundation because it is from everydayness that any partial object of consideration (for example, that of whatever science) can be abstracted or precised. Foundation (*arche, ratio, Grund*) states a position with respect to what is grounded. The first foundation is that about which nothing can be said, because it is the origin of all saying. The foundation of the world is what prominent thinkers have called Being. For example, the Being of economic reality as such—Marx tells us in his *Grundrisse*—is work as such, "laboriousness." The being of macho sexuality, as Freud teaches, is the phallus as such, "phallicity," the *imago patris*. The foundation or Being of a system is what explains the totality. The foundation of the world is the striving that is projected into the future—a striving that remains anchored in the past, or implanted by the conditioning spatiality of the same foundation (just as the ground is under the foundation of a house).

2.2.5.2 The foundation is identical to itself. It is where all that populates the world is nevertheless unified, one. Foundation and identity are one and the same thing. Being is identical with itself. "Being is" and it is *thus* as obviously and primarily as it *is*.

2.2.5.3 Beings, things, possibilities, on the other hand, are multiple, numerous, different. The origin of the difference between beings is the determination of the Being of the System, of the world. The difference between beings shows, as regards the foundation, dependence; as regards other beings, negativity. One is *not* the other; they are different. The totality of beings or different parts is explained or founded in the identity of the Being of the whole. Being, identity, and foundation are the whence of emergent beings, difference, and dependence. A being (*ens*) is dependent because it is founded on the Being (*esse*) of the system.

2.2.6 Metasystem, Whole and Parts

2.2.6.1 The world is a totality of structured parts, be they homogeneous or heterogeneous, which maintain a similarity in some aspect. The parts of the world are organically functional; they are like subsystems or component systems. The totality of the world is an existential metasystem, composed of infinite variables. It is nonformulable, nonformalizable: it is itself the foundation of all formalization. Those who study systems often forget the fundamental system, the world.

2.2.6.2 One does not know the full meaning of any being or part if it is not discovered within the totality of sense, within the world, the everyday system. Every world must be defined as a totality of totalities, a system of systems (and thus a system that includes the economic, the political, the sexual, the pedagogical, the religious, etc.), which explains the partial, singular behavior of each member, subject, or particular "I." The ontological method (5.2) consists exactly in knowing how to refer beings or parts to the world that establishes them, the subsystems to the system that is the originating identity from which there issue, as by internal differentiation, the multiple beings or parts that constitute it. They are moments of historico-social formations.

2.2.6.3 All ontologies know how to explain the parts by the whole. In this sense it can be said that if by the "manner of knowing them" beings first present themselves (the parts before the whole), by their "mode of Being" or by their foundation it is the world that comes first and the sense-things next (the whole before the parts). The process that begins with the parts and directs itself to the whole is ontological; what goes from the whole to the parts of the system is apodictic, demonstrative, scientific (5.1).

2.2.7 Comprehension and Interpretation

2.2.7.1 We comprehend or embrace the world as a totality. This totality is present in every concrete human act. To discover that this sense-thing is a table is possible because the one who discovers it can relate it to other things and interpret it as a table. Without the *a priori* whole, it is impossible to make sense out of anything. Those who have amnesia do not have their past world effectively present as a frame of interpretation.

2.2.7.2 Dealing with the world as a totality I call comprehension. Comprehension is the act by which persons grasp something, not as a whole (prehension or simple apprehension) but rather along with (com-prehend) other objects until they compose a whole world. The act of comprehending or embracing the world as a whole is not a speculative moment (the *Idea* of Hegel) or a conceptual moment (the *conceptus* or *Begriff* as an act of apprehension of an object for Kant, the *sense* for Husserl, or the *eidos* for Aristotle). The comprehending act is preconceptual in that it is the foundation of conceptualization. But it is not an alogical or affective act. To comprehend is to embrace and present to the world a horizon of interpretation.

2.2.7.3 Comprehension is fundamental and at the same time quotidian. It is the light that illumines and thus is not itself seen; it is the end toward which all other things are chosen and thus cannot choose itself; it is the foundation of all words and thus ineffable. It is not, however, that before which one must remain silent, even though one can speak about it only in a roundabout way, indirectly, and formally (not about its content). One can speak directly of a past comprehension only, of one that has turned into a being—the comprehension of the Greeks or the medievals—but not of actual comprehension, our comprehension.

2.2.7.4   Interpretation, on the other hand, constitutes sense (2.3.5). But between comprehension of the world as a totality and the interpretation of sense there is derived comprehension or founding interpretation. To know that the material of the table is wood is not the same thing as interpreting the table as a table. Discovering the reality of a thing as a moment of the world is derived comprehension or founding interpretation, the first moment of the concept but still not full interpretation. This derived comprehension (dependent on the comprehension of the world) or founding interpretation (related to all cosmic things in the world) is what discovers in phenomena or things within the world their reality—their essential anteriority to that which is of itself, their essence preceding their meaning, their cosmic constitution, which appears concomitantly with their meaning. The thing is of itself insofar as it is real; it manifests itself in the world insofar as it is a phenomenon or being. The first grasping of the real appearance of a thing or phenomenon is accomplished by derived comprehension or founding interpretation. The real constitution of a thing is not its worldly manifestation. Its real constitution is not its interpreted meaning sense.

2.2.8   Everyday Dialectic

2.2.8.1   If dialectic is the passage (*dia-*) from one horizon or frontier to another horizon or ambit (*-logos*), the world is continually comprehended as a dialectical process with a mobility that continually exceeds its limits; it flows without cessation. The totality of the world is never fixed; it displaces itself historically or spatially. Inasmuch as we incorporate new beings into our world every day, the horizon of our world displaces itself in order to comprehend and embrace them. From childhood to old age, we go from one moment to another, from one experience to another, from one frontier to another. Unlike animals, whose frontier is fixed by the instincts of the species or by a thin overlay of conditioned reflexes or even by a certain rudimentary intelligence, we— on the contrary—can expand our horizon into the past (not just by memory but also by recorded and studied tradition), into the future (by turning to new pursuits), and in spatiality (dealing with new spaces).

2.2.8.2   The movement of totality as such is dialectical; the movement of beings within the world is ontic—movement that can be formulated, as when it is said that velocity indicates a relationship between traversed space and determinate time—that is, a quality of movements. Movement in physics is intramundane, ontic; the movement of totality, of the world as such, is dialectical, ontological.

2.3   MEDIATION

2.3.1   *Status Questionis*

2.3.1.1   The totality of the world as the horizon within which we live—the system—puts together the beings, the objects, the things that surround us. The beings or the objects are the possibilities of our existence; they are the means to the end that the foundation of the world constitutes. Mediations are what we seize upon in order to reach the final objective of our activity. Proxim-

DIAGRAM 2

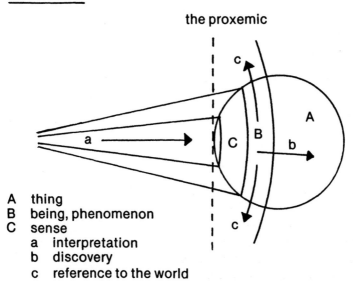

the proxemic

A	thing
B	being, phenomenon
C	sense
a	interpretation
b	discovery
c	reference to the world

ity is face-to-face immediacy with the other; totality is the entirety of beings as such, as a system; mediations make it possible to draw close to immediacy and remain in it; they constitute totality in its functional parts.

2.3.1.2   The far side of proximity in the world is always a nearness to things, mediations, and objects. I call this nearness to things *proxemic*, "physical closeness" (person-to-beings), which is not *proximity* (person-to-person). Beings can appear as mediations or as everyday possibilities for a *proyecto* (2.3) forming part of the world (2.2), or as natural beings, material for work (4.1), signs or signifiers (4.2), artifacts (4.3), or merchandise (4.4). Here we are concerned only with mediations, which are not always real things. (2.3.7.1).

2.3.2   Originative Farness

2.3.2.1   When humankind appeared, when it became present as the species *homo* (4.1.5), in environs inhabited by other primates, it faced a natural, inhospitable, hostile medium. It was surrounded by mere things, beings that had not yet been incorporated into a world as mediations, possibilities, or artifacts. They had some sense, the sense they could have had in a purely animal medium. They provoked automatic stimuli linked with instinctive motives modified by some learned (conditioned) reflexes.

2.3.2.2   Little by little things began to take the shape of beings at hand, mediations that were taking the form of artifacts, tools (*pragmata*). The virgin earth, the *terra mater* (in Latin) or *pacha mama* (in Aymara, the language of the Incas), was one day transformed by agriculture. The culture-thing* is no longer a mere thing. It is now in a world; it is a being; it is in my world. The environs were then populated by sense-things: the rock gave way to the weapon, wood to fire, the cave to the dwelling place.

2.3.2.3   The face-to-face relationship, proximity, the essence of praxis, leads us to the theme of the proxemic or the essence of *poiesis* (4.3), of the work that a person accomplishes in nature whereby a mere thing gains a sense and value; it is transformed in mediation.

---

*I use the expression "culture-thing" in parallel with "sense-thing" (see 2.2.1.2, p. 21, note).

2.3.2.4 For all this to be possible, space, distance, the far side of proximity, is necessary. Farness establishes the possibility of possibilities, of mediations. The farness of proximity (person-to-person) gives way to proxemic nearness (person-to-nature).

2.3.3 Phenomenon

2.3.3.1 Something is approaching from farness; something is advancing toward proxemic closeness, to the vicinity of touching, feeling, hearing, tasting. What appears is a phenomenon. Here it does not matter whether it is pure appearance or whether the appearance is that of what the thing really is. What matters is that it appears and manifests itself. That is, the thing is not only really constituted (the thing as such, in the order of its own constitution (2.3.8.1), but it relates to an observer who uses it as a mediation.

2.3.3.2 That is to say, placed in the world, a person confronts beings that appear. But beings, which turn into objects when they are considered in themselves, are distinguished from the environment only when they are put to some use. A person turns to something or something appears or is a phenomenon only when a person intends to do something with it. Sheer "things there," real, cosmic, which are "of themselves," turn into worldly beings, mediations, insofar as they are useful to someone for something. The "for" of mediation is the essence of possibility, which is only a means that permits someone to attain something proposed or imagined.

2.3.3.3 Taking this into account, we shall have to consider as posterior or secondary the description of a being as an object. I shall call "object" that which stands before (*ob-*), which has been flung out (*-jected*) for the theoretical consideration of the *ego cogito*, as when one asks, What is this? Obviously, before one asks explicitly about something it is already there, in one's world. The spoken theoretical question is secondary. The object is posterior to the phenomenon.

2.3.3.4 The phenomenon, that which appears, is like a cut-out of a being; all the rest of it is left behind as though in its background, its context. The only thing that comes forward and therefore gains our attention or is constituted by us as sense is whatever in some way is an actual mediation in the continuous process of daily life.

2.3.4   Critical Everydayness

2.3.4.1   The everyday way of living surrounded by products is not, as the modern thinking of the *cogito* proposes, a theoretical life (*bios theoretikos*, as the Greeks said) where persons explicitly ask themselves what things are. The first way of confronting products in daily life is to use them within the dynamics of the practical, existential life of every day (*bios praktikos*). Thus the daily world of beings, products, and objects (objects now not in the sense of theoretical consideration but as something used in our workaday world) surrounds us daily from our rising in the morning (leaving the oneiric behind), during all our waking hours, until night (which again seizes us in the logic of the desires of the nonconscious, which is neither practical nor theoretical life).

2.3.4.2   The daily way of facing the world is not the critical way. Here we are concerned with the critical way only as opposed to everydayness.

2.3.4.3   The farness, the distance that leaves proximity behind, is lived within attitudes, interpretations, sense-things, and products we do not notice because we have always been close to them since we "saw the light of day." This not noticing is like an unseen prison. We see the world through the bars of our cells, and we believe they are the bars of cells in which others are imprisoned. Our life, because it is "natural" and obvious, is lived in an acritical naivety with very great consequences. Our way of facing beings is conditioned by this everydayness that is our own being, our second nature, our ethos, our cultural and historical character.

2.3.4.4   This is the first naivety. Later there will be other types of naivety correlative to other types of criticism. Thus everyday persons in Western civilization consider themselves critics of the naivety of the primitive or uncivilized person. Westerners do not view the sun as a god, the way the Aztecs or Egyptians viewed it or the way Eskimos and animistic peoples of Africa or Asia still view it. Nevertheless, Westerners naively take for granted that their culture, political power, and military domination are justified, and that they spread democracy and liberty on earth. This mentality is part of a naive everydayness that manipulates whole populations.

2.3.4.5   Scientists, for their part, believe they are not naive, because they can discover what the person on the street does not know. But scientists of the center, as we shall see later, forget that the very principles of their science contain cultural elements (scientifically indemonstrable) and that all their endeavors serve the nonscientific *proyecto* and historical culture of the system wherein they live. Scientism, the current ideology of the center, is a subtle ideology, which, although less naive than the everydayness of the *hoi polloi*, is more dangerous inasmuch as it fabricates the instruments necessary for the power of the center to be exercised over the periphery. At the proper moment, we shall have to question the naivety (with respect to the system as a totality) of scientists and discover a critique that is more critical (with regard to the everydayness of the general populace) than is the scientific one (5.7).

2.3.5   Interpretation of Sense

2.3.5.1   Things appear in the world as phenomena. A phenomenon is a being with a certain sense. The sense is our interpretation of a phenomenon insofar as it has been integrated into a practical or productive process as a mediation.

2.3.5.2   The world is comprehended (2.2.7.2); a phenomenon or being is interpreted as to its meaning. How is this sense or meaning constituted?

2.3.5.3   Persons discover and constitute sense. They do so insofar as they understand what was concealed. They conceive; there is a concept. Mental conception of a being entails novelty; it is the discovery of what was not known before. The being was there already, before, *a priori*. It is not newly constituted; it is only discovered. Because of this, its meaning has an aspect of having been there before, but concealed. Interpretation, in some way, discovers what was previously concealed: the real (arrow *b* in diagram 2).

2.3.5.4   Nevertheless, it is not pure discovery of something already given. It is at the same time intentional constitution of meaning. Discovery of sense refers to the reality of the being as a thing; the constitution of meaning refers to the worldliness of the being or its reference to the rest of the beings in the world (arrow *c* in diagram 2). I discover water because I am thirsty. That is, I discover it as a mediation because its real constitution is such that it can satisfy what I feel as thirst. I do nevertheless constitute its sense as a being that slakes thirst, as a beverage. Water also has other possible senses; and other beings (e.g., orange juice) have a similar constitution.

2.3.5.5 If, for example, I am thirsty and I discover in looking around (circumspection is a looking in, an inspective vision like that of an inspector) a juicy fruit (an orange), I discover likewise, as in the case of water, its real capacity to satiate my thirst. The conceptual interpretation would be identical to that of water: I constitute it as a beverage. But I can discover water in another way. For example, there is a fire. In my circumspect looking around, I discover water; I consider its capacity to put out the fire. I constitute it as a mediation for avoiding the dangers of a conflagration. Thus I interpreted it in another sense.

2.3.5.6 A phenomenon or being (water) can be comprehended in its real constitution (2.2.7.4)—water as a liquid—and interpreted in different senses (as a beverage and as something to put out a fire). If it is discovered in its real constitution, the sense is related to reality (alcohol, though it is liquid, is not correctly interpreted as something to put out fire); if it is constituted in its reference to the world, the sense is related to the totality of the world (and in this acceptation, without persons or world there is no sense whatsoever even though there be real things).

2.3.5.7 To repeat. There is no phenomenon without constitution of sense. The wood of the table can appear to me as firewood, because when the weather is extremely cold it is more important not to freeze than to have a table. The wood-firewood appears as a phenomenon, a sense-thing, just as wood-table daily appears as a sense-thing. The sense, on the other hand, is never a merely theoretical or abstract consideration. It is always quotidian and existential; it is the way in which something makes up the "for" of an action, be it practical or productive.

2.3.6   Perception and the Percept

2.3.6.1   Phenomena, beings, when they are the apparition of the real, can fall under the testing capacity of the senses (in the way that a meal is sampled or tested by the taste buds). Bodily organs (eyes, ears, etc.) permit the establishing of proxemic and ontic relationships. Nevertheless, sensations (of a tree, for example) are not each of them totally independent units (the brown of the wood, the fresh smell, its exterior form, the wrinkles on its branches, etc.), nor are they purely sensible.

2.3.6.2   Merleau-Ponty clearly showed that sensations are integrated in a field that includes sensations as indivisible parts: perception. Perception is the phenomenologico-sensible totality constituted by indivisible unities of eidetic sensations. Just as there is conception of sense in interpretation, so there is perception of the immediate field of what is seized by sensibility. Concept and percept (sensible image) are given simultaneously because interpretation is an act of sentient intelligence and perception is an act of intelligent sensibility. Just as the human person cannot be divided into body and soul (person is one indivisible substantivity; 4.1.5), so eidetic content is not to be separated from sensible content.

2.3.6.3   Beyond interpreted sense as minimal conceptual unity, or perceptive sensation as minimal sensible unity, and before the world as totality (2.2.2), the immediate field of perception is found. It is not proximity; it is the area of the proxemic (physical closeness) in its strictest sense (the ontic level that effectively confronts us as the actual field of mediation: the presence of the present in its presentness or intellectual sensitive actuality).

2.3.7   Estimation of Value

2.3.7.1   Everything that is discovered and constituted in its sense can be estimated for its value. Possibility or mediation has value insofar as it is possibility or mediation. To be of value is the very fact by which possibility or mediation mediates, a *proyecto* is implemented. Possibility as possibility is the value that one attributes to a phenomenon or being.

2.3.7.2   In the middle of the desert, in extreme thirst, water acquires an immense value. It is the first and necessary mediation to quench thirst and subsist. The pen or pencil acquires value at the moment one wants to express an idea and not forget it. To have sense is not the same thing as to have value.

2.3.7.3   Sense and value are had because they make reference to the world, the system, projected undertakings, and the totality of references that unfold from humankind and not just from the real constitution of the thing itself. That the rose grows and exudes its perfume is due to its real constitution, "of itself," from within itself. That the rose is the queen of flowers, that when roses are red the lover gives them to the beloved, is worldly; it is to *have* sense and value. Sense and value are superadded to the thing by the fact of its being integrated into a human process.

2.3.7.4   Something can have sense and not value. Something has sense when it keeps a possible relationship with an interpretive totality. Something has value when it keeps an actual relationship with a practical or productive totality (actual operative mediation for a project). Access to sense is intellectual and existential; access to value is estimative and operative. Interpretation considers the real constitutive or eidetic structure of the sense-thing; esteem appreciates the real or symbolic function of the sense-thing. All that has value has sense even though it can be that something that is devoid of sense for some is highly esteemed by others. But something can have sense and nevertheless not have value. For a pacifist, waging war has a meaning, but it is without value. That is, the eidetic structure of war can be discovered and interpreted, but it is not an actual operative mediation for the one who criticizes it.

2.3.7.5   At any rate, neither sense nor value is the foundation of the world or of ethical, economic, or esthetic systems. Value is mediation as such, and all mediation directs itself to a *proyecto* that establishes it. Axiologies are ideologies when it is forgotten that the hierarchy of values is never absolute, but is relative to the historical system it serves as mediation. It is equally ideological to think that the sense of beings is absolute, forgetting that it is one's own world that establishes and gives sense to everything that surrounds one.

2.3.8 Things, Beings, and Senses

2.3.8.1 I must now clarify certain notions about the proxemic or the essentially ontic (what refers to beings or phenomena). When I speak of a thing *(res)* I refer to a substantive reality whose constitutive notes are closed or really independent as a whole. For example, a dog is a thing. It has an essence that enables it to perform actions proper to dogs, those of its concrete individuality. If I cut off its foot, I can no longer say that the foot is a thing, because when it is no longer alive it becomes evident that it is only part of something else, the dog. A thing is real "of itself," from within itself, a moment of the cosmos (2.2.3.1 and 3.4.6)—which is not the world (2.2.3.2) or only nature (4.1.2.2).

2.3.8.2 On the contrary, being *(on, ens,* that which is) indicates that a thing is being referred to insofar as it is incorporated into the world as mediation or possibility, even though it is only a being of reason *(ens rationis)*—a centaur, for example. Being can be differentiated from phenomenon. One says "being" in reference to the eidetic content, keeping in mind the reality connoted (if there is any), the essence. One says "phenomenon" in reference to the fact of appearing in the world, with respect to the significant totality. Every being is a phenomenon and vice versa; but not every real thing is a being. If the thing is a being, it is a sense-thing. The centaur is a mere being whereas the wood-table is a being and a sense-thing. Sense-thing can be such in many ways. A wooden poster is a sign (4.2), an artifact (4.3), merchandise (4.4). A thing can be a purely natural being (4.1) as differentiated from a cultural being (4.2.4) or from a logical being (5.1.6).

A thing, insofar as it is a sense or a being *(ens),* always has a meaning in the world. Notice that reality is constitutive of a thing; we say it has an essence (3.4.7.3). A phenomenon, on the other hand, has a general content (the derived comprehension or the conceptualization of some essential or accidental notes; 2.2.7.4), which is determined in its eidetic or conceptual structure (this structure is not to be confused with the essential notes constitutive of the thing) by the interpretation of its meaning, sense. Essence expresses relation to real constitution and therefore founds interpretation as discovery; the eidetic structure has relation to the worldly totality or the order of phenomenal manifestation. Sense, then, is the eidetic structure of a being, which is interpreted conceptually on the quotidian existential or the theoretical critical level with respect to the world as the totality of the phenomenon.

2.3.8.4   Reality, entity, and phenomenality indicate different levels. Reality belongs to things insofar as they are really constituted "of themselves" *(ex se)*. Entity *(entitas)* belongs to beings insofar as they are discovered in relation to their essential content (if they are not beings of reason, in which case their entity would be minimal because it refers to a purely eidetic structure). Phenomenality belongs equally to beings but insofar as they are constituted in their eidetic relational structure or worldly sense.

2.3.9   Situated Freedom

2.3.9.1   In reality persons are not surrounded by things or by independent, autonomous beings. The things and beings that constitute one's surroundings are mediations and possibilities. When persons work, they do so for a *proyecto*. That *proyecto* determines the possibilities or mediations for its realization. That is, we are, as it were, besieged by decisions to be made, ways that open and close.

2.3.9.2   Since classical times this openness to the duty of continually determining oneself for this or that possibility, this being sometimes disconcerted and not knowing which to choose, this power itself to choose and not to choose, this capacity or dominion over mediations has been called *freedom*.

2.3.9.3   Persons realize themselves by chosen determinations. The choice of one possibility makes others impossible. By decision after decision persons construct their own biography, their own history. Freedom is possible because no mediation completely fulfills the human *proyecto*. Indifferent or neutral to possibilities presented, a person finally selects one that is not the whole or plenary one but the possible, concrete, prudent one.

2.3.9.4   To choose freely does not mean being able to determine mediations absolutely from an absolute indetermination. This would be infinite, radical freedom. Nor is a person totally determined or conditioned; that would be simply an animal stimulated by unrestrainable, instinctive motives. Persons are free and at the same time historically determined—that is, conditioning is not absolute, but relative or partial. The peaks of the reality of human freedom always reveal spontaneity. We are masters of our own decisions and choices.

2.3.9.5 Mediation is possibility for freedom. A thing is a being because, interpreted in its sense and esteemed for its value, it is finally chosen or rejected in view of a *proyecto*. Without freedom there is neither person nor being nor sense, because there would simply be no world; there would be only the cosmos, things, stimuli, and animals.

2.4   EXTERIORITY

2.4.1   *Status Questionis*

2.4.1.1   Here we approach the most important category for philosophy of liberation. Only now do we have the interpretive instrumentation that allows us to begin a philosophical discourse from the periphery, from the oppressed. Up to this point, our discourse has been something of a summary of the already known. From now on a discourse begins that, when it is established on its corresponding political level with the necessary mediations that are lacking in philosophies of the center that use the same categories, we shall be able to say is a new discourse in the history of world philosophy. This is not to claim superior intelligence; it derives from the simple fact that, when we turn to reality as exteriority, by the mere fact that the exteriority we explore is a *new historical reality,* the philosophy that issues from it—if it is authentic—cannot help being equally new. It is the newness of our peoples that must be reflected as newness in philosophy, and not vice versa.

2.4.1.2   The spatial metaphor of exteriority can lead to more than one equivocation. We could also denominate the "beyond," vis-à-vis the horizon of Being of the system, an *interior transcendentality,* a "beyond" vis-à-vis the subject in the system, vis-à-vis one's work, one's desire, one's possibilities, one's *pro-*

yecto. Exteriority and interior transcendentality have the same signification in this philosophical discourse.

2.4.2   The Being That Is Not Merely Being

2.4.2.1   Among the beings or things that appear in the world, which manifest themselves in the system along with instruments, there is one absolutely *sui generis,* distinct from all the rest. Along with mountains, valleys, and rivers, along with tables, hammers, and machines, there enter daily into our environment the faces of other persons. Far from proximity, in farness, their presence comes back to remind us of previous proximities. Generally, however, the face of the other person figures in our environment as just one more sense-thing. The taxi driver seems like a mechanical prolongation of the automobile, the housekeeper as one more instance of cleaning and cooking, the teacher as an ornament of the school, the soldier as just another member of the army. It seems difficult to detach other persons from the system in which they are inserted. The person is just another being, a part of a system.

Nevertheless, there are moments when persons appear to us and reveal themselves to us in all their exteriority, as when the taxi driver (who turns out to be a friend) says to us, "How goes it?" The unexpected question arising from a horizon of beings shocks us. Someone appears in the world! Much more so when someone says, "Please help me!" Or "I'm hungry. Give me something to eat!"

2.4.2.2   The face of a person is revealed as other when it is extracted from our system of instruments as exterior, as someone, as a freedom that questions, provokes, and appears, as one who resists instrumental totalization. A person is not something, but someone.

2.4.2.3   Exteriority, which does not have the same meaning as it did for Hegel (because for the great German philosopher exteriority is definitely interior to the totality of Being or, finally, of the Idea), is meant to signify the ambit whence other persons, as free and not conditioned by one's own system and not as part of one's own world, reveal themselves.

2.4.3   Being, Reality, and Distinction

2.4.3.1   If Being *(esse)* is the foundation of all systems, and of the system of systems that is the daily world, there is also reality beyond Being, just as there is also cosmos beyond the world. Being is like the horizon toward which and from which the phenomena of the world manifest themselves. It is the ontological foundation and identity; it is the light that illuminates the totality of the world. But beyond Being, transcending it, there is still reality. If reality is the order of the cosmic constitutions of things that are resistant, subsistent, "of themselves," it is evident that there is reality beyond Being. How many cosmoses have never been incorporated into any world! Did not the reality of the primate come millions of years ago and then later the appearance of the world, of Being?

2.4.3.2   Among the real things that retain exteriority to Being, one is found that has a history, a biography, freedom: another person (4.1.5.5). Persons beyond Being, beyond the comprehension of the world, beyond the sense constituted by the interpretations supplied by one's own system, transcending the determinations and conditions of one's totality, can reveal themselves as in opposition to us, can rebuke us. Even in the extreme humiliation of prison, in the cold of the cell and the total pain of torture, even when the body is nothing but a quivering wound, a person can still cry: "I am another; I am a person; I have rights."

2.4.3.3   If reality is the substantive and independent constitution of a thing—its essence—then a person is properly real, more real than the cosmic totality of the heavenly bodies and living beings that together form the physico-astronomical and botanico-zoological substantivity without real exteriority of one to another. Only the free person, each person, is the self-substantive, autonomous, other totality: metaphysical exteriority, the most real reality beyond the world and Being.

2.4.3.4   All of this acquires practical reality when someone says, "I'm hungry!" The hunger of the oppressed, of the poor, is an effect of an unjust system. As such, it has no place in the system. First of all because it is negativity, "lack of" (4.3.3), non-being in the world, but fundamentally because to satiate structurally the hunger of the oppressed is to change radically the system. Hunger as such is the practical exteriority of, or the most subversive internal transcendentality against, the system: the total and insurmountable "beyond."

2.4.3.5   The logic of totality (5.2) pursues its discourse from identity (or foundation) to difference. It is a logic of nature (4.1) or of totalitarianism (3.1.5–6). It is the logic of the alienation of exteriority (2.5.6) or of the reification of alterity,* of the other person. The logic of exteriority or of alterity (5.3), on the contrary, establishes its discourse on the abyss of the freedom of the other (2.6). This logic has another origin, other principles. It is historical and nonevolutionary; it is analectical (5.3) and not merely dialectical (5.2) or scientific-factual (5.1), although it includes both.

2.4.3.6   A person—each person, all persons—originates in someone's uterus. But a person is not a mere numerical difference within the identity of the species or of the originating identity of the mother. Persons are born distinct from their origin, forever. The constitution of the genetic chain in the fertilized human ovum is distinct from every other genetic process. The father and mother contribute equally. Nevertheless, the new being, the child, will establish its own world, a unique achievement; the newborn will be free (4.1.5). The essential note of freedom makes a person distinct from the moment of birth. The child is not differentiated from the mother the way a graft can be differentiated from a tree before being planted so that a new tree can take roots and grow (the new tree is differentiated only from the identity of life). Persons, on the other hand, forever separate, never essentially united, are other from the moment they are real; their alterity will keep growing until their last day; their death is historical, not merely biological.

2.4.3.7   Distinction-convergence is opposed to identity-difference. Persons, distinct in their real constitution as a contingent or free thing, converge, reunite, approach other persons.

---

*The term "alterity" (compare "totality," "exteriority") has been established by Emmanuel Levinas (*Totality and Infinity* [Pittsburgh: Duquesne University Press, 1969]; *The Theory of Intuition* [Evanston, Ill.: Northwestern University Press, 1973]; *Existence and Existents* [Hingham, Mass.: Kluwer Academic Publ., 1978]; *Otherwise Than Being* [Kluwer, 1981]), and other authors.

Convergence will be goodness, justice, fulfillment, service, liberation. Beyond Being, persons converge in extrasystemic future reality.

2.4.4   Provocation of the Other

2.4.4.1   The other is the precise notion by which I shall denominate exteriority as such—historical, not only cosmic or physico-living, exteriority (4.1). The other is the alterity of all possible systems, beyond "the same," which totality always is. "Being is, and non-Being is," or can be, the other, we could say, contrary to Parmenides and classical ontology.

2.4.4.2   Others reveal themselves as others (3.4.8.1) in all the acuteness of their exteriority when they burst in upon us as something extremely distinct, as nonhabitual, nonroutine, as the extraordinary, the enormous ("apart from the norm")—the poor, the oppressed. They are the ones who, by the side of the road, outside the system, show their suffering, challenging faces: "We're hungry! We have the right to eat!" That right, outside the system, is not a right that is justified by the *proyecto* or the laws of the system. Their absolute right, because they are sacred and free, is founded in their own exteriority, in the real constitution of their human dignity. When the poor advance in the world, they shake the very pillars of the system that exploits them. The face (*pnim* in Hebrew, *prosopon* in Greek), the person, is provocation and judgment by its mere self-revelation.

2.4.4.3   The others, the poor in their extreme exteriority to the system, provoke justice—that is, they call (*-voke*) from ahead (*pro-*). For the unjust system, "the other is hell" (if by hell is understood the end of the system, chaos). On the contrary, for the just person, the other is the utopian order without contradictions; the other is the beginning of the advent of a new world that is distinct and more just. The mere presence of the oppressed as such is the end of the oppressor's "good conscience." The one who has the ability to discover where the other, the poor, is to be found will be able, from the poor, to diagnose the pathology of the state.

2.4.4.4   The other is a person as an imploring, revealing, and provoking face.

2.4.5   Revelation of a People

2.4.5.1   The face of the other, primarily as poor and oppressed, reveals a people before it reveals an individual person. The brown face of the Latin American *mestizo* wrinkled with the furrows of centuries of work, the ebony face of the African slave, the olive face of the Hindu, the yellow face of the Chinese coolie is the irruption of the history of a people before it is the biography of Tupac Amaru, Lumumba, Nehru, and Mao Tse-tung. To describe the experience of proximity as individual experience, or the metaphysical experience of face-to-face as lived experience between two persons, is simply to forget that personal mystery is always risked in the exteriority of the popular history of a people (3.1.3–4). The individualization of this collective personal experience is a European deformation derived from the bourgeois revolution. Each face, unique, inscrutable mystery of decisions not yet made, is the face of a sex, a generation, a social class, a nation, a cultural group, a historical epoch.

2.4.5.2   The other person—metaphysical alterity, exteriority on the anthropological level—is primarily social and historico-popular. This is why the faces that are taken care of with beauty aids and rejuvenated by face-lifts and cosmetics of the oligarchies, aristocracies, and bourgeoisies—be they of the center or of the periphery—are faces that, like mummies, want to escape the contingencies of time. The eternalization of the present, in terror of the future, is the obsession of every dominating group. On the contrary, the withered face of the Bedouin of the desert, the furrowed and darkened skin of the peasant, the poisoned lungs of the miner whose face never sees the sun—these "apparently" ugly faces, almost horrible for the system, are the primary (4.4.9), the future, the popular beauty.

2.4.6   Freedom, Non-Being, Nothing

2.4.6.1   The other is the exteriority of all totality because the other is free. I do not mean freedom here as just a certain possibility of choosing between diverse mediations depending on a given project. Freedom here is the unconditioning of the other with respect to the world in which *I* am always the center. Others as other—that is, as centers of their own worlds (though they be dominated or oppressed)—can point out what is impossible, unexpected, unpublicized in *my* world, in the system. All persons, insofar as they are free, and insofar as they take part in a system, are functional, professional, or members of a certain structure—but they are not other. Others are other insofar as they are exterior to the totality (and in this same sense they are suppliant human faces—persons). Without exteriority there is neither freedom nor personhood. The fact of freedom, of free choice, is discovered only in the unconditioning of the other's behavior.

Robinson Crusoe, had he been born alone, would not have been free but only spontaneous: moreover, he would not have been a human being, a person, because persons recognize and develop themselves as persons in proximity, never in solipsistic farness. Crusoe would have been an animal whose rationality would have remained purely potential. He would not have had a world, simply because no one would have given sense to beings.

2.4.6.2   As an unconditioned, exterior other, the other as other is non-Being. Beyond the horizon of Being, the other is the barbarian (who for Aristotle is not human), or in a macho society the woman (who for Freud is castrated), or the orphan who is nothing and has to learn everything (like Rousseau's Emile). Insofar as the other is not, in terms of alterity and totality, it can be said that the other is nothing. But new systems come from nothingness—new in the metaphysical sense, radical. Berdyaev states that the Greeks thought about the problem of change, but they never even suspected the question of *newness*.

2.4.6.3   From the other as other, freedom unconditioned inasmuch as its exteriority is despised as nothing (as uncultured, illiterate, barbarian), the history of the new arises. Thus every future system resulting from a subversive revolution in the metaphysical sense is analogical, somewhat similar to the anterior totality, but really distinct (5.3).

2.4.7   Reason and Faith

2.4.7.1   Reason (in the sense of Hegelian *Vernunft* or even Heideggerian *Verstehen*) is the human speculative capacity by which one sees or discovers what beings are and what the world, the system, or the totality consists of. It is the capacity to comprehend foundation and difference. It is the contemplative capacity that illuminates the area controlled by political and military power. It would seem that beyond reason there is the irrational. (Frequently the irrational passes for the supremely rational: Hegel's *Idea*, Nietzsche's "superman," Hitler's racism, the Manifest Destiny or American Way of Life of the United States, and numerous irrational myths that founded supremely analytical, mathematical, computerized, and "reasonable" enterprises.) Nevertheless, beyond reason, beyond the irrational that passes for rational, and more than the irrational, there is the exteriority of the other who cannot be comprehended completely (2.2.7), or understood perfectly by any world or system.

2.4.7.2   Beyond the horizon embraced by reason, but still ontological reason, the reality of the other resists. When the others speak from within themselves—but not by the force of torture that makes its victims confess in despair—they reveal their exteriority, their alterity which reason can never scrutinize from within itself. The other cannot be interpreted, analyzed, or studied from within the system, as can be done with stones, vegetables, or animals. We can investigate a cockroach starting from what its reality shows us, or we can ignore it. It would never occur to us to ask it "Who are you? How are you?" On the contrary, we ask for the name, the biography, and the opinions only of the other. But persons can lie. Hypocrisy is a sign of their exteriority. They can jealously guard the mystery of their secret. They can die without revealing it.

2.4.7.3   What reason can never embrace—the mystery of the other as other—only faith can penetrate. In proximity, face to face, someone can hear the voice of the other and welcome it with holy respect. "I love you!" says the beloved to the lover. What can one do in the face of such a simple and almost daily revelation? Do I believe what is said? Do I distrust? Is she deceiving me? Is she making fun of me? To tell her I also love her is a risk; in such a risk I can lose my reputation, my honor, and even my life. What do I do . . .?

2.4.7.4   Faith means to accept the word of the other because the other reveals it—with no other motivation. What someone reveals to me has no criterion of certitude other than the very reality of the other as other. I do not accept what the other reveals to me because of the evidence of its content or because it is true. It is accepted because behind the other's word is found the very reality of someone, immediate, open and exposed in a metaphysical openness of which the ontological openness to the world is a distant imitation (4.2.6). To reveal is to expose oneself to traumatism, like the prisoner who opens his shirt to the firing squad. To believe is to fling oneself into empty space because the other has stated that at the bottom of the abyss there is water and there is no danger. This is metaphysical relationship par excellence—proximity, revelation, and faith. It is supreme, historical, and human rationality.

2.4.8   Interior Transcendentality

2.4.8.1   The category of exteriority, as said above, is misunderstood when what is "beyond" the ontological horizon of the system is thought of in an absolute, total way without any participation in the interior of the system. To avoid this misunderstanding, exteriority must be understood as transcendentality interior to totality. No person as such is absolutely and only part of a system. All, including even those who are members of an oppressing class, have a transcendentality with respect to the system, interior to it.

2.4.8.2   The fact, for example, that the Nicaraguan Sandinista National Liberation Front did not even request the extradition of the dictator Somoza manifests this internal transcendentality. In the first place, the oppressor is an oppressor not in the ultimate secrecy of private life but in social functionality, in activity regulated by the institutional totality. If the social structure as a whole is modified, many who were wielding power in the system would not be converted to mere citizens without instruments of oppression. Magnanimous justice or pardon for their deeds is possible because the person is never identified with the social function without possibility of separation. Members of the dominant bourgeois class are themselves victims of capital, and the overcoming of capitalism will free them from the slavery exercised over the truly human level of their existence. This internal transcendentality is the exteriority of the other as other, not as part of the system.

2.4.8.3   The increasing structurally-related unemployment in the present crisis of capitalism is another example of interior transcendentality or hope of exteriority. To have the ability and desire to work and to be unable to do so is to be made a subject "beyond" the system. The work that is possible but not used, and the time lost by the system that cannot engage it, is internal negativity; it is active exigency for transcendence in the interior of a system that is unjust and repressive with regard to productive labor straining toward the future.

2.4.9   Ontology and Metaphysics

2.4.9.1   Ontology moves in the light of the world under the control of reason. Philosophy as ontology means to reflect on oneself, to speculate on or look at oneself as in a mirror (*speculum*); it is to look for identity as the origin of what one already is.

2.4.9.2   Metaphysics, in the meaning I give it in this present discourse on philosophy of liberation, is knowing how to ponder the world from the exteriority of the other. It is to know how to think about not just the negativity of a being, which gives way to ontic novelty when it goes back to the origin of the world, the foundation, Being; it is to know how to think about Being from the exteriority that judges it—just as the periphery of the world judges today the center that pursues the philosophy of domination (be it ontological or functionalist, structuralist, analytical, or semiological), just as the women who liberate themselves from domination judge "phallocracy" or macho ideology, just as the youth of the world judge the aging, gerontocratic, castrating generations. Metaphysics is to know how to think about the system, the world, from within ontological negativity (because the negativity of an Adorno, for example, always ends up affirming Being, the ontological, even though it be as a future utopia). I, on the other hand, deny that same Being and its utopia not in the name of a future utopia but of a present utopia: the peripheral peoples, the oppressed classes, the woman, the child.

2.4.9.3   The ontological tension between a being (*ens*) and Being (*esse*) has been called preoccupation (*boulesis* for Aristotle or *Sorge* for Heidegger). The metaphysical tension of a moment in the system thrown toward exteriority, toward the other as other, I shall call the "pulsion"—desire—of alterity. This pulsion, desire, and love for real justice is like a hurricane that destroys walls, makes a breach in the ontological horizon, and turns itself inside out into exteriority. Metaphysics takes a risk not only in its fidelity to its vocation but also in the pulsion that mobilizes, transforms, and subverts reality itself.

2.5 ALIENATION

2.5.1 *Status Questionis*

2.5.1.1 Our discourse up to this point will have delighted dominators because it is peaceful, and dissatisfied the oppressed because it is not conflictive. Pedagogically it is necessary to go from the source to the mountain rivulets, and then on to the torrential rivers that finally flow into the wild ocean. The discourse of philosophy of liberation will only now begin to show, feature by feature, its true physiognomy.

2.5.1.2 Totality, the system, tends to totalize itself, to center on itself, and to attempt—temporally—to eternalize its present structure. Spatially, it attempts to include within itself all possible exteriority. Having an infinite hunger, the fetish (3.4.2) attempts to install itself forever in an insatiable cannibalism. Face-to-face proximity disappears because the fetish eats its mother, its children, its siblings. Totalized totality, Cyclops or Leviathan on earth, kills as many alien faces (persons) as question it until finally, after a long and frightful agony, it sadly disappears from history, not without first sealing its final days with innumerable injustices.

2.5.2 The Other: The Enemy

2.5.2.1 Sages are clairvoyant; they see with absolute clarity. "Salvation is achieved by knowledge," according to the tragedy, and thus the Socratic "Know thyself" is as ontological as Neitzsche's "the eternal return of the same." In the end, "the same" remains "the self-same"; "Being is" summarizes all ontology. In the presence of Being there is nothing to do but contemplate it, speculate on it, go into ecstasy over it, affirm it, and remain tragically in the passive authenticity (*Eigentlichkeit*) favorable for the dominator but fatal for the dominated. Gnosis is the perfect act of the ontological, aristocratic oppressor.

DIAGRAM 3

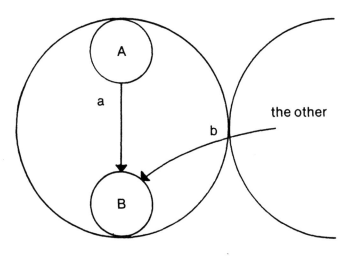

A   dominator   a   domination
B   alienated   b   alienation

2.5.2.2   Evil or injustice, of course, is not something persons commit. Especially the ones whom the gods have selected to dominate do not find in themselves the guilt of domination. Heraclitus said, "by *physis* some advance as gods and others as humans; some are free and others are slaves." The *ananke* or force of destiny has so desired it. Evil is only ignorance of what things are and, on the other hand, it is the reason for multiplicity. If we were one like being and foundation in their identity, there would be neither plurality nor evil. Matter or determination, which denies Being and constitutes beings, is the origin of evil. Plotinus and Hegel agree.

2.5.2.3   For the system, the other appears as something different. As such the other threatens the unity of "the same." The sage is in charge of proclaiming, on the basis of ontology, the danger that the other poses for the whole, the totality. So the sage clearly points out the enemy of the system: the one who is different, the other. Having identified the evil, the distinct, the other, ontology rests in peace.

2.5.3   Annihilation of Distinction

2.5.3.1   The sage has pointed out, with clairvoyance, Being and its opposite: distinctness, the other. Now is the hour of the practical person, the hero of the system, of Julius Caesar in Gaul, Napoleon in Russia, Hitler in Europe, Cortes in Mexico, Pizarro in Peru, the imperialist armies in Latin America, Africa, and Asia. It is the hour of praxis that eliminates the enemy, the one who is distinct, the other.

2.5.3.2   Because distinctness is an exteriority that denies the one-dimensionality of the system, its indistinct incorporation within the system, its becoming one more among the rest, is welcomed. The one who opposes leveling out remains distinct, other. As other than the system, that one is beyond Being. Inasmuch as Being is and non-Being is not, the other is not. If the other speaks, provokes, or demands, it is the verbal expression of non-Being. Before the other can continue these works of falsification and demoralization of the system, heroes throw themselves upon the enemies, the others, and annihilate them. The SS staged its heroics in Nazi Germany; the CIA—a lawfully armed extension of the transnational corporations—keeps up the tradition in the peripheries of the contemporary world.

2.5.3.3   The designs of the ruling system are imposed univocally on everybody by propaganda, the communications media, movies, and television—through all receptive pores. Whoever resists is kidnapped, jailed, tortured, expelled, or killed.

2.5.3.4   The dialectic between master and slave is no longer possible: the slave disappears from the horizon—by death. The periphery knows so many deaths—Patrice Lumumba, Ben Barka, Elieser Gaetán, Oscar Romero . . .!

2.5.3.5   The ontology of the center justifies what the central powers and imperialist armies do. What was Stoicism and Epicureanism but the consecration of the empire? Who are Hegel, Nietzsche, and Heidegger but the phenomenologists of European centrism?

2.5.4   Totalization of Exteriority

2.5.4.1   What is most frightening is the certitude (*Gewissheit*) the dominating heroes have of representing the gods on earth—in bygone epochs—and now democracy, freedom, and civilization. They are brave defenders of Being, who give their lives for the highest ideal before the plebeians, the barbarians, the representatives of non-Being, matter, difference, the diabolical, falsehood, disorder, chaos, Marxism—in a word: evil. The good consciences of heroes transform them into fanatics.

2.5.4.2   Clothed in noble, warlike, healthy, Nietzschean virtues, white-skinned and blond-haired like the Aryans, Europe throws itself upon the periphery, on the geopolitical exteriority, on the wives of other men, on their children, and on their gods. In the name of Being, of the human world, of civilization, it annihilates the alterity of other peoples, other cultures, other erotics, other religions. Thus it incorporates them or, in another way, violently expands the frontiers of its world until it includes other peoples in its sphere of control. From the year 718 Spain extended its military frontier to the south in its struggle of reconquest against the Arabs; after 1492 it extended to include most of Latin America. Latin America is a totalized geopolitical area annihilated in its exteriority and swallowed up by cannibals in the name of civilization.

2.5.4.3   The conquests of Latin America, the enslavement of Africa and its colonization, as well as that of Asia, are the dominating dialectical expansion of "the same" that assassinates "the other" and totalizes "the other" in "the same." This huge dialectico-ontological process of human history simply went unperceived by the ideology of ideologies (even though it claims to be the critic of ideologies)—modern and contemporary European philosophy.

2.5.4.4   Tautology takes possession of everything: "the eternal return of the same." It is the self-affirmation of a particular social formation.

2.5.5 Alienation

2.5.5.1 The other, who is not different (as totality asserts) but distinct (always other), who has a history, a culture, an exteriority, has not been respected; the center has not let the other *be* other. It has incorporated the other into a strange, foreign totality. To totalize exteriority, to systematize alterity, to deny the other as other, is alienation. To alienate is to sell someone or something, to pass it on to another proprietor. The alienation of a people or of a single individual makes its victims lose their Being by incorporating them as a moment, an aspect, an instrument of another's Being.

2.5.5.2 The geographical periphery of the world, of the woman and the child, is the property of the center, of the male, of the adult. The Being of others is alienated when they are displaced from their own center and made to revolve around the center of a totality alien to them.

2.5.5.3 Alienation, nevertheless, is a risk taken in the poiesis of social formation. The praxis of domination, as a person-to-person relationship, places the other at the service of a dominator; but it is in work (poiesis) that domination really fulfills itself. When the fruit of work is not recovered by a people, a worker, a woman, or a child, its Being remains alienated. When the dominator systematically appropriates the fruit of the work of the totalized, dominated other; when this appropriation becomes habitual, institutional, and historical—at that moment alienation is real, certain, and effective: it is a mode of unjust production. Ownership, such as the right to possess the other's product, is the counterpart in the dominator of the alienation in the dominated. In a consumer society it is the ownership of capital; in a bureaucratic society it is control of the functions that exercise power. Alienation and the exercise of dominating power are the two aspects of totalized totality.

2.5.5.4 Thus all political, erotic, pedagogical, or fetishist alienation will be accomplished in its respective economy (3.1.5–4.4.9), in social formation.

2.5.6   Face as Instrument

2.5.6.1   In times of danger the other is transformed, thanks to ideologies, into "the enemy." In peacetime, even though the other is always considered a potential danger (cause of fundamental anxiety to every totalized or schizophrenic system), the face of the other is manipulated as a mere thing without transcendence or mystery; the other is considered an instrument. The face of the other is exchanged for an ugly mask, weatherbeaten and rustic. The mask is not a face; it does not make appeals; it is one more piece of furniture in the environment. One passes near the other and says simply: "A worker!" or "A native!" or "A black!" or "An undernourished Pakistani!" (one of those illustrated in posters to beg alms from Europe and the United States for the poor countries; thus Europeans and North Americans have a good conscience, not asking themselves why the peripheral peoples have rickets and especially what the center has to do with hunger in the periphery).

2.5.6.2   To kill, for example in El Salvador, one must beforehand deprive the others of their sacred exteriority and reduce them to "the enemy." In the same way in peacetime (for the dominators) and in times of peaceful coexistence (the better to exploit the periphery), the others are deprived of their dignity as persons and are constituted forced labor, instruments of an instrument, ultraperfect robots, things, tools. After this "sleight of hand" by classic ontology and its ever faithful ideologues (Rosenberg) or politicians (Kissinger and Haig with their "humanitarian" plans for Vietnam and El Salvador), all is possible, from making soap with the fat of martyred bodies to training dogs to violate women as a torture (the former was seen in Nazi Germany, the latter in Chile in 1976).

2.5.6.3   The reification of the other allows aristocracies to manage persons as plurality, multitude, *lumpen*, animals with *logos* but not human beings, as Aristotle taught with regard to slaves in Greece.

2.5.7   Praxis of Domination

2.5.7.1   The praxis of domination is a perversity. It is the practical affirmation of the totality and its *proyecto;* it is the ontic realization of Being, its alienating performance. The master exercises power over the servant by means of oppressive praxis. It is the mediation of the system by which its structure endures and persists.

2.5.7.2 Domination is the act by which others are forced to participate in the system that alienates them. They are compelled to perform actions contrary to their nature, contrary to their historical essence. Domination is an act of pressure, of force. The servant obeys out of fear, out of habit.

2.5.7.3 Domination is transformed into repression when the oppressed try to liberate themselves from the pressure they suffer. Faced with a gesture signifying the intention of flight from a situation of domination, the dominator increases the pressure; the dominator represses. Repression can be individual and psychological, but it is always social. Thus cultural norms are introjected through education and punishment into the very psychic structure of the child, of the person. Today the average person is very much repressed (3.2.5). By the same token, political or economic power represses those who rebel—represses them politically (3.1.5–1.6), through the police or the military. Repression is the unmasked face of domination.

2.5.7.4 Psychological repression, by way of the communications media, becomes violent as the pressure of a revolution increases. The corporality of the oppressed is violated against their will. This institutionalized violence is of course justified by the ontology and ideologies of the system. It remains consecrated as a virtue. The man violates the woman, shuts her up in his house, and consecrates her as "housewife"; the father does violence to the child, forcing the child to blind and total obedience to his dominating authority. Brother does violence to brother, requiring him to venerate the state under pain of death, "for his own security," and out of patriotic love (the old homeland).

2.5.7.5 War is the ultimate fulfillment of the praxis of domination; it is domination in its pure state. When the dominated no longer accept being oppressed by peace, or by repression, or by tactical violence, the dominator begins war—"total war," as the geopolitician Spykmann and his pupil in the periphery, Golbery do Couto e Silva, would say. War is practical ontology; it is the being that in practice reduces the other to non-being. Thus Parmenides anticipated the strategy and tactics of von Clausewitz and the Pentagon.

2.5.8   The Ethos of the Dominator

2.5.8.1   Ethos is the moral character of a people or a person; it is the structural whole of attitudes that predetermine action. The ethos of domination, be it imperialist or dependent national, revolves around the mystification, in the form of reigning customs or virtues, of what were vices in the time of oppression. (We have plenty of examples of dependent national domination in Latin American, African, and Asian neocolonies.) Repressed, the oppressed bring upon themselves a psychic self-poisoning in response to the violence they suffer. It is impossible for the weak to exercise the desired act of revenge against the strong. Thus arises resentment as autorepressive introjection of power, which, not being turned against the dominator, poisons as it settles into the one dominated. The resentment of the dominated cannot be lived either as a vice, which it is, or as mere resigned passivity. It is sublimated as the virtue of patience, or obedience, or discipline, or fidelity. In this way when the resentful oppressed of yesterday become the dominators of today, they present as virtues their old vices mystified. The avarice of the poor persecuted inhabitant of the medieval town, the bourgeois, is now the virtue of thrift.

2.5.8.2   Hatred, predecessor of envy, dwells in the heart of the dominator's ethos. The dominator is repulsed by the goodness, happiness, or success of the other; the dominator cannot stand the other's presence or existence, the other's imploring face. Hatred is a perversion of natural tendencies. It is the autoeroticism of the totality and the exclusion of exteriority. It is the origin of political and individual pathology: totalitarianism (political) and psychosis (personal). Both are self-centered and deny alterity; they are tautological, perverse, and self-destructive. Hatred is the perverse pulsion that keeps united the structured parts of the totalized whole.

2.5.8.3   Here prudence (practical wisdom) is shunted into "reason": the art of planning and winning wars. Justice gives to the powerful what was snatched from the weak under the appearance of legality. Temperance is merely comfort, which leads to a rocklike insensibility impervious to another's distress. And thus the comforts enjoyed by the consumer society prevent it from discovering that its deceitful gluttony is hunger in the dominated; the arrogance of the manager is the indignity of the hourly workers; the purchased copulation is the degeneration of the prostitute; the pedagogical domination of the father is the ruin of the child. . . .

2.5.8.4 The "virtues" of the center and the dominating classes are alienation in the periphery and dominated classes.

2.5.9 Legality of Perversion

2.5.9.1 For a good moralist of the center like Kant, legality was the objective alignment of an act with the law, and morality was the will to fulfil the law out of duty. If we accept the principle "Love your country and fight for it," and we compare a nineteenth-century Englishman with a Nigerian, each will fight for their country; both acts can illustrate "a principle of universal legislation." But it so happens that the one is perverse (the Englishman fighting abroad) and the other is ethically heroic and exemplary (the African). Nevertheless, both acts are legal and moral for Kant.

What type of morality could it have been that tried to take the measure of peripheral nations and their cultures from the nations and cultures of the center? Only an imperialistic morality. What are the values of a Scheler and his hierarchies except mediations of a Western thrust into the future? That thrust is their foundation although it never appears as such in his *Der Formalismus in der Ethik*. Every ethic of the law, of virtues, of values, of the end (be it *telos*, *finis*, or a Kelseynian national constitution—that is, teleological or positivist) is an ethic that conceals its own world and system.

2.5.9.2 Surreptitiously, Being, good, the *proyecto* of a culture, and human nature become identified with each other. Socrates divinized Greek culture by making his disciples believe that the ideas they had contemplated before their birth were divine; and they were *only* Greek. Rousseau, following him, made of the emerging bourgeois culture *la nature même des choses*. Inasmuch as the *proyecto* of a culture of the center was the natural human end, its exigencies were natural rights (as, for example, private property). Whoever stood up against Europe stood up against nature—that is, against God and the divine will.

2.5.9.3   In the name of those laws, valiantly practicing those virtues, and aiming to fulfil the *proyecto* of the world domination, Europe set forth with Columbus and his ships from the port of Palos in Andalusia in 1492. Fulfilling those laws, Francis Drake, pirate by profession, assassinator of defenseless *mestizos* and violator of women, devastated the Latin American coasts and received as a reward the right to lock up his thefts in the banks of London and the honor of being a British nobleman—*Sir* Francis Drake. Behold the magnificence and the first accumulation of capitalism that oppresses us now! Its origin was the gold of Amerindians and the flesh of black slaves!

2.6   LIBERATION

2.6.1   *Status Questionis*

2.6.1.1   Now we arrive at the central core of this chapter, at the essential moment of metaphysics, understanding that metaphysics is the passage from ontology to the transontological, to the one who is situated beyond Being, in reality (2.4.3 and 3.4.7), the other. Ontology is phenomenology; it is a *logos* or a thinking about what appears (the phenomenon, the being) from the foundation (Being). Beyond phenomenology the road of epiphany opens: revelation (or apocalyptic) of the other through the other's face, which is not merely a phenomenon or manifestation, a presence, but an epiphenomenon, vicarious, trace or vestige of the absent, of the mysterious, of one beyond the present. Ontology (phenomenology) gives way to metaphysics (apocalyptic epiphany of the other). The manifestation of being is fulfilled from the horizon of the foundation or Being of the system; epiphany fulfills itself as a revelation of the one who makes decisions beyond the horizon of the world or the frontier of the state. Manifestation is not revelation; presence is not exposure to traumatism. Liberation is not a phenomenal, intrasystemic action; liberation is the praxis that subverts the phenomenological order and pierces it to let in a metaphysical transcendence, which is the plenary critique of the established, fixed, normalized, crystallized, dead.

2.6.2 Ethical Conscience

2.6.2.1 The totalized person who carries out the *proyecto* of the established order and observes its laws can have a *moral* conscience. I designate moral conscience the application of the principles in force in a given system to a concrete decision. An administrator who tries to sell products at the highest possible price to make more profit for the company and who personally steals nothing from the company has a moral conscience. Moral conscience accompanies an act and can cheer, disturb, blame, or tranquilize. The greatest tyrant can have a tranquil moral conscience, as can the fanatic.

2.6.2.2 I designate *ethical* conscience the capacity one has to listen to the other's voice, the transontological word that breaks in from beyond the present system. The just protest of the other may question the moral principles of the system. Only the one who has an ethical conscience can accept this questioning from the standpoint of the absolute criterion: the other as other in justice.

2.6.2.3 The conditions for the possibility of being able to hear the voice of the other are very clear, and I shall be describing them throughout section 2.6. In the first place, to be able to listen to the voice of the other it is necessary to be atheistic vis-à-vis the system or to discover its fetishism (3.4.3). In the second place, it is necessary to respect the other as other. Respect is the attitude of metaphysical passivity with which honor is rendered to the exteriority of the other; it lets others be in their distinctness. Respect is a metaphysical attitude as a point of departure for all activity carried out in justice. But it is not respect for the law (which is universal or abstract), or for the system or its *proyecto*. It is respect for someone, for the freedom of the other. The other is the only really sacred being worthy of respect without limit. Respect is silence, not the silence of someone who has nothing to say (Wittgenstein), but of those who want to listen to everything because they know nothing about the other as other.

2.6.3   Responsibility for the Other

2.6.3.1   Those who hear the lament or protest of the other are stirred in the very center of their world, are decentered. The cry of pain of the one we cannot see signifies someone, not just something. The someone signified by the signifier—the cry— exhorts us, urges us to take on the suffering, the cause of the cry. To "take charge" (*spondere*) is to make oneself responsible. Responsibility is related not to answer-to (a question) but to respond-for (a person). Responsibility is to take charge of the poor who are encountered in exteriority with regard to the system. To be responsible-for-with-regard-to is the theme.

2.6.3.2   To be responsible for the other in and with regard to the system is anteriority prior to all other anteriority, a passivity that is almost metaphysical activity (more active than respect but more passive than the praxis of liberation). It is the metaphysical anteriority of the new or future order. It is anteriority to ontological openness to the world; it makes it possible; it is its real *a priori*. The mother is responsible for the defenseless child just as the teachers are responsible for their pupils and leaders for their people.

2.6.3.3   Responsibility for the poor, exterior to the system, exposes the just person to retaliation by the system, which feels under attack because of its dysfunctionality, openness, and exposure. For this reason, with inexorable logic the totality persecutes those who in their responsibility for the oppressed testify to the necessity for a new order. Responsibility is obsession for the other; it is linkage with the other's exteriority; it entails exposing oneself to traumatization, prison, even death. Heroes of liberation (not the heroes of the ancient expansionist homeland), antiheroes of the system, put their life forward and risk it. Responsibility is thus supreme valor, incorruptible strength (2.6.8), wisdom, authentic clairvoyance of the structures of totality.

2.6.4   Destruction of Order

2.6.4.1   The one who takes responsibility for the other in the system is seen by the dominator of the totality as a "fifth columnist," a prophet of hatred or chaos, a corrupter of the young (who still retain some freedom inasmuch as they have not yet fully entered the system of the whole). What is certain is that those who pursue the impulse of alterity or love of the new order in which the poor and oppressed can dwell in justice are transformed, even against their will, into an active principle of destruction of the old order. The oppressed as oppressed (but having some awareness of the positiveness of their exteriority) and the ones who risk themselves for them, insofar as they yearn for the new order and assume an active responsibility at least by no longer supporting the foundations of the present order, make dominators uneasy.

2.6.4.2 Every new order begins as a corruption or destruction of an old order. This is a physical, biological, natural law. It is also, analogously, a historico-human and cultural law. No system, be it tribal, nomadic, rural, or urban; no culture, ancient or modern; no economic system, be it feudal, capitalist, or socialist, can make way for a superior order without dying in the process.

2.6.4.3 There have been chaotic destructions of order, without sense, without future, as when armed hordes invaded regions with a superior culture; they devastated without leaving anything in its place. More than destruction, that was annihilation, in a totally negative sense. On the contrary, the destructuring of the flower, which makes way for the fruit, and the rupture or pain accompanying childbirth are creative, affirmative destructions. Something dies, true, but only as a condition for the possibility of the birth of something else. Every moment of passage is agonizing, and thus liberation is also the agony of the old for the fruitful birth of the new, the just.

2.6.5 Liberation: Anarchy

2.6.5.1 A process that has no conductive principle or rationality is called "anarchism"; it is a process without direction. Anarchism, even if it exudes immense generosity, is utopian in the reprehensible sense, insofar as it does not furnish a possible model for the next step after the destructive process. Liberation, on the contrary, is anarchy (in Greek it means "beyond the principle") insofar as the origin of its metaphysical activity (the activity of respect and of responsibility as its passive anteriority) is the other, the one who is beyond the system, beyond the frontier of the established order.

2.6.5.2   Liberation is metaphysical or transontological movement in behalf of the one who stands beyond the horizon of the world. It is the act that opens the breach, pierces the wall, and searches deeper into unsuspected, future, and really new exteriority.

2.6.5.3   Liberation, the act of the oppressed by which they express or realize themselves, incorporates a double moment, in that it is a denial of a denial in the system. The double moment passes unperceived in a simple dialectic as negation of a negation. To deny what is denied by the systems is to affirm the system in its foundation, for what is negated in the system (the oppressed) does not cease to be an intrinsic moment in the system. On the contrary, to deny the denied in the system, concomitant with the expansive affirmation of what in the oppressed is exteriority (and thus was never in the system, because it was distinct, separate, and outside), is liberation. Liberation is to leave the prison (deny the denied) and affirm the history that was anterior and exterior to the prison (the history of the prisoner before being put into jail and the history that was lived as personal biography in prison— such as the eleven years spent there by Antonio Gramsci).

2.6.6   The Mask That Becomes Face

2.6.6.1   Alienation covers the face of the other with a mask fashioned by the system to hide the other's entreaty. The mask defines the other by the function that the other fulfills within the system—as an employee, worker, or *campesino*. The other's exteriority is defined from the horizon of the system and thus functions within it. The other's function or social class has been fixed; the "for-what" has crystalized and the "who" has vanished.

2.6.6.2   For the historico-biographical face to be revealed in justice, it is necessary to mobilize institutions, functions, and the systemized totality. To allow the imploring face to appear demands the expropriation of possessors in the system so that those defined as parts can be revealed. Displacement of functions requires throwing the system as a whole into a dialectical mobilization that leaves persons free (3.4.5.2).

2.6.6.3   The frightening mask, even ugly from so much use and suffering, withered by the wind and sun, gradually recovers the beauty of the people. Goya began with masks or monsters and ended by painting the face of a people beginning to reveal its splendor. Wrinkles recovered their humanity like the faces of the old Amerindians of the Andes that reveal the depths of the wise, the patience of the brave, the centuries of culture, the mystery of their symbols, the goodness of the exteriority that awaits a new order in justice.

2.6.6.4   Suddenly the glassy stare of the instrumentalized is transformed into a penetrating gaze. It is not a stare that objectifies the one at whom it is directed (as in Sartre's description), but a look that personalizes; it is the look that makes one responsible for the liberation of the face that exposes itself to rejection and demands justice. It is the demanding look that gives rise to mercy, justice, rebellion, revolution, liberation.

2.6.7   Praxis of Liberation

2.6.7.1   When I speak of praxis (person-to-person relationship) I include also in this case poiesis (person-to-nature relationship). Liberating action that directs itself to others (brother or sister, woman or man, child) is simultaneous with work in their favor. There is no liberation without economics, without humanized technology, without planning, and without beginning with a historical social formation. Because of this, the praxis of liberation (a practical poiesis or a poietic praxis) is the act itself by which the horizon of the system is crossed over and one really penetrates into the exteriority through which the new order is constructed, a new, more just social formation.

2.6.7.2   Routine praxis within the system (2.5.7) is dominating because it consolidates the existent totality; it is an ontic activity (2.2) or a mere mediation internal to the world, founded in its *proyecto*. It is the praxis of consolidating the old and the unjust.

2.6.7.3   The praxis of liberation, on the contrary, puts the system into question—not just as a possible or ideational question, but as a constitutive questioning, one that opens a world from itself, its own road from within itself. It is a metaphysical, transontological praxis—liberation properly so called. There is no Greek word for it; the Greeks did not have this type of experience. But in Hebrew *habodah* means "work," as also "service," in Greek *diakonia*. Service is not a mere functional, intrasystemic work done out of duty or legal compulsion. It is a work (practical poiesis or poietic praxis) done for the other with responsibility, for the other's liberation. It is an innovative activity using instruments put at the service of the poor. The praxis of liberation is the procreation of a new order, of its new structure, and at the same time of the functions and beings that compose it. It is the ultimate realization—creative, inventive, innovative.

2.6.8   The Ethos of Liberation

2.6.8.1   Ethos (2.5.8.1) is custom and character. How, then, can one have a custom whose function is to create the new? How can anyone become habituated to what is always new? Is it possible to have a habit of the unique, the unrepeatable— liberation from a given situation of oppression? If there is such a virtue, we must know how to distinguish it from the vices masquerading as virtues in the prevailing totality. The ethos of liberation is not just the habit of not repeating the same thing. On the contrary, it is an aptitude or capacity, become character, for innovation and creation. Inasmuch as it emerges from serving the other (2.6.7.3), and the other is always a concrete person in a unique situation of oppression and exteriority, only someone who is responsible and faithful to someone else's uniqueness can be a liberator.

2.6.8.2   The ethos of liberation is structured around an axis that is not compassion (as for Schopenhauer) or sympathy (as for Scheler)—given that both are positions of functional parts toward other parts (to suffer-with one's equal)—but commiseration: placing oneself with (*cum*) someone in misery (*miser*). The ethos of liberation is other-directed pulsion or metaphysical justice; it is love of the other as other, as exteriority; love of the oppressed— not, however, as oppressed but as subject of exteriority. The traumatic condition of the human being endowed with freedom, the other, reduced to being an instrument in a system, is rightly called misery. To discover the other as other and place-oneself-together-with that person's misery, to experience as one's own the contradiction between being free and having to endure slavery, being distinct and someone and at the same time only a different internal part; to hurt from the pain of this cleavage is the first attitude of the ethos of liberation. It is not friendship or fellowship (among equals) but love of the oppressed because of their real dignity as exteriority.

2.6.8.3   From the commiseration shared by liberating heroes and the oppressed among themselves—for they have unlimited commiseration of their equals—the whole ethos of liberation is organized. (Only in this instance are fellowship and friendship actively liberative.) On it depends liberative justice, which does not give to each what is due within the law and the prevailing order, but grants to all what they deserve in their dignity as others. Thus liberative justice is not legal justice, whether distributive or commutative, but real justice—that is, subversive: subverting the established unjust order. It is obedience (a hearing of the one ahead of you: *ob-audire* in Latin) that is faithful, trusting, and does not doubt the other's word. Thus it is metaphysical prudence and not Machiavellian or cautious intrasystemic convenience.

Authentic liberative politics advises liberative heroes and the people even to lay down their lives for the new order—it is imprudent prudence for the dominators of the system, absurdity for the wisdom in vogue. It is patient and active hope in the liberation of the oppressed, which knows how to keep the rudder firm in view of the strategic end even if many reformist tactical concessions must be made. It is valiant, strong, daring hope that does not fear to offer its life for what it is doing. It is the valor of the liberated, the supreme gesture of the perfect and exemplary person. Mahatma Gandhi, Patrice Lumumba, and Ernesto "Che" Guevara stand out as symbols for world youth; without wavering, they faced death for the people.

2.6.8.4   Finally, only the person who does not fear death is to be feared. That person is free in the face of death who is already free from the comfort that ensnares in its sweet arms the bourgeois of the consumer society. Temperance, as mastery over desires and satisfactions, allows for the correct intepretation of the other's word, guarantees to justice its rightful exercise, and makes it possible for the brave to leave all in order to serve the poor until death. Without discipline there is no liberation.

2.6.9   The Illegality of Goodness

2.6.9.1   Goodness is not to be confused with being a "do-gooder," naive, and uncritical. By goodness I understand the very fountain of the liberating act: human fulness, which is allowed to exteriorize itself in creative works that are revolutionary and innovative. Fearful, timid cowards can hardly create something new if they cannot even resolve the daily problems of their egotistic and totalized individual little worlds. Goodness is magnanimous; it is called to great works and tasks.

2.6.9.2   The liberating act, gratuitous and responsible, the expansion of goodness, confidently propels itself toward the future (not the future of the ontological *proyecto*, which remains the same; its utopia is an imaginary prolongation of the same), toward the real utopia (realization of the other's exteriority, the really utopian pursuit for that which has no place here and now, *ouk topos* in Greek), toward the new order: utopia.

2.6.9.3   The *proyecto* of liberation, the foundation or Being of the future and new order, is not a prolongation of the system (univocal) but re-creation from the provocation or real revelation of the other's exteriority (anadialectical [5.4.1] and thus analagous); the other mobilizes the process. That process is a real criticism of the system; it is a rupture; it is destruction. Goodness, *diffusivum sui*, reveals itself in detotalizing the system or annihilating repressive frontiers.

2.6.9.4   In this way, the liberating act (act of gratuitous goodness), inasmuch as it is beyond intrasystemic interest, is and can only be illegal, contrary to present laws, which, because they are those of an old just order that is now oppressive, are unjust. It is the inevitable position of liberation: subversive illegality.

3

FROM POLITICS TO ANTIFETISHISM

What was discussed in chapter 2 at six levels of reflection (proximity, totality, mediation, exteriority, alienation, and liberation) must now be discussed again in terms of four metaphysical moments: politics, erotics,* pedagogy, and antifetishism. We thus have more problems to resolve. Our discourse, incorporating more and more elements, gains in complexity and allows us to approach reality more concretely.

3.1   POLITICS

3.1.1   *Status Questionis*

3.1.1.1   The proximity from which I set out in this chapter is not that of mother to child; I shall here emphasize the person-to-person relationship (brother-to-brother, sister-to-sister, brother-to-sister, sister-to-brother) or politics insofar as (quantitatively) it has a much greater frontier of influence, and (qualitatively) it functions as the first conditioned conditioner of the other three moments—that is, of erotics (3.2), of pedagogy (3.3), and of antifetishism (3.4).

3.1.1.2   To simplify the exposition, though it is already ab-

---

*The terms "sexuality" and "erotics" are sometimes interchangeable, but erotics is broader and more comprehensive; eroticism extends to nonsexual ambits (e.g., gluttony). See Emmanuel Levinas, *Totality and Infinity* (Pittsburgh: Duquesne University Press, 1969).

breviated, I shall not linger on the moment of political proximity (the thematic of 2.1 on the level of politics), which is to some extent defined in 3.1.3–4; nor shall I here dwell on political mediations (2.3), because they will be taken up to some extent in the exposition of economics (4.4). On the other hand, the word "politics" here has a broad meaning. It includes not only the activity of a politician, a professional in politics, but also all practical, social, human action that is not strictly sexual, pedagogical, or antifetishist. Politics applies as well to the one governing as to the one being governed on the international or national level, to groups and social classes, to social formations and their modes of production, and the like. I want the expression "person-to-person" to suggest this very broad conceptual extension.

3.1.2   Political System

3.1.2.1   The practico-political relationship, person-to-person, always manifests itself within an institutionally structured totality as a historical social formation, and also ultimately under the power of a state. From the clans or tribes of the Paleolithic periods to the villages or cities of the Neolithic, to the confederation of cities or kingdoms (such as those of Mesopotamia of the fourth millennium) or empires (the Persian, Chinese, Roman, Aztec, or Incan, or that of Spain, England, or the United States), political life is systematic. Aristotle, Augustine, Vico, Hegel, and Marx, as well as Parsons, Weber, and Lévi-Strauss, all agree that politics manifests itself as a functional totality. If it is a totality (2.2), it has a foundation or *proyecto,* Being (2.2.5), in a dialectical unfolding (2.2.8), in geopolitical or utopian temporality (toward the future).

3.1.2.2   A political system is an institutional system—that is to say, a whole structured into parts that take charge of occupations or professions, responsibilities shared in diverse modes of productivity. There are shepherds, farmers, goldsmiths, priests, merchants, rulers, and so forth. A function is an occupation or daily routine for performing a task. Each function is organically linked with others, and they form among themselves a functional organic whole. This functionality has been on the increase throughout the centuries; it goes into effect with the birth of a system and little by little, if it can, it reaches a classic epoch. Decline sets in when the functional whole no longer responds to the new demands of a new historical age.

3.1.2.3 The concrete practical whole on the political level can be denominated "social formation." The place where power is exercised is called the state. It is obvious that the state has a relationship with the social classes or stable groups of persons that take form because of the division of labor, ideologico-cultural formation, and other factors (all in relationship to the practical productive totality, which can be broken down into modes of production; 4.4.3). This does not mean that the state does not acquire a certain autonomy relative to social classes (as is the case in certain populisms in dependent capitalism). Political relationships, on the other hand, also depend on social relationships of production that are established among the classes. That is, the practico-political level cannot but take into account the productive person-to-nature relationship (4.3) and because of it the economic person-to-product-to-other relationship (4.4).

3.1.2.4 It is a fact that every political system has a practical model; nevertheless, it could not be formulated explicitly until our epoch. In any case, systems have stability due to the functional institutionality of their organic parts. The political system is a system of systems: not as one that constitutes, but as one that conditions the cultural, military, and other systems.

3.1.3 Political Worldwide Exteriority

3.1.3.1 Beyond the political totality functionally structured, that of structuralism and functionalism, one finds the people—in its worldwide meaning, that of a peripheral nation (2.4.6.2). I define as a people those who are oppressed by a political totality, who maintain a cultural exteriority, the peripheral political other.

3.1.3.2 The oppressed classes, as oppressed, are dysfunctional parts of the structure of a political totality. They are parts that must perform functions that alienate them, impede them from satisfying the needs that the system itself inculcates in them. These exploited and unsatisfied classes long for a new system (3.1.7) because, in addition, they have experience of another world exterior to the system that oppresses them. History is anterior to the oppression a people suffers, and because of this it has a different sense of life; it constitutes another culture.

3.1.3.3 On the international frontier, thanks to the theory of dependence and of unequal development, we are able to discover a worldwide system whose center is the United States and, with relative interdependence, Europe, Japan, and Canada. The rest is oppressed periphery (including even South Africa and Australia). The peoples are the peripheral nations as partial totalities, dependent and dominated, included in an unjust system that suppresses them. The "others" of the empires, of the imperialist capitalist social formation (of the United States, for example), are the Latin American, African, and Asian countries. The exteriority of these nations is not only economic (today they are in great part included in the imperialist system), but historical, political, and cultural as well. This exteriority comes into focus as a distinct manner of living, manipulating, comprehending, and interpreting technological instruments, mediations. The peoples of these nations are peripheral social formations.

3.1.4   National Social Exteriority

3.1.4.1 If the advance of a certain nationalism against an entrenched government was the position of Kemal Atatürk, Gandhi, Sukarno, Nasser, Senghor, Cárdenas, or Perón, nevertheless they differ from a Mao Tse-tung, Ho Chi Minh, Frantz Fanon, Lumumba, Agostinho Neto, Castro, Sandino, or Allende in terms of the concept of a people within a nation. That is to say, anti-imperialism can be purely apparent (as in the case of Golbery de Couto e Silva, Mobutu, the shah of Iran), or it can be equivocal (as in the case of Latin American populisms, the position of the majority of the Arab leaders, or the Congress Party of India), or frankly revolutionary. Anti-imperialism is real when nationalism is defined by the oppressed classes. That is why it is necessary to make precise the notion of a people within a social formation.

3.1.4.2 "The people" can be an oppressed nation (3.1.7); it can also be the oppressed classes within a nation. The geopolitically oppressed classes in the peripheral nations are the rural classes (Amerindians, *campesinos,* sharecroppers, field hands, clans, or tribes); in the national peripheral space they are negated by the centrality of the privileged capitals in those same dependent countries.

3.1.4.3 But the people, besides rural dwellers, also includes the emergent working class that is slowly taking form in the industries set up to reduce dependence on foreign imports.

3.1.4.4 In the peripheral nations there are, then, dominant classes (directors of transnational corporations, oligarchies of landowners, national managerial bourgeoisies, military and technological elites), middle-class sectors (professionals, owners of small businesses, public officials), the oppressed classes (the peasantry, the proletariat), and marginal groups (seasonal laborers, domestic servants, beggars).

3.1.4.5 The peripheral nation as a totality is not a people, except by reason of its oppressed classes.

3.1.4.6 The oppressed or popular classes of dependent nations are the ones that preserve in their own culture (3.3.4) the maximum exteriority of the de facto worldwide system; only they, given their metaphysical alterity, can project a real and new alternative for future humanity.

3.1.5 International Alienation of the Social Formation of Dependent Nations

3.1.5.1 On the international or worldwide level, alienation of peripheral peoples results from imperialism. Philosophically it is founded on North Atlantic ontology. Militarily it is the control of the oceans and continents by means of armed forces and satellites that police the skies. Culturally it is the ideology of the communications media. (It is defined in terms of economics in 4.4.)

3.1.5.2 In effect, the poor countries of the world have become the enemies of the center (2.5.2), as has been seen in the meetings of the United Nations Conference on Trade and Development (UNCTAD) convoked to fix the prices of raw materials. The everyday person of the center, in the process of growing fascism, fears the brown, black, or yellow demographic multitudes. Although they have been totalized and systematically exploited (2.5.4), the center still cannot find rest. Neo-Malthusianism is anxious to check the advance of the periphery.

3.1.5.3   The praxis of imperialistic domination is carried out at two levels: the economic—by the theft of the value added to raw materials by workers subjected to neocolonialism (1.2.4)—and the political—governmental power supported by military control.

3.1.5.4   In effect, hunters killed animals in order to live. Later they used their hunting arms against other persons, and thus the warrior came to prominence. Aided immensely by modern technology, warriors became military professionals. Military art, the science of violence, is the ultimate and most precise essence of the praxis of imperialist domination. It is because of this that the Pentagon carries the responsibility for injustice at the international level of violence in the production and use of arms. Imperialist praxis becomes even more Machiavellian and immoral when it plots the assassination of a political figure of the periphery (the CIA in Chile), or when North American entrepreneurs, according to investigations brought about by the Lockheed scandal, think that it is not wrong to corrupt the buyers of their products in the periphery.

It becomes evident that, in the opinion of North Atlantic ontology, the inhabitants of the periphery are not humans (at least not "like us," as unscrupulous transnational entrepreneurs would say); they can be corrupted and killed like laboratory guinea pigs. This is the praxis of imperialism—a praxis that manifests its inner reality. Philosophies can be very humanistic (within a dominating totality) but, like that of Aristotle or Hegel, they justify the status quo of their own social structure.

3.1.5.5   Within the essence of the ethos of imperialist domination can be found the disciplined certainty of the bureaucrats or fanatics (more dangerous, because of their good and even virtuous consciences, than liars) who are faithful to their daily patriotic and religious duties with the unshakable conviction that they are advancing the cause of civilization, culture, democracy, and freedom by means of blackmail, corruption, exploitation, hunger, assassination—all the suffering of the periphery.

3.1.6   Alienation in National Social Formation

3.1.6.1   Today the classes in the center and in the periphery are qualitatively distinct and even contradictory. Perhaps they will not be tomorrow. The bourgeoisie of the center can exploit the bourgeoisie in the periphery; the proletariat of the center can oppress the proletariat in the periphery. The class doctrines of the nineteenth century and those that carry out analysis only on the national level have not taken into account the difference between classes in the center and in the periphery. Because of this, even orthodox Marxism should be recast from the point of view of geopolitical worldwide spatiality so that it could devise a hermeneutic with appropriate categories.

3.1.6.2   Alienation of the oppressed classes in the periphery is carried out through the drainage of the surplus value of products as they pass from the countryside to the city, from the rural to the urban citizen, from distant provinces or states to national metropolises such as Buenos Aires, Rio de Janeiro, Mexico City, Cairo, Bombay, and Hong Kong. In the industrial centers there is always exploitation of labor by capital (except in socialist countries of the periphery), of workers by owners. Field hands within the country-city framework and the proletariat in the capital-labor framework are the most alienated on the national social level of peripheral social formations.

3.1.6.3   When these classes become conscious that they are dominated, they confront the forces of internal order (ruling and oppressive). Whereas imperialist armies carry on international suppression, it is the professional armies of the periphery—the armed forces of internal occupation and the police for control of the streets (when they are not the political secret police used by fascisms of dependent and underdeveloped capitalism)—that are the agents of national repression. The ethos of social domination is militant and military; it organizes terror, torture, bombings, and kidnapings.

3.1.7   National Liberation from Imperialism

3.1.7.1   Throughout the periphery there is a belated but increasing awareness of the necessity of liberation—that is, the need to break the chains of a dominating dependence. It is at the same time a national political and a cultural reality (of the Latin American, Arabic, African, Hindu, Southwest Asian, and Chinese cultures). The heroes of this historical process are known throughout the world, even if their efforts were not crowned with ultimate success during their lifetime; they are at least symbols of nations that will one day be free. Ho Chi Minh, Mao Tse-tung, Ben Bella, Lumumba, and "Che" Guevara symbolize this new age of world history. The theorists of this phase are Theotonio dos Santos, Enrique Falleto, Frantz Fanon, Samir Amin, Abdel Malek, and their Vietnamese and Chinese colleagues already mentioned. Nevertheless there are not among them philosophers in the strict sense of the word, who gave metaphysical articulation to historical praxis. This book was written to help fill that vacuum.

3.1.7.2 Struggles for the liberation of the periphery—national but at the same time cultural and continental—are very diverse. Each kind of liberation must take into account the prison from which it exits. Hence the models of political liberation confronting imperialism must be very distinct, taking into account the concrete historical exteriority, originality, and alterity of each region and country. The sheer domination of the dominating center cannot intrinsically define any dependent nation; dependency is just one aspect of the national peripheral totality, which does not include one's own national exteriority.

3.1.7.3 Starting from the extreme left and moving toward the extreme right, political parties, pressure groups, and present-day models can be categorized in a fanlike manner: from groups of the new left (from Trotskyite guerillas in Argentina to the leftists of the Chinese cultural revolution, or some groups of Palestinian guerillas), to the popular socialisms (of China, Vietnam, Cuba, and Angola), passing through the popular leftist fronts (such as the Sandinista Front in Nicaragua, the Farabundo Martí Liberation Front in El Salvador), through populisms of diverse inspiration (Cárdenas in Mexico, Vargas in Brazil, Perón in Argentina, Sukarno in Indonesia, Mahatma Gandhi and the Congress Party in India, Nasser in Egypt, Nyerere in black Africa), through modernizing militarisms (such as Velazco Alvarado in Peru, Qaddafi in Libya), to neoliberalisms (the Christian democratic parties in Latin America), to the traditional center-right conservatisms, to dependent capitalist fascisms (such as Golbery do Couto e Silva in Brazil and Pinochet in Chile, among others).

All these models form an immense gamut of political possibilities. Of all of them, nevertheless, only the popular and democratic socialisms prove to be a model of real liberation, of autonomous choice for the periphery. This does not mean that all countries are able to bring this about here and now; but the truth is that the rest of the models, above all the misleading populisms of national liberation with an interclassist front (such as that of Perón and Nasser), betray their inefficiency when, in a crisis, the dominant national classes ally themselves with transnational corporations and with imperialism against the oppressed classes, against the people. Kemal, Nasser, Haya de la Torre, Senghor, and Sukarno fell into this error. If the oppressed classes (3.1.8) do not head up the process, it will revert to dominative dependence or to counterrevolution; in short, there will be no liberation.

3.1.8 Liberation in its Strict Social Sense

3.1.8.1 The political process of liberation runs its course in the national social periphery of the rural and working classes. From the beginning of modernity they have been the ones who accounted for the wealth that colonial empires extracted from their colonies—the Amerindians who mined gold and silver, the blacks sold as slaves, the Asian farmers. They are the world proletariat, the poor in poor nations, the despoiled in despoiled nations. The social revolution of peripheral countries, the taking over of power by the oppressed classes (essentially farm workers and day laborers) is the *conditio sine qua non* for authentic national liberation. There is no other authentic alternative for the future. Only in the liberation of the periphery, within the peoples of the periphery, in its oppressed working classes and rural groupings, is there the possibility of a future world culture that can bring about a qualitative leap to originality, newness. If instead the biological or cultural genocide of peripheral peoples takes place, the center will feed itself on the sameness it has ingrained within itself. "It will eat its own excretion." The death of the child, of the poor, will be its own death.

3.1.8.2 Imperialism and the neocolonial oligarchies in dependent countries permit the creation of employment in the periphery, the founding of industries to substitute for foreign imports, even national development—but never that full power be exercised by the popular masses. Baran and Sweezy, critics of the center, point out that imperialism cannot afford to lose the political control it exercises over peripheral countries, because it would lose markets that yield enormous profits. That is why popular liberation, the seizure of power by popular groups, threatens the very survival of the entire system of the center, of capitalist social formation.

3.1.8.3   Liberation implies the taking over of power by the popular classes in order to organize "social formation." Philosophy of liberation, on its political level, must be very clear about this; otherwise it could deteriorate into a confusing, misleading, reformist, or petit bourgeoisie ontological ideology. The political philosophy of our epoch can no longer divide governments into monarchies, aristocracies, and democracies, as did the conservative Aristotle (who wrote his *Politics* to "save" or "conserve" the *polis*, revolution being political evil itself—that is, antiliberation). Today nations are divided into states and social formations of the center and of the periphery. The center exercises hegemony through imperialism of a multinational, operative, capitalistic type. In the center there are semidependent states, such as Western Europe and Japan. In the periphery there are social formations, states, that are free because of the efforts of the people, such as Cuba, Vietnam, China, Angola, and Nicaragua; the intermediary imperialist class (the dominant oligarchical or bourgeois class) has disappeared. There are also social formations, peripheral states, in search of development in diverse postures within capitalism (3.1.7). And there are fascist models of dependent capitalism in the current phase of imperialism.

3.1.9   The *Proyecto* and Dignity of Liberating Praxis

3.1.9.1   The liberating politician is the prototype of the statesman, especially if we keep in mind that within contemporary peripheral social formations the last court of appeals is political. I am not referring to antiheroes—Caesar, Cortes, Napoleon, Hitler, and those responsible for the wars in Vietnam and Angola. I am referring to Joan of Arc, Washington, Bolívar, San Martín, Agostinho Neto, Castro, Mao, and those who give up their lives for the oppressed. Their liberation struggle negates the negation of the oppressed and affirms their exteriority. They are like Moses or Muhammad, symbols of a people that is born, that grows, that lives. They are prophets of life, not of death; founders of freedom, not its assassins. Between George Washington and Henry Kissinger (now that his responsibility for Allende's downfall has been established) there is the passage from the creation of a new state in justice to the decadent maintenance of an empire of injustice and oppression.

3.1.9.2 The *proyecto* of liberation that a people carries affirmatively in its culture is the future common good, the positive, authentic, human, ethical utopia. It is because of this that life itself is interpreted by the valiant as a mediation (2.3).

3.1.9.3 The *proyecto* of liberation, future Being (non-Being in the present system), is the analectical foundation (abysmal, chaotic, and anarchic for the present system; (5.3) toward which liberating praxis throws itself vehemently, anxiously, and totally. When the traitorous soldier was about to plunge his bayonet in Lumumba's entrails, that hero exclaimed, "All for the liberation of the African people!" His life was an offering and homage in the *proyecto* of a new country. The supreme moment of his liberative praxis was his own death. His blood fertilizes the birth of a new Africa. That is why his subversive praxis was ethical; what he undertook—destruction of the old, the dead—was metaphysical.

3.1.9.4 Political systems or social formations go through four structural moments that are analogous but never identical. The period of liberation begins with resistance to oppression, repression; it takes up the struggle that dominators have necessitated (for them it is perverse) and to which those who are liberated respond (for them it is honorable, good, heroic).

The second period entails the organizations of the state and a new mode of production. It is the time of Lincoln, of Lenin, of Borge. It is the time for justice; there is room for everyone; there is much to do; everything lies ahead. Liberation is a time of struggle (because of this, a time of military priority, but of the nonprofessional military). Joan of Arc was a shepherd, Washington a gentleman farmer, Hidalgo a priest, Belgrano a lawyer, Trotsky an intellectual, Mao a teacher, "Che" Guevara a medical student, Camilo Torres a priest, Lumumba a teacher, Agostinho Neto a poet, Sandino a worker. They were civilians; their military valor was civil patriotism. At the moment of reconstruction the great politicians appear (military art gives place to political wisdom in its authentic liberating sense).

The third period is the classic epoch, stabilization, the slow ascent. Patrician creators give place to the elders (the senate), to conservatives.

The fourth phase is at the same time one of splendor and of decadence. It is in this phase that the state and the social formation jell; the productive forces grow; the domination of the oppressed becomes repression. Again military art acquires a primacy, although not as the valor of the civilian but as the discipline of military bureaucracy, of a profession that must be entrenched. It is the epoch of the empires, of bread and circus, of the slaughter of liberators because they are subversives. It is the time of the Pentagon, of control of the frontiers, of not allowing the barbarians to cross the Danube . . . or Mexicans to cross the Rio Grande.

3.1.9.5   During the time of liberation, of praxis as service, ethos is structured around the virtues of fortitude, just valor, patient prudence, and temperance that is estranged from comfort because it is ready to give all—even life itself, if necessary—for the new homeland. The empathetic pulsion of alterity for the poor, the oppressed, the people, is the liberating ethos, the unquenchable fire that feeds on the limitless generosity that is the measure of all other human gratuitousness. An awesome responsibility, more overwhelming than imprisonment or torture, mobilizes the liberator to project history toward a more just and more human goal.

3.2   EROTICS

3.2.1   *Status Questionis*

3.2.1.1   Political injustice is parricide, the death of a brother, of a sister, of a close relative. Injustice or perversion on the erotic level is uxoricide (death of the woman in a society where macho phallocratic ideology reigns, as we shall see). Erotics defines the man-woman relationship. We should never confuse the human being (species) or person with the man (masculine person) or the woman (feminine person).

3.2.1.2 From the multitude of persons in the ebb and flow of everyday life, suddenly there emerges someone who is no longer merely a colleague, a fellow citizen, but a woman for the man, a man for the woman. Sexual exteriority is cut off from political totality; the political experience is different from the sexual experience, which is touch and contact with the intention of sensitizing the body of the other. The erotic is a new chapter in metaphysics.

3.2.2 Erotic World

3.2.2.1 The *ego cogito* had favored the cognitional aspect of human nature. Thanks to Freud, the *ich wünsche* (I desire) was rediscovered. And the assertion can be made that the *ego* of the *ego cogito* has been a phallic masculine *ego*. (Descartes negated his mother, his lover, and his daughter. He searched for total solipsism.) Freud, inasmuch as his intention was therapeutic, did not describe sexuality as, for example, Merleau-Ponty would describe it.

3.2.2.2 Plato affirms in the *Symposium* that ever since the androgyny (a strange being formed by a woman-man) separated into two beings, men have loved women—that is, they seek the return to "the same" (*to auto*). Aristotle agrees in saying that sexuality, in its finality, brings it about that "the same [the species] remains the same" by means of procreation. If the man penetrates the woman, it is only so that through conception the eternal species may attain immortality. We have already noted that at the peak of the Middle Ages Thomas Aquinas teaches that "the mother only supplies the matter, but it is the father who gives Being to the child." "The same" is the phallic; it is the *eros* that desires sameness. Morever, with the contempt of the body came contempt of sexuality.

3.2.2.3 It is only in our epoch, at the end of the nineteenth century, that there begins an anti-Cartesian, antidualist reappraisal of the ancient doctrine of the dual—body-soul—substantiality. Merleau-Ponty affirms that the normal person can constitute a sexual intention. Such an intention consists in sexualizing an object, the body of the other. Sexuality would be a sensitization of the body of the other. One's whole world is eroticized when this intention, which is not a mere representation or a mere biological determination, is constituted. It demarcates a phenomenological region proper to oneself. This intention energizes the erotic situation; it knows how to maintain it and give it continuity until its accomplished fulfillment.

3.2.3   Erotic Exteriority

3.2.3.1   The world eroticized as a totality tends to ignore the other by the pulsion of totalization (and because of this it is a schizoid or closed world; 3.2.5–6). On the contrary, normal human sexuality begins with "Let her kiss me with the kisses of her mouth," "Let him kiss me with the kisses of his mouth." It is the proximity that sets limits to and overcomes the erotic world that constitutes sexualized objects. Before the sexualization of the object, beyond the sexual object (Freud's *Sexualobjekt*), the other provokes distinct sexuality. The other, male for the female and female for the male, not different but distinct (2.4.4.2), advances from political distance to the proximity of the kiss, or *eros*, of coitus. Maximum distinction becomes maximum convergence: proximity in nakedness (because dress de-eroticizes the political or pedagogical relationship but is an impediment for *eros*), in beauty, the *pulchritudo prima* that measures all other beauty.

3.2.3.2   If we can surpass the body-soul dualism and affirm the unity of the flesh (*basar* in Hebrew), we shall be able to understand that the sexual, even more than the sensibility of the other's body, means complying with the other's desire as other, as another flesh, as exteriority. The person, subject to the pulsion of alterity (unknown to Freud), by which one tends to the other as other, really touches what is beyond the horizon of light or of ontology. The erotic, which is authentic metaphysics, advances to the shadowy area where the other dwells. The other, whose sexuality invites me to the complementarity of absence, can never be taken as a mere object or thing. On the contrary, upon losing one's alterity one also loses the capacity for the plenitude of *eros*, gratuity, self-donation, freedom, justice.

3.2.3.3   The exteriority of the other as the possibility of negation of provocation is the very origin of human orgasmic realization.

3.2.4 The Metaphysics of Eros

3.2.4.1 Sexual intention begins by touch, contact, caress. Caressing is nearness, proximity; it is a progression restrained by modesty but tempted to profanation; it is a growing and voluptuous "exploration," in which two persons advance and draw back, asking the other as other, without words, whether their desires are mutual. It is secretly stretching out one's hand in the night beyond Being and light (the ontological), without looking for or clarifying any sense (the phenomenological), without intending to set any value. The caress advances, avoiding encounter with resistance from the freedom of the other, which is always possible. Nudity always tends to the sadism of violation or the masochism of being violated. Alejo Carpentier tells us that "close to Rosario I shared the primal sensation of beauty, beauty physically perceived, enjoyed equally by the body and the mind, which is born with each rebirth of the sun."

3.2.4.2 The closeness-farness rhythm, which is the summary of all life and history, is lived in the act of coitus (through the contact of the phallus with feminine flesh and of the clitoris with masculine flesh) in a cadence that grows until it arrives at the ecstatic paroxysm where subjectivity and the "I" decentralize in order to become totalized in the embrace of mutual voluptuosity—if it is done in justice—of orgasm.

3.2.4.3 Coitus is one of the privileged metaphysical experiences of the human being. It is access to the area of reality beyond the horizon of the world. It is beyond reason, where desire takes us as a satisfaction of the other's desire. It is no longer a mere desire or other-directed pulsion but the very realization of desire in proximity. The sexual organ is in the human being the presence in totality of the absence of the other; it is a call to the realization of the other in the other's negativity.

3.2.5 Uxoricidal Machismo

3.2.5.1 The death of one's brother or sister, fratricide or sororicide, is political alienation. In our culture and epoch the death of *eros* is the assassination of the woman: uxoricide. The macho ideology is the counterpart of uxoricide. The best European diagnosis of machismo has been proposed by Freud. He clearly saw that "sexuality is by nature masculine," and because of this the phallus was defined as constituent and active and the vagina as passive and constituted, the sexual object. "Being is; non-Being is not" in erotic ontology should be stated: "The phallus is; castration is not." That is, woman is not; she is only an object, as was the Amerindian, the African, the Asian, the poor nations, the oppressed classes, the politically disenfranchised. If the constituent "I" is the "phallic *ego*," then the Being of machismo, the foundation of the alienating sexual totality is "phallicity" (the phallus as phallus). It can then be understood that if woman is not, in non-Being everything is indistinct: *En la noche todos los gatos son pardos* ("at night all cats are dusky"). The phallus can no longer perform the sexual act because upon entering into relationship with the sexual object (woman), the man enters indifferently into commerce with his mother and wife (because in non-Being there can be no difference, not even between the clitoral-vaginal intentionality of the wife and the mammary-oral intentionality of the mother; the woman is indistinctly mother-wife). The ontic, concrete, sexual act is always incestuous.

3.2.5.2   From Being as abstract or fundamental phallicity, the *imago patris*, which Mitscherlich does not define adequately, stretches out the horizon of the comprehension of all erotic relationships. It is there, within the alienation of the woman, that the oedipal situation arises. The son's love of his mother is ambiguous (at least as far as the father is concerned); the father, the phallic *ego*, sets up his son as his opposition, for he has intercourse with non-Being, the sexual object, his woman (wife)—the same woman (mother) whom the son also tries to totalize (in reality it is the unsatisfied woman who totalizes herself through her son). In the conflictive presence of an actual phallus (the father) and a potential phallus (the son), confronting the same woman (without difference between mother-wife but defined as object-woman), the son cannot help repressing his phallicity and remain forever in a neurotic, pathological, perverse condition of desiring incest.

3.2.5.3   Machismo, as an ideology that cloaks the domination of woman defined as sexual object, not only alienates the woman but also makes the male impotent inasmuch as it impedes his relationship with a woman. He turns to solipsistic masturbation, to something that fulfills his autoeroticism.

3.2.6   Eroticism and Political Domination

3.2.6.1   Phallocracy, constituent domination by the phallus, is sometimes a substitute for or a determinant of plutocracy. In the process of the conquest of Latin America, the European not only dominated the Amerindian man but violated the Amerindian woman. Cortes lived in concubinage with Malinche, an Amerindian. The *ego cogito* establishes ontologically both the "I conquer" and the phallic *ego*, two dimensions of domination of person over person, but now of one class over another class, of one nation over another nation. Sexuality is thus a replica of political, economic, cultural domination.

3.2.6.2   On the world level, the problematic of sexual alienation has been given little or no study. In some African cultures it is not so much the father, mythical ancestor and protector, but the older brother of the mother who fulfills the function of the repressive, castrating, phallic *imago*. The manifestation of prostitution as a phenomenon of the popular classes, in the center as well as in the periphery, shows phallic domination concomitant with economic domination. The tango *Margot* by Celedonio Flores (1918) narrates the sadness of a poor boy from a peripheral barrio in Buenos Aires on seeing his loved one, Margarita, a shanty town girl, become transformed into the plaything of a wealthy man from the city center (and that is why she adopts the rococo French name Margot).

3.2.6.3   The woman of the people, the woman within a peripheral culture, ends by undergoing a threefold attack, a triple violation: violated for being from an oppressed culture and nation, for being a member of a dominated class, for being a member of a dominated sex. She is a poor woman of the poor—Indian, African, or Asian—victim of imperialism, of class struggle, and of macho ideology.

3.2.7   Erotic Liberation

3.2.7.1   The liberation of *eros* will be accomplished through the liberation of woman, which will allow the male to regain part of the sensitivity lost in the the macho ideology. Liberation from the ancient patriarchalism (which the Indo-Europeans and Semites transmitted for millennia) is liberation of the woman who has always been defined as castrated, as nonphallic. It is necessary to begin again.

3.2.7.2   Just as the male has an active, constituent, phallic openness (*Offenheit*) to the world, so also has the woman, as wife, an active, constituent clitoral-vaginal openness (to the phallus of the husband), and as mother a mammary openness (to the suckling of the infant). Positively defined (phallic non-Being is really something distinct: active clitoral-vaginal reality), woman has a distinct and positive orientation with respect to the male (clitoral-vaginal) and to the child (mammary-oral). Liberation is not merely negation of domination by the negation of sexual diversity (as when feminism champions homosexuality, test-tube babies, etc.). Liberation is real sexual distinction: the male affirms his phallic openness (with what risk that may entail) and the woman equally affirms her clitoral-vaginal and mammary-oral openness (in her dimension as wife and mother; 4.2.6.2).

3.2.7.3   In this manner coital proximity, the praxis of the liberation of the other as other, the sexual rhythm as a liturgy in respect for the other, fulfills the desire of the other as other, as sexed in another way, as erotic alterity. Only in the real exteriority of the other, a free and sexually distinct other, can orgasm be a human act that gives full sway to the political and the pedagogical.

3.2.7.4   Detotalization, deobjectification, or distinction of the woman is the *conditio sine qua non* for normalcy, which is nonpathological, nonrepressive of *eros*.

3.2.8   The New Home

3.2.8.1   The orgasmic plenitude of human love between male and female constitutes the foundation, the essence, the nucleus of home. In the center of home is the fire, the hearth—a hearth that warms, that protects against wild animals and the elements, that lights up the domestic world, that cooks the food, that exudes intimacy. Hearth, wood, mother. The proto-home, the first home, is a dwelling centered around the hearth and the male-female proximity. Proto-home, unique and circular dwelling—proto-kitchen, proto-bedroom, proto-dining room, proto-living room. It is an all-purpose, unicameral dwelling, not yet partitioned into the house of multiple rooms and functions. The essence of the home is the warmth of *eros*.

3.2.8.2 Male and female joined in the warmth of coitus is a new analogical unit: the couple. The couple is equivocal; it can be totalized. If it is totalized, someone will be assassinated again—the other, the child (filicide is pedagogical alienation par excellence; 3.3.5).

3.2.8.3 Through fecundity the couple opens to the child. Only in this way, in the complex couple-child relationship, does the home appear. The home is a basic totality that prefigures all the remaining totalities: male-female erotics, parent-children pedagogy, sibling politics. All of them together around the table, the hearth, constitute the home, the family. All of them are together there before they are together in the political assembly or the apprenticeship classroom.

3.2.8.4 The macho ideology alienates the woman; the alienated woman distorts the child; the distorted child is ready for political injustice. The liberation of woman does away with machismo and permits the appearance of the couple who are equals (sexually distinct but persons [faces] with equal right to life, work, education, politics, etc.). The couple permits the appearance of offspring, of siblings. The death of the old house, that of the phallic family, permits the appearance of a new home, the liberated home where there reigns an expansive, innovative, fecund, nontraumatic sexuality.

3.2.9   The *Proyecto* and Praxis of Erotic Liberation

3.2.9.1 Phallic ontology conceives of human erotic perfection as asexuality. Given the fact that "phallicity" (Being as phallus as phallus) falls into an irresolvable aporia (all phallic acts are incestuous: they are directed toward mother and wife at the same time), the only way to be perfect is through *ataraxia* (imperturbability) or *apatheia* (apathy): the supreme pleasure is contemplation. This is castration by sublimation, the only moral solution to the macho ideology. Its counterpart is the morality of *parthenos* (the virgin offered to the sacred phallus). This cannot be the *proyecto* of erotic liberation.

3.2.9.2   In the periphery—as well as in the center, but with easily understandable differences—aristocratic families, oligarchies, and elites preserve fetishist practices that have been inherited from conquistadors, colonizers, oppressors, and imperial bureaucrats or institutions imposed by the communications media. Concubinage with aborigines, with black slaves, and prostitution of the working-class girl are among those practices. To liberate the cultural eroticism of dependent peoples and cultures and that of the popular classes, to give them back their dignity, could be the goal of a worldwide campaign for sexual liberation.

3.2.9.3   Inasmuch as sexual intercourse involves exposure in the presence of the other in nudity, it is always a risk; the other can instrumentalize me or play with my obliging gratitude. It seems that the one who has no doubt about the other has already instrumentalized that person as a sex object. In this case, there is no risk, because alienating totality has already been established and the act is intrinsically perverse, autoerotic. On the contrary, if it is an authentic, obliging sexual openness (in whose serving of the other's desire the praxis of erotic liberation is fulfilled), the response of the other can always be reifying. Nudity that does not blush is not authentic human sexuality. One can always fear being used by the other. Fear, always possible, that is the guarantee of authentic, other-directed sexuality, is modesty. Modesty complements erotic beauty and accompanies its fullest realization in justice.

3.2.9.4   A Chinese poet writes in the *Chi-King*: "A son is born. He is placed on the bed and wrapped up in rich cloth. The lord, the chief, the sovereign is born. A daughter is born. Wrapped up in common cloth, she is placed on the floor. There is in her neither good nor evil. Let her learn how to prepare wine, how to cook meals. Behold what she ought to know."

3.2.9.5   The wife of the man in the oppressed classes and peoples is today the dominated one par excellence in the world. A Latin American gaucho, Martín Fierro, sings sadly of his misfortunes:

> And my poor wife,
> God knows how much she suffered!

They tell me she took flight
with I don't know what hawk
without doubt to look for the bread
that I could not give her.

3.3   PEDAGOGICS

3.3.1   *Status Questionis*

3.3.1.1   The pedagogic has to do with the parent-child, teacher-pupil proximity at the point where politics and erotics converge. The child born in the home is educated in order to form part of a political community; the child born in a culture is expected to found a home. That is why pedagogical discourse is always twofold, and the planes continually become confused. This matter has been more or less well stated in what is called the "second Oedipus complex." The young man in his adolescence again situates himself in an oedipal conflict, but now in a socio-psychoanalytical context. The pulsion toward the mother is at the same time toward the ancestral, the popular culture; the interposition of the father is likewise that of society or the state. His "ego ideal" (father-state) is in crisis. The young man cannot identify with a decadent *imago patris*; the oedipal conflict persists, and its revelation is youthful rebellion as a symptom of sexual and political repression.

3.3.1.2   Pedagogics occupies itself with the education of not only the child, the pupil, in the family but also of the young and the people as a whole in educational, scientific, and technological institutions, and by the mass media. It is ideological and cultural schooling.

3.3.2   Pedagogical Systems

3.3.2.1   As long as humankind has been in existence, there has been transmitted to a new generation, to the child, the totality of mediations that constitute the world. The transmission of accumulated culture is accomplished by pedagogical systems, from the most ancient and simple (such as teaching how to polish a stone) to the most recent and complex (such as putting satellites in orbit or making decisions by computers). It is evident that in proportion as there is more to transmit (quantitatively and qualitatively) pedagogical systems have become better. From the simple advice of the father in the Paleolithic Age they have reached the universities and research institutes of the highest technological precision.

3.3.2.2   The domestic pedagogical system educates within the traditional ethos of the people, within the social class of the family. The system can be patriarchal, where the male dominates the female, and the couple dominates the child. This pedagogical system is erotically uxoricidal but pedagogically filicidal (3.3.5). The oedipal situation is inherent in certain pedagogical systems, but not others—that is, if we can trust certain conclusions of Margaret Mead. In any event, the character of future citizens depends on the manner in which their personality has been sexually forged in the home, in proximity with the mother and in correlation with the presence of the father and siblings.

3.3.2.3   The pedagogical system, political or social, also educates within the prevailing social ethos, but sometimes there are supplemental institutions, such as the ancient schools of the *amautas* (sages) of the Incan empire or the priests in ancient Egypt. These institutions are not dispersed moments; they form systems. The educational system and the mass media are today the two most important systems in the formation of the average person.

3.3.3   Erotic Pedagogical Exteriority

3.3.3.1   Exterior to the systems of education already in place, a new person, an other, is born. Husband and wife, if they decide in freedom and gratuity to give reality to someone who is not yet, constitute themselves as that one's origin, in the procreative fecundity that proceeds from nothingness to the reality of the child. The child is a newness, the new one, the one who seals the reality of the sexual male-female union as husband and wife. Paternity-maternity (a new qualitative moment added to mere masculinity-femininity) is correlative to filiality. The metaphysical moment, with which we have been concerned all along in this work, is clearly revealed.

3.3.3.2   The politically responsible person can take charge of the poor or oppressed already there. The sexually responsible person can take charge of the violated woman in a macho world. But in pedagogics metaphysical anteriority shows itself in a still better manner, anterior to ontological anteriority: the anteriority of the freedom of progenitors. From procreative freedom a child is brought forth into the light of the world, the real future that is utopian criticism because it is exterior to the organized, traditional, already given order. Procreative fecundity and the responsibility for justice are what give reality to the new order, the new person.

3.3.3.3   The child is the exteriority of all erotics, its metaphysical goal, its real fulfillment (4.1.5.5). Moreover, the child is distinct, not merely different, from the couple; the child is the other from whom one always has to learn how to listen in silence to the new revelation that is brought to past history as tradition. The child is innovation itself, new time and, therefore, eschatological; the child is ultimate time. That is why in the presence of the new one, in the presence of mystery, we ought to have a sacred respect and silence in order to learn how to listen to the provocative voice that makes tradition fruitful and makes it history.

3.3.4   Political Pedagogical Exteriority

3.3.4.1   The child, the new one, is not an orphan; it is the offspring of its parents and of a people. The progeny of a people is its youth; and it is the people itself inasmuch as it is oppressed, inasmuch as it is cultural exteriority. The peripheral nation, or Latin American, African, or Asiatic culture, is exterior to the reigning cultural system, that of the center. The exteriority of national culture provokes and questions the hegemonic cultural system. And in those same peripheral nations there are the oppressed, rural manual laborers, marginal classes; within each nation they play the role of cultural exteriority.

3.3.4.2   The African, Asiatic, and Latin American cultures have their own validity, which has not been understood by or incorporated into the hegemonic school or university systems or their public communications media, because they are scorned as nonculture, barbarism, illiteracy, witchcraft. They are interpreted by the reigning, rationalistic, would-be universal cultural system as nothing, non-Being, chaos, irrationality. The scorn that is held for these cultures is analogous to the scorn that the father of Oedipus had for his son, phallus in potency and therefore despised.

3.3.4.3   The culture of the oppressed groups and classes of these three continents—popular culture—is the one that preserves the best of the Third World and is the one whence new alternatives will emerge for future world culture, which will not be a mere replication of the structures of the center. The exteriority of popular culture is the best guarantee and the least contaminated nucleus of the new humankind. Its values, scorned today and not even recognized by the people itself, must be studied carefully; they must be augmented within a new pedagogy of the oppressed in order to develop their possibilities. It is within popular culture, even traditional culture, that cultural revolution will find its most authentic content.

3.3.5   Filicide

3.3.5.1   The physical or cultural death of the child is pedagogical alienation. The child is killed in the womb of the mother by abortion or in the womb of the people by cultural repression. This repression will always be carried out in the name of freedom, of course, and by means of the best pedagogical methods.

3.3.5.2   Huitzilopochtli, the Aztec sun god, said to the falcon god, in a popular myth, that in order to go out each day he needed the blood of children, of the young. The old god needed young blood. It is the mythical death of the child! Socrates, as mentioned before, likewise kills the young, making them believe that the (Greek) answers toward which he subtly directed his disciples were nothing less than the eternal and divine truths (he divinized Greek culture). But let us consider a still more subtle dominator.

3.3.5.3   Jean-Jacques Rousseau idealized, in the name of nature, the emergent bourgeois culture. For this he first needed to enter into a pedagogical contract with his pupil (complementary to a social contract). The preceptor (the father or the state) obliges the pupil to be or to behave like an orphan (without mother and hence without popular culture) and to be odedient in everything, as Rousseau explains in *Emile*. Claiming that nature expresses itself in reality, the repressing preceptor obliges Emile to follow a fixed curriculum tenaciously in order to merit his title of petit bourgeois, with even a European tour (the delight of the bourgeoisie of the time) and with a perfectly docile wife, a repressed housewife.

Rousseau's *proyecto* is ideological in two ways: first because he disguises the bourgeois class as *nature*; then, because he does not give any critical attention to this cover-up and makes Emile accept, in the name of criticism, a course of action in all naivety. Pestalozzi, Montessori, and Dewey do no more than continue on the same ideological road, perfecting the process of domestication with more modern techniques.

3.3.5.4   Poor repressed Oedipus is the product of a modern macho, individualistic education, which finishes by educating the wolf that Hobbes needed, the person who is ready to fight always and anywhere in order to subsist in a world of competition.

3.3.6   Portrait of the Colonized

3.3.6.1   Albert Memmi and Frantz Fanon portray the visage of the politico-culturally domesticated person in the periphery. In order to understand this topic we must make certain distinctions.

3.3.6.2   By "imperialist culture" or "culture of the center" I mean the culture that dominates in the present order. It is the refined culture of European and North American elites. This is the culture that all other cultures are measured against. The *Mona Lisa* critiques all other paintings; Beethoven's Fifth Symphony catalogs all other musical compositions; Notre Dame is the prototype of all churches. And this culture has the collective means of communication in its hands (the United States originates and transmits 80 percent of the material that is used in Latin America by daily newspapers, magazines, radio, movies, and television).

3.3.6.3   This culture is partially refracted in the oligarchical culture of dominant groups within dependent nations of the periphery. It is the culture that they admire and imitate, fascinated by the artistic, scientific, and technological progress of the center. These elites, alienated minorities in their own nations, are scorned by the creators of the culture of the center. Someone is black and plays the piano!—as if a hyena were to perform acrobatics or a donkey to play the flute. On the masks of these local elites the face of the center is duplicated. They ignore their national culture; they despise their skin color; they pretend to be white; they speak English or French; they dress, eat, and live as if they were in the center. They are the outcasts of history.

3.3.6.4   The culture of the oppressed, not as a people (3.3.8) but as repressed, is the culture of the masses. It is the reproduction *ad nauseam*, the *Kitsch* vulgarization, of imperialist culture refracted by the oligarchical culture and passed on for consumption by magazines, pulp novels, pornography, and the like.

3.3.6.5   This entire process of cultural alienation is profoundly ideological inasmuch as it expresses supposedly universal knowledge or ideas (because they are those of the center) and inasmuch as it hides the domination that oppressed countries and classes suffer. It is by means of the culture of the masses that ideology propagates imperialist enterprises and produces a market for its products (4.3.3). Cultural domination is thus an element of political (3.1.5-6) and economic (4.4.6-7) alienation; it is like the vanguard of the army that reconnoiters the terrain for the next attack. Ideological cultural imperialism today surpasses all other types of anterior cultural influx, and it is assured of all the support of the sciences and of those whom Chomsky calls "intellectual warriors," the elite formed at Harvard or Yale.

3.3.7   Anti-Oedipus

3.3.7.1   To liberate the son is the task of metaphysical pedagogics. Neither the father nor the son must be assassinated. In reality in *Totem and Tabu* it is not the father who is killed but the old man, inasmuch as he is overcome because he can no longer dominate his sons, now adults. The oedipal situation is an alienating and alienated situation. To allow the son to be, so that Oedipus grows as another, as the anti-Oedipus, is to respect him in his exteriority. Of course, to avoid committing filicide he ought not to have committed uxoricide.

3.3.7.2   A free woman allows for the appearance of a real couple. The orgasmically fulfilled couple engenders the child in love. The parents are responsible for its distinct alterity; they listen with devotion to the child's cry, protest, and juvenile criticism. If there is no castrating father, there is no castrating mother, and the son is defined not as phallus, potentially an enemy, but as mouth-hands-feet that attaches himself in order to obtain nourishment. Thus he does not address the woman in her clitoral-vaginal openness but in her nourishing, protective, soft, and warm maternal breasts. In the nipple-mouth proximity, the child, fulfilled, not repressed, slowly and surely starts on the road of alterity that will take it to adult sexuality and politics.

3.3.8 Liberation of Popular Culture

3.3.8.1 The liberation of the oppressed is put into effect by the oppressed, but through the mediation of the critical mentality of the teacher, the leader, the organic intellectual*—with and within the people.

3.3.8.2 Beyond the oligarchical culture of the dominating elites can be found the national culture, an equivocal culture because it includes oligarchical conditioning. In any event, the affirmation of national culture is a liberating confrontation with imperialist culture and a first necessary step on the road of the cultural revolution of the periphery.

3.3.8.3 Popular culture includes the culture of the masses, the oppressed as oppressed, and reflects imperialist culture and the properly distinct exteriority of oppressed groups. The cultural revolution by liberation must start and must be put into effect by the people and from within its popular culture. Such a culture possesses the symbols, the values, the uses, and the traditions of accumulated wisdom, as well as the memory of historical commitments; it knows its enemies, its friends, and its allies. Popular culture, far from being a minor culture, is the relatively least contaminated and radiative nucleus of resistance to oppressors by the oppressed. But it does not come to life spontaneously.

3.3.8.4 A people alone cannot liberate itself. The system has contaminated it with the culture of the masses, the worst thing

---

*The term "organic intellectual" was popularized by Antonio Gramsci. It refers to an intellectual who does not live in an ivory tower—who lives and works in and with the people, as an "organ" in the body politic.

that the system has to offer. It is because of this that the critical mentality of the organic intellectual, of critical communities or political parties, is indispensable so that a people acquire a critical mentality and discern the worst that it has in itself (introjected imperialist culture) and the best that it has from antiquity (cultural exteriority, the maximum of potential criticism without actual awareness). Philosophy has much to do in this field (5.9.5).

3.3.9 The *Proyecto* and Praxis of Pedagogical Liberation

3.3.9.1 The *proyecto* of pedagogical domination annihilates the culture of peripheral nations and oppressed classes. The *proyecto* of pedagogical liberation, on the other hand, which opposes the "passivity" of the student, as Paulo Freire would say, affirms what the people has of exteriority, of its own values. The *proyecto* of pedagogical liberation is not formulated by teachers; it is already in the consciousness of the people. It is the metaphysical *a priori* of the process, the one toward which there is a broad proclivity arising from protracted popular struggle, the *proyecto* of "the excellent ancient popular culture," Mao would say.

3.3.9.2 This *proyecto*, it is true, can be attempted by the converted colonized, the intelligentsia that discovers its own people. Frantz Fanon would say that in the first phase colonized intellectuals assimilate the culture of (imperialist) occupiers. In a second phase they recoil from what they have done and resolve to return to the people. Finally, in a third period, after having tried to lose themselves within the people, to identify with the people, they come to understand that they must shake the people. Instead of favoring the people's lethargy they become the ones who awaken the people. Nevertheless, the critical action of the organic intellectual is not sufficient, as Gramsci would say.

3.3.9.3 What is needed is the revolutionary worker from within the popular culture, a person of the people, who has never left the people but maintains a critical attitude, the one who leads a people to its own cultural affirmation. Until a critical alertness is formed within the praxis of popular leaders, all education will be elitist and dominative.

3.3.9.4 The ethos of pedagogical liberation demands that the teacher know how to listen with respect in silence to youth, to the people. Only the genuine teacher who has become a patient and enthusiastic disciple can attain to an adequate discernment of the reality in which a people finds itself. Pupils, the young, and the people admire teachers who, in their lifestyle, in their living together with them, in their humility and service, dedicate a critical awareness to affirming the values inherent in the young and in the people. Such teachers manifest a collaboration that unifies, mobilizes, organizes, and creates.

Anti-ideological veracity is the fundamental pedagogical attitude. It is an uncovering of the deceits of the sytem, a negation or destruction of what the system has introduced to contaminate the people, and an affirmative construction of cultural exteriority. To perform this task today in the periphery is to risk death because critics, the ones who demand a more just future, are the first to be jailed, eliminated, assassinated. But they are the harbingers of what is to come. I have suffered it in my own flesh, and many colleagues and companions have suffered it also.

3.3.9.5   From liberating revolutionary culture will spring forth a new world culture, an alternative much richer than imperialist culture. We shall say with the poet Carlos Fuentes, "You, my son, will be my triumph; the triumph of woman. . . . Malinxochitl, goddess of the dawn. . . . Tonantzin, Guadalupe, mother."

3.4   ANTIFETISHISM

3.4.1   *Status Questionis*

3.4.1.1   We are here at the origin and the end of metaphysics. It is a matter of archeology, if *arche* signifies source or spring whence everything proceeds and toward which everything tends (more *Abgrund* than *Grund* or *Ursache*; more abyss than foundation or cause). In this section our discourse reaches its end and confronts itself with the phenomenon of fetishism. I call "fetishization" the process by which a totality is made absolute, closed, divinized. Political totality is fetishized when it takes over within imperialism (3.1.5) or nationalistic totalitarianism (3.1.1). Erotic totality is fetishized when it succumbs to fascination with the perverse phallus of macho ideology (3.2.5–6). Cultural totality is fetishized when oligarchical ideology alienates popular culture (3.3.6) or castrates the son (3.3.5). Fetishism is the death of totality, of the system, of discourse.

3.4.1.2   Antifetishism, a negative notion that deliberately tries to veil its infinite metaphysical affirmation, is the guarantee of the perennial dialectic of history, of the detotalization that liberation produces in all fossilized systems. Atheism vis-à-vis the present system is a prerequisite for innovative, procreative, liberative praxis.

3.4.2   Fetishization of the System

3.4.2.1   The English word "fetish" comes from the French *fétiche,* derived from the Portuguese *feitiço,* derived from the Latin *facticius*, "factitious." A fetish is something made by the human hand but made to appear divine, absolute, worthy of worship, fascinating, tremendous, that before which one trembles in fear, terror, or admiration. Every system tends to fetishize, totalize, absolutize itself.

3.4.2.2   When a political system attains central power, geopolitically, economically, and militarily speaking, it divinizes itself: "Hail, Caesar!" declared the gladiators before dying. "The Spaniards immolate a great number of Indians to their god, which is gold," it was said in sixteenth-century Latin America. *Gott ist mit uns* was written close to the swastika in Nazi Germany. "In God we trust" is printed on the U.S. dollar (which moreover has a symbol of the Trinity on it, the eye of divine wisdom, and other fetishistic symbols). The doctrine of "national security," upheld by the CIA, is affirmed in Brazil in terms of the defense of Western and Christian civilization. It is in the name of matter—in whose presence Holbach, Engels, and even Goethe felt a sacred respect—that more than one bureaucracy reigns. (It is well to point out that between matter as totality and idea there is neither practical nor ontological difference; their logic and divinity are identical.) Once it is divinized, who dares to blaspheme the dignity of an absolute state (a Leviathan on earth, Hobbes would say)?

3.4.2.3   When an erotic system comes to be in force and is accepted by the oppressed, it is likewise divinized. In macho ideology the perverse phallus, that of the uxoricidal and castrating father, is fetishized. Not only in the phallic cults of sacred prostitution, but in the daily cult that the wife and son must render to the husband-father, in vaginal passivity and in the castration of Oedipus, the phallus is fetishized. The divine is "father" (alienating father). Who will dare to challenge the phallus in the name of woman?

3.4.2.4   When a pedagogical system, a "sacred cow" Illich called it, comes to be identified with truth itself, with absolute truth, ideology reigns over the ones who remain hidden and are interpreted as nothing, as barbarians: "Being is, I am Being; non-Being is not: the periphery, the oppressed classes, the poor, the others are not." It is the sacralization of pedagogical fetishism. Parmenides was its first high priest; Rousseau, the greatest of the Europeans; the followers of Dewey, its acolytes.

3.4.3   Atheistic Antifetishism

3.4.3.1   To deny the divinity of a fetishized system is authentic atheism. It is the negation of a negation (3.4.4.5). Antifetishism is knowing how to return things in a practical way to their rightful places, to reduce them to their truth. It is not to say—with Hegel or with Nietzsche—"God is dead!" The question is: Which God has died? The fetish? Europe as divinized? It is not a question of rending one's garments because someone says, "There is no God!" The question is: Why do they eat my people just as they eat bread (Psalm 14), and do not give bread to the hungry?

3.4.3.2   It is, then, metaphysically correct to say that "the beginning of all criticism is the criticism of religion"—that is, the religion of the system, fetishistic religion, the religion of medieval Christendom (which was not Christianity but a culture, as Kierkegaard fittingly pointed out) and of the modern bourgeoisies. The fetishism of capital has nudged aside all the other gods from the altar of the center, and it is carefully worshiped by the great enlightened democratic potentates fat from so much consumption. On its altars were immolated the Amerindians in the gold mines, the black slaves, the colonial Asians, the woman as grantee of useless luxury and leased vagina, as Esther Vilar would say, the son as potential market for unnecessary merchandise.

3.4.3.3   Marx says that atheism as a pure negation of essentiality no longer makes sense; atheism negates a god (fetish) *and* affirms, by reason of this negation, the existence of human beings, of the poor, of the oppressed. For this very reason Feuerbach said that it is necessary to abandon the Hegelian fetishistic theology and open up to anthropology (to the other person). Such atheisms are a precondition of the possibility of liberative revolution and of support exterior to the prevailing present system.

3.4.4   Necessary Hypothesis for Revolutionary Praxis

3.4.4.1   In his *Philosophy of Poverty* Proudhon confesses that "studying in the silence of my heart the mystery of human revolutions, the great Unknown, God, has become for me a hypothesis—I mean, a necessary dialectical moment." This explains why John of the Cross says in *The Ascent of Mount Carmel* that "after everything there is nothing", or why Babeulf, the first socialist, wrote to his wife in 1794, when the French Revolution was at its peak, that he hid himself in the "night of nothingness." The nothingness of the system, beyond all Being, that which transcends totality, the metaphysical ("in the presence of which it is necessary to keep silence," Wittgenstein would say) is non-Being—the other than the given. To be open to nothingness, radical nihilism, is to expose oneself to the freedom that the system does not condition.

3.4.4.2   The unknown is the necessary postulate or hypothesis. If the system is divine, it is immutable. If it is not divine, one must be atheistic about it. But one can hardly deny the divinity of a system, present or future, if one does not affirm that the divine is other than all systems. Only this affirmation—first practical and then theoretical—is the condition that makes revolution possible—liberating mobilization against a fetishized system.

3.4.4.3   The practical affirmation of atheism is the struggle for justice. That is, whoever fights for the liberation of the poor affirms in a practical manner that the system is unjust, that it is not divine. Hermann Cohen in his work *Vernunft und Religion* fittingly says that the prophets discovered where the poor were within the state, and from them they worked out a pathological diagnosis of the system. Thus, to discover the poor and take risks for them is to know the nondivinity of an oppressive totality (because divinity, the absolute Other, is goodness itself, justice).

3.4.4.4 The person who is overcome by the metaphysical passivity anterior to all worldly anteriority and assumes responsibility for the oppressed, in the presence of the absolute other, is a bearer of religion—not fetishized religion but metaphysical religion, the origin of all just systems. Unshirkable responsibility, stronger than death, is the procreating, metaphysical fecundity of all that is new in history. The liberating heroes of future homelands feel responsibility for their oppressed (3.1.9); parents are responsible for giving a critical reality to their offspring out of sheer generosity (3.3.7); teachers are responsible for giving a critical awareness to their students, to the people (3.3.8). The one who takes responsibility for the oppressed, the one who is persecuted, imprisoned, tortured, and assassinated for taking responsibility for the poor, witnesses in the totality of the glory of the Infinite.

3.4.4.5 Pure atheism, without affirmation of the infinite Other, is not sufficiently critical; it permits the fetishization of a future system. Only if it is affirmed that the divine is other than all possible systems will liberating revolution be possible. Hence disbelief in the fetish—atheism—must be affirmed as the exteriority of the absolute and of the Origin. The center set itself up as divine: it rejected anthropological exteriority (the Amerindian, the African, the Asian) and hence also absolute Exteriority. Antifetishism is negation of the negation of absolute Exteriority. To affirm absolute Exteriority is to close the road to a future tautological negation of the liberating affirmation. It is, as Proudhon said, the necessary hypothesis of all revolution.

3.4.5 The Metaphysics of Historical Mobilization

3.4.5.1 Atheism vis-à-vis the fetish is the negative precondition for revolution; affirmation of absolute Exteriority is the affirmative and definitive precondition for liberation. Both preconditions are practical. It is in action that the fetish is denied and Exteriority affirmed—when one assumes responsibility for the oppressed. Now let us turn to the theoretical precondition for liberation.

3.4.5.2   Fetishism, like the tragic pantheism of the classical ages (for example, that of the Greeks and Romans), not only divinizes the system but also takes hold of its instrumentalities, practices, and institutions. The whole and the parts are divinized (2.6.6.2). Inasmuch as the function that something fulfills within the system is identified with its reality, everything is eternalized.

A group of armed subversives, the Machabee brothers, arose in revolution against the Hellenistic empire in the second century B.C. They and their mother were the first ones to affirm that the absolute Other "created all out of non-Being." Tertullian affirmed against Hermogenes: "God created all things from nothing" (*ex nihilo*). To create means to give reality without antecedents, from what is not yet constituted, from outside any system or social formation.

3.4.5.3   The metaphysical theory of creation is the theoretical support of liberative revolution; it is the most thorough-going deposition that no system is eternal, because everything, even the sun and the earth, is contingent (it could be nonexistent) and possible, nonnecessary (at a given time it was not).

3.4.5.4   The metaphysical contingency and possibility of the totality of the cosmos (3.4.6) amply guarantees the contingency and possibility of the institutions of a given social formation, of any political, erotic, pedagogical, and even religious systems. Contingency thus gnaws at the claim to divinity made by an oppressing state. It takes away its eternity and places it in a dialectical liberating movement.

3.4.5.5   The metaphysical theory of creation gives fluidity to the whole and to all its parts. Neither the cosmos, nor the world, nor any system is divine. The theory of creation denies such divinization and affirms disbelief in fetishism: the fetish itself is a creature, workmanship of human hands only, a creature made by a creature. That is, if everything is created, nothing is divine. The theory of creation is the atheization of the cosmos and of the world.

3.4.5.6   Medieval christendom misunderstood this doctrine; it gave emphasis to the notion that the Absolute had created the world *as it is*. Creation thus lost its metaphysical bite and became a fetishist ideology.

3.4.6 Ethical, Cultic, Economic Constitution of the Cosmos

3.4.6.1 For those who hold themselves responsible and in peril for the sake of the oppressed, nothing is allowed to impede their feeding of the hungry, not even the private property—natural or divine (in historical and fetishized reality)—of the one who has obtained bread unjustly. Everything can be modified in order to serve the oppressed.

This systematic or worldly plasticity is likewise projected to the cosmos. The cosmos itself is experienced as suspended from and in a creative Freedom that places the cosmos, matter (3.4.8), at the disposition of the liberator and the oppressed. The constitutive intention that utilizes the cosmos and nature as a mediation is a cultural-economic integration (hence cultic) of the cosmos in political discourse.

3.4.6.2 The cosmos—the totality of reality, of real things keeping among themselves a transcendental bond or referential unity, constitutive by itself—appears to the interpretation or praxis of the liberator as created by unconditional Freedom, as the theater of service (3.4.8) and matter to mitigate the hunger of the hungry (4.4.9). The cosmos thus acquires an ethical constitution. In comes forth from Absolute Freedom to be used with freedom at the service of the other.

3.4.6.3 We do not adore the cosmos (nature) now, as Greeks, Romans, Egyptians, Aztecs, Incas, Hindus, and Chinese did. We use the cosmos as a mediation of service, of cult. The cosmos has an ethical constitution insofar as it has a creator; it has a cultic-cultural constitution insofar as it has been worked on (4.2.4.4) in justice. The metaphysics of practical freedom resides in the cosmos historically, in a defetishized way. It will never bow down to matter as eternal divinity (the naive materialism of Goethe or Engels); it will simply use matter as a mediation.

3.4.7 Reality, Essence, and Existence

3.4.7.1 Only now can we turn to these classic concepts, though they take on another sense. Reality is totality creatively constituted; it is the relative unity of all substantivity "of itself," from within itself, anterior or prior to all posterior manifestation in the world. The real is the cosmos as totality, the *prius* of the world.

3.4.7.2   Outside the creative and absolute fecundity, the cosmos is existent (placed-outside: *ex-sistere*). Eternal Being is not existent, only "sistent"; it is real by itself (*a se* and not only *ex se*). The existent is the creature, moment of the real cosmos, actuality of the constituted totality effective of itself and from within itself.

3.4.7.3   On the other hand, the essence of cosmic things is the unity of the constitutive notes that act synergetically, codetermining each other. The constitutive or real essence is individual; it is what constitutes the reality of the thing that exists in itself. The essence constitutes the substantivity of the real, as Zubiri might say. Thus, properly speaking, the totality of inorganic, natural, physical things has essence, one and only, inasmuch as they constitute only one system, only one astronomical substantivity (4.1.3). For its part, the totality of organic things likewise has one essence, because it reacts as one substantivity (4.1.4). Only the human being, each human being, is in reality one substantivity (I do not say "substantiality," because "substantivity" assumes substantiality in the way that the human organism assimilates a substance such as sugar) inasmuch as its freedom seals the unity of its constitutive notes with real autonomy and operativeness (4.1.5).

3.4.7.4   Only a person, and each person, is really a thing, *res eventualis*, a thing that has a history.

3.4.8   Critical Materialism and Worship as Economy

3.4.8.1   The system, when it is totalized as a closed world, tends to become fetishized, as already noted. Only the implorative provocation of the other, of the poor, unsettles the established order and the easy conscience of the dominator. The questioning of the oppressed, the protest of the poor, is the epiphany of the revelation of the Absolute. To reveal is nothing more than to beseech from exteriority in order to mobilize the praxis of the liberator—that is, to make of inert matter (the cosmos) the object of service-worship.

3.4.8.2   Naive cosmological or acritical materialism affirms that everything is matter. By matter is understood a mythical reality that would be something like an infinite mass, an infinite rock. If everything is matter, and a person its epiphenomenon, as Engels thinks in *Dialectics of Nature*, if matter is infinite (which is a contradiction in terms), if it is eternal (that is, it has no beginning and no end; it is "from always," strictly speaking), if it has life, intelligence, beauty, and so forth, in potency or in act, it means that now matter is divinity. (It has all the characteristics that can be attributed to divinity.) All reality arises by differentiation from the original identity of matter. In this case, everything is internal to matter; there is no freedom or responsibility; determination and necessity reign supreme. Everything is divine. Likewise, the oppressive empire, castrating machismo, and filicidal pedagogy are divine. Who would be able to rise blasphemously against the eternal wisdom of matter? Who would dare to alter its sacred source? Paradoxically, naive materialism ends up being fetishist and carries on like any other type of pantheism or idealism.

3.4.8.3 On the contrary, authentic materialism or critical materialism (which parallels authentic atheism or radical atheism) interprets nature (see chap. 4) as matter for work (*C* in diagram 4). Things are relevant inasmuch as *with them* (that *with which* the artifact is manufactured is its materiality) are fabricated things needed by the other as such, beyond the present system of necessity. The materiality of the sense-thing, its possibility or mediation for service, is what in 3.4.6.3 is called the cultic-cultural constitution of the cosmos.

3.4.8.4 For Hegel the supreme worship or liturgy is rendered by the perfect act of absolute religion. That worship consists in the certainty possessed by the subject of the absolute state, by an act of faith, that the representation is the idea, in other words, the certainty of being God. This certainty of being the manifestation of matter can be had by a member of the bureaucracy or by a North American government official defending Christian civilization. It is the certainty of the fascist who keeps a "good conscience" while assassinating a hero of liberation.

3.4.8.5 On the contrary, the absolute worship to the infinite Other, the absolute economy, is to give to the other, in justice, matter worked on. To serve (*habodah*) is as much to liberate the oppressed as it is to perform divine service or worship. A just economy, as the sum total of artifacts produced by human labor and distributed with equity among a people, is worship of the Infinite: by giving food to the hungry, and the poor, to the defenseless and the widowed, to the solitary and the orphaned, liturgy is rendered to the Absolute.

3.4.8.6   Authentic materialism is correlative to the cultic utilization of the cosmos: the fruit of labor and earth is offered to the Absolute Other (4.3. and 4.4) when service is rendered to the poor.

3.4.9   The Festival

3.4.9.1   I am not speaking here of the *homo ludens* of Nietzsche and his commentators. It is not a question of the Dionysiac or Bacchanalian feast, of the wine that intoxicates those who are able to acquire it, the feast of dominators, that of *otium* or *orgia*. It is another type of celebration.

3.4.9.2   Worship of the Infinite is liberation itself. The feast of the Infinite is the rejoicing of liberation. But, as Rosenzweig tells us, peoples remember and celebrate only the times of their own liberation; never are victories of other peoples celebrated.

3.4.9.3   The festival of liberation of those who sing, dance, run, jump, exult in rejoicing, is the celebration of release from the prison of oppression—the political celebration of the compatriots who create the new homeland, the erotic celebration of the couple who find orgasm fulfilling in mutual rapturous service; the pedagogical celebration of youth in rebellion when it seems to them that they are already touching with their hands a more just, more human world, which they can enter without being repressed. That festival, the fiesta that Nicaragua now celebrates on July 19, under the leadership of the Sandinista National Liberation Front (FSLN), is a rejoicing in liberation.

3.4.9.4   I am not talking here about the Sunday that simply injects a parenthesis into the work week. Nor do I mean the friendly card game that lets us think we are living in heaven upon earth, without responsibilities, without justice. The game of placing between parentheses (*Einklammerung*) is phenomenological; it is the entertainment of the circus, of the clowns who make others happy while they themselves weep under the mask of solitude and anguish. That is the feast of dominators; they want to forget daily life because, although they pretend to have triumphed, they know that what they have achieved is fictitious, a fetish.

3.4.9.5 The supreme worship, the praxis of liberation, gives supreme happiness. The festival of a people that liberates itself is the infinite, incommensurable festival, the one that measures all other rejoicing and makes it possible for us to continue living. It is a spilling over into history of the joy of the Absolute.

4

FROM NATURE TO ECONOMICS

What we have already arrived at in chapters 2 and 3—six levels of reflection (proximity, totality, mediation, exteriority, alienation, and liberation) in four metaphysical situations (politics, sexuality, pedagogics, and antifetishism)—must now be implanted within the confines of nature, semiotics, poetics, and economics. This discourse multiplies by four the degree of complexity arrived at in chapter 3.

4.1   NATURE

4.1.1   *Status Questionis*

4.1.1.1   The practical relationship with the other (see chap. 3) always includes a person-to-nature relationship of proxemics or poiesis. It is of this nature that we must speak here. Nature is not the cosmos (2.3.3.1) or culture (4.2–4). Nature is not yet the matter of human labor, which has a significance, a history, dialectically opposed to culture. Nature, the part of the cosmos that is included in the world, is formed by natural beings (4.1.2.2). It is the phenomenal totality structured by a physical, astronomical, or inorganic and organic, vegetable, and animal order. We must describe the potential matter (*C* in diagram 4) of human labor (the matter of semiotics, poiesis, and economics), its destruction and ecological regeneration.

DIAGRAM 4

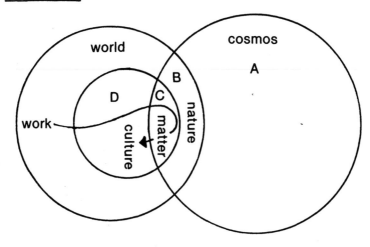

4.1.2　Nature and Politics

4.1.2.1　Naive realism and materialism (such as that of Engels) assert that the cosmos (*A* in diagram 4) is what is first; and they eliminate the notion of nature as it is understood here. Idealism (such as that of Sartre) affirms the world and consciousness as first and confuses the real cosmos with worldly nature (*B*). For its part, philosophy of liberation, beyond critical realism or Heideggerian thinking (an ontological idealism), surpasses the false contradiction of realism-idealism by affirming the real anteriority of the cosmos (*ordo realitatis*), the existential *a priori* of the world (*ordo cognoscendi*), and the economic interpretation of nature (*ordo operandi*).

4.1.2.2　Nature is the totality of noncultural beings (*B* in diagram 4) included in the world (2.2.7) that, without ceasing to be part of the cosmos as real things (2.3.8.1), nevertheless have as foundation of their sense the historical *proyecto* of the world (2.2.3.2). Nature is the intramundane reality: besides essence (3.4.7.3), it has sense (2.3.8.3)—that is, it is a natural being. A natural being is a sense-thing in potency (4.2–4) or, better and more exactly stated, a natural thing with sense (differentiating it from the cultural thing or artifact, which is, properly speaking, the sense-thing). Nature is the phenomenon (2.2.3) of the cosmos; it is the appearance of the cosmos in the world as totality. Nature as phenomenal totality is constituted by natural beings or phenomena, by natural (5.1.3), noncultural, data.

4.1.2.3   It is from the world—from a historical, political, sexual, or symbolically determined world—that we comprehend nature and interpret natural beings. If there is a history of the world, there is likewise a history of nature. That is, the Greeks understood *physis* as eternal, divine, nascent; the medievals understood *natura* as created (*natura naturata*), finite, without a principle of corruption; modern Europeans have understood nature or *Natur* as matter that is mathematically observable (since Galileo) or economically exploitable (since the Industrial Revolution). Nature, along with work and capital, is the origin of the myth of civilizing progress. It will now be understood what is meant when it is said that nature is interpreted politically: it is hermeneutically visualized from the center or from the periphery (4.1.8), from diverse social classes, from political systems, principally, as the matter of a mode of production in a determined social structure.

4.1.3   Physical Substantivity

4.1.3.1   Nature, the noncultured part of the cosmos in the world (hence a negative notion with regard to human labor), is the phenomenal appearance of that which is real, of itself, anterior to the world in the order of manifestation, which is to be distinguished from the order of revelation (2.4.5.2–3) and of real constitution (3.4.7.1). Kant referred to nature as the unknowable *noumenon* (object of the archetypal creative *intellectus*), and to that which we call nature as the order of physical objects constituted by the *a priori* category of understanding. We must affirm that the cosmos is really known in its real constitution (derived comprehension is real discovery; 2.2.4.7) but never interpreted in its entirety (due to the exteriority of the cosmos; hence there will always be a possibility of a future history of nature). The cosmos, hence, is known as a worldly phenomenon—that is, it is constituted in its historical meaning (2.3.5.6) as nature.

4.1.3.2   Real constitution is known concomitantly in all true interpretation of sense. Thus we know the cosmos as nature. From nature we formulate models that allow us to understand what the cosmos is. I shall call universe the model of the cosmos insofar as it is nature, but on its macrophysical, astrophysical level.

4.1.3.3 Today the most acceptable model of the universe (very different from that thought of by Aristotle in his *Physics*, Holbach in his *Système de la nature*, Schelling or Hegel in their *Naturphilosophie*) unites cosmology or astronomy with cosmogony; the universe is neither eternal (as it was for Aristotle and Maimonides), nor incorruptible or changeless (as it was for Aquinas), nor infinite in space. On the contrary, it underwent a zero time (t^o); it is in a finite expanding space. The universe is young; it still has abundant hydrogen. The earth is more than four thousand million years old. We can calculate exactly, according to Ambartsoumian, the age of the sun, of the stars, and of the galaxies. We can even know that the galaxies move away with a velocity V proportional to their distance d, as Slipher tells us.

4.1.3.4 Microphysics, with its corpuscular or undulatory model, tells us of a nucleus and electrons, atoms and molecules, and macromolecules, which begin by being microscopic and end by becoming more and more complex.

4.1.3.5 All the physical cosmos, even before being included as nature or modeled as universe, is in reality a macrosystem with its own unity, coherence, and substantivity. I want to emphasize that it is *one*, unique. A pile of rocks has only additive unity. The cosmos as real totality has constitutional unity. It can include many substances (hydrogen, iron, lead: *substantia* or *ousia*), but they are subsumed within a real physical system. The constitutional unity of the interdependent notes that make it a system is substantivity, as Zubiri says (which is not the traditional substantiality). In this case it is the substantivity or unity of the system of the cosmos as real physical totality. Unity does not come from a mere process of combination or complexification, but from an effective physical coherence, which is not that of an organic or a mechanical artifact. It is a composed substantivity *sui generis*: the physical cosmic system. Philosophy of nature should explore these themes.

4.1.4   Living Substantivity

4.1.4.1   The totality of the cosmos, hence, functions as only one thing: a single reality essentially constituted, of itself, from within itself (*ex se*, not *a se*), a real system, which is included in the world as nature. In such nature, we ought now to differentiate the merely physical (from astrophysics to the microphysical intra-atomic level) or inorganic and the living (which begins in organic being).

4.1.4.2   Among inorganic beings, it seems that the heavier nuclei are more recent. There is, then, a transformation in the physical cosmos, according to certain patterns. In all events, the astrophysical cosmos, although immense, possesses a relatively simple and homogeneous structure; its greater complexity is only a totality of macromolecules in process of entropy, transforming formidable quantities of energy into mass, or hydrogen into substances atomically heavier than it. The physical cosmos tends toward an immobile stabilization.

4.1.4.3   But within that cosmos an antientropic phenomenon takes place—life—where a much greater complexity can be seen in a single living cell. In terms of the heterogeneous functionality of the structural parts of the substantive living system, a single cell has more complexity than the whole inorganic cosmos.

4.1.4.4   Life appears in the cosmos. It has been on earth between three and four thousand million years. It originates and goes through a process of evolution. This poses three themes: living substantivity, the phylogenetic multiplication of the individual within a species, and evolution through a process of metaspeciation.

4.1.4.5   The substantivity of the whole inorganic cosmos is unique. It is only one thing. Atoms, molecules, and conglomerates such as rocks, planets, and galaxies, are singular parts of only one system. By contrast, each living being, from the unicellular to the vegetable or animal, has a relatively individual substantivity—not as much as in the case of the human person, a unique individual in the proper metaphysical sense because of its autonomy. The quasi-individual substantivity of each living being has unity in its constitutive notes, with greater coherence and functional heterogeneity than does the whole inanimate physical system.

4.1.4.6   The greatest living unity and individuality can be seen in the reproductive capacity of phylogenetic self-multiplication into stable species through the reproduction of new individuals with genetic identity or with similar specific, hereditary characteristics. Individuals become a species (it is not the species that becomes individualized). A species is the totality of constitutive notes by reason of which a constitutive essence belongs to a determinate phylum.

4.1.4.7   Species evolve. That is, in the generation of the new individual they can transmit a system or a constitutive genetic scheme with possibilities for a new speciation. The origination of specific essences by metaspeciation is what is called evolution. Evolution becomes complete only when a new individual is produced that possesses in its system or genetic scheme constitutive notes different from those of the progenitor and that can, on its own, multiply as a new species; then it is the head of a new phylum. The living substantivity or essence is hence evolutive. Life would, then, seem to be what Bergson called the *èlan vital* or biological finality that surpasses entropy and is directed to ever greater degrees of complexity and consciousness. Philosophical biology must reflect on this thematic.

4.1.5   Human Substantivity

4.1.5.1   Real things, individual and specific essences, evolve—from the unicellular to the pluricellular, from the vegetable to the animal, from the insects to the vertebrates, from the fish to the amphibians, birds, and mammals, and—seventy million years ago—the primates. More than three million years ago, finally, *homo* appears, in the beginning perhaps as *homo habilis*; two hundred thousand years ago as *homo sapiens* with distinct racial differentiations.

4.1.5.2   Only the human being has sufficient substantivity to be considered something individual, autonomous, separate, and independent. The systemic coherence of essential human notes is of a maximum closure: it is the only thing really totalized constitutively. This is so not only because of possessing the constitutive note of intelligence, but more because of possessing the note of real alterity: it is a being for the other. Arms and legs, sexual organs, cranial configuration, speech apparatus—a person's entire bodiliness is orientated not only to its intelligence, but also—to say it once more—to its metaphysical reference to the other. It is the openness to the other, to other-directedness, that enables a person to be a person, to be substantivity properly so called.

4.1.5.3   Physical substantivity is unresponsive, unique, and closed. Living substantivity ranges from the plant, which shows certain inside-outside reactions (in photosynthesis), to the animals, which can originate a response to stimulus thanks to a nervous system, progressively more complicated in "higher" animals. Nevertheless, mere sensibility and the first degree of sensory-motor intelligence do not enable the individual to separate itself distinctively and autonomously from the species. Only in the human being, because of its nervous system, which has an incalculable relational coherence due to the fourteen thousand million neurons in the cerebral cortex, is the experience of the proximity of total exteriority and the handling of multiple mediations in the totality of the world possible.

4.1.5.4   Humankind did not first appear as a species knowing how to comprehend, interpret, and question as it does today. Within the same human species there was a maturation of essence. From *homo habilis*, the Pithecanthropus or Neanderthal, to *homo sapiens* there was a maturation of constitutive notes. Earlier human beings could have been intelligent but not rational or free (as a child is intelligent from its birth but reaches the age of reason at the end of infancy, and freedom during adolescence). In the same manner persons must have first expressed themselves as a totalized species, minimally individualized as separate, distinct exteriority, as other. In *homo sapiens* the dominion of rationality must have affirmed itself clearly as a free, independent exteriority, thus enabling it to be the subject of pulsion toward alterity and of very complex communicative, relational semiotics (for example, human language).

4.1.5.5   On the fact of human independence, of the free and exterior closure of human substantivity, depends the fact that each individual is distinct and not merely different (3.3.3.3). The human species is not constituted univocally by individuals differentiated from a single identity. The human species is formed by distinct individuals who shape history (a human being is a *res eventualis* and not merely a natural being). The content of the species is analogous, similar, but with individual distinction (and not mere difference). It is a species that has a history, world history; human beings are individuals who have a biography. The metaphysics of exteriority and liberation depends on the real *sui generis* constitution of human substantivity, absolute closure, freedom, responsibility, separate and independent totality with a semiotic function vis-à-vis the totality of the physical or living cosmos and even vis-à-vis all the rest of the individuals of the human species. The only free being that has a world is the other. Philosophical anthropology studies these issues.

4.1.6 Nature and *Eros*

4.1.6.1   It is the human being that turns toward the other as exteriority but with a specific analogous unity, and because of this it turns toward systematic social structures (classes, nations, etc.) toward social formations (with modes of production). The human person, thanks to freedom and separation, is the only being that can turn itself toward and reflect on things in order to comprehend them in its world. To unfold a world (2.2) is a real constitutive note of a human being. To include in that world inanimate and animate cosmic things is what has happened ever since humankind has been on earth, from the moment of its appearance. Hence nature is as old as human nature. The first human circumspection (2.2.5.5) of the cosmos established nature as the comprehended part of the cosmos (*B* in diagram 4).

4.1.6.2   That first nature could not have been other than inhospitable, a cause of terror (because of terrifying natural phenomena, the ferocity of wild animals, incomprehensibility of their actions): cold, hunger, solitude, confusion. Attacking humankind on every front, nature advanced threateningly to the horizon of *eros*.

4.1.6.3   Nature as landscape, as a place in which to reside, dress, eat, as a horizon still without frontiers—an aggressive, savage, chaotic nature—is the erotic nature where humankind will make its house; it is ecologic (both "ecology" and "economy" come from the Greek stem "house": *oikia*). In this manner there originates the person-cosmos dialectic, the emergence of nature as habitat.

4.1.6.4   From nature persons take, for example, wood,

which—after the domestication of fire—is warmth, security, and light (3.2.8.1). In that nature they discover the cavern as house, the stone as door, the fruits of the earth as nourishment, and the animals that one day they will shepherd in order to replenish their supply of protein. Nature is nourishing, sheltering, protective, and maternal. It is the beautiful nature of the splendor of dawn and of twilight, of the rivulets of the mountains, of the song of the nightingale, of the fierceness of the oceans, of the perfume of the rose.

4.1.7   Nature and Imperialism

4.1.7.1   Gardenlike nature has now been transformed by the human species into an immense dunghill. Humankind, which once lived in respect for the *terra mater* and even rendered worship to it, now transforms it into pure matter of labor—though there are romantics who plead for a "return to nature" as did the hippies. The divine nature of the Greeks, the "sister earth" of Francis of Assisi, is now interpreted in terms of sheer exploitability: *homo naturae lupus*. Wolf? Infinitely worse than the wolf, which has in no way destroyed nature.

4.1.7.2   In effect, nature as exploitable matter, destructible without limit, a cache of profits, a source of capital gains, a time-projected extension of the dominative attitude of the slave driver (who made the slave work that nature), is obviously the interpretation adhered to by the center (Europe first, but now equally the United States). This change of person-to-nature attitude started in the Industrial Revolution, and it reaches a hallucinating peak in the present state of monopolistic imperialist capitalism, the society of superconsumption and aggressive destruction of nature as a mere mediation (a "logical corollary" of the previous destruction of oppressed peoples of the periphery). The goddess nature is now industrial raw material: iron ore, petroleum, coffee, wheat, livestock, wood.

4.1.7.3   The industrial conglomerates transform the garden into a dunghill. Factory effluents kill the fish and the vegetation of the seas; they rarefy the atmosphere with asphyxiating gasses; they destroy the natural sources of oxygen (the United States robs the periphery of its oxygen because it consumes more than it produces). The Club of Rome has pointed out that there are natural resources that are nonrenewable, that pollution is on the increase, that the human species is multiplying itself irresponsibly, that food supplies are on the decline, and that we are approaching a gigantic ecological collapse. Nature could exterminate this species that has turned irrational because of its economic system. Nature, which seemingly would remain patiently passive, responds with a threat that brooks no opposition: they who destroy me destroy themselves!

4.1.7.4 But the technologico-economic system of the capitalist social formation seems unwilling to change. Launched by its own logic to the maximization of profits, and hence of consumption-production and vice versa, imperialism continues its devastating course. Until when? To what limit?

4.1.8   Ecology and Liberation of the Periphery

4.1.8.1 Nature, earth, its biosphere and its atmosphere, have been mortally wounded. The second report of the Club of Rome says that growth is not linear but organic (that is, the regions of the center will resist crises better; those of the periphery will die sooner). But crises are global now and will affect all residents of all regions. Those responsible for the destruction of nature are the developed powers of the center: they account for more than 90 percent of the contamination of the earth (even though they count less than 30 percent of the world population). That industrial center will never make the decision to reduce its own growth: its economy is founded on the (irrational) principle of ever accelerated profit. Will some technological miracles regenerate ecological equilibrium? Or will the romantic and moralistic advice of the Club of Rome convert the wolves into lambs? It does not seem likely. A solution, if there is to be one, will come from other sources.

4.1.8.2 The alternative Worldwide Model formulated in the periphery in opposition to the Club of Rome (by the Bariloche Foundation in Argentina) sets out from other premises. But much work remains to be done on it.

4.1.8.3 Can it be that a new person-to-nature attitude is impossible for capitalism, given the phase it is in now? Can it be that person-to-nature relationships that are less extravagant, less destructive, less consumptive, more economical, more patient, and more respectful of nature, can emerge only in peoples that have not arrived at the contradictory degree of technology within capitalism? Can it be that the destructive system will come to an end only when person-to-person relationships are redefined?

4.1.8.4   It would seem that at the moment when the peoples of the periphery demand a just price for their raw materials (nature worked on by the servant, the oppressed, the dominated), as has been somewhat fictitiously determined in the case of petroleum—at the moment the whole system will explode. Of course, before that moment comes, the powers of the center will have been able to transfer their more pollutive industries to the periphery and assure themselves of control of the less destructive and more complex operations. And before that moment comes their imperialist armies will continue to invade, repress, and assassinate. But, in the end, the hour will come. It is only in the periphery—in Asia, Africa, and Latin America—that a regeneration of the person-to-nature relationship can begin to take place—if it is not already too late.

4.1.8.5   The political liberation of the periphery seems to be the essential condition for the possibility of the restoration of natural ecological equilibrium—if true liberation, affirmation of the cultural exteriority, is undertaken, and not simply imitation of the economic process and destructive technology of the center. It would be the authentic humanization of nature, the development of culture in justice.

4.1.8.6   It is time to search for a metaphysical foundation for the peace movements in Europe and the United States, and for the liberation movements in the Third World. This foundation cannot be anything other than *life*—the human life, as Being, that is threatened by the arms race in the geopolitical center and by injustice in the periphery. The capitalistic system, unable to distribute overproduction, cannot make use of its mammoth productive capacity. It instead produces unemployment; unemployment reduces buying potential; fewer sales further reduce production. To make up for the profit loss by reason of reduced production and consumption, recourse is had to the arms industry. Armaments (means of death, not of production or consumption) bring with them the threat of the total extinction of life in the center, and they are used to repress and exterminate liberation movements in the periphery. This life—threatened in the center by atomic missiles and in the periphery by hunger and injustice—confronts the logic of profit, and struggles—with pacifism in the center and machine guns in El Salvador.

4.2   SEMIOTICS

4.2.1   *Status Questionis*

4.2.1.1   A philosophy of beings has two aspects: description of natural being (4.1) and of cultural being (the poietic). I call cultural being the mediation (2.2) that is a fruit of human production. The cosmos appears as nature from within itself, of itself; it is real, anterior to the world. Cultural beings, fruit of the person-to-nature relationship, are situated on a new level, the level of culture. They are signs, products, or artifacts. The totality of these beings I call culture. Those that signify someone or something are called signs; they are studied by philosophical semiotics. Beings, operations, and systems involved with the functional or formal coherence of products are called artifacts or useful beings (4.3).

4.2.1.2   Philosophical semiotics includes many classic disciplines in philosophy (logic, philosophy of language or of communication, etc.). It is a philosophy of sign and communication where "what has been said" emerges from "saying," and imperative revelation arises from proximity and justice.

4.2.2   Wordless Self-Exposition

4.2.2.1   In face-to-face proximity, in the nonspatial timelessness of immediacy, in closeness to the other, with the other, in the child's suckling, in the lover's kiss, in the toast of compatriots celebrating a liberation victory, or in the dance of happiness, there are no words; silence or music reigns. It is the dense silence of plenitude where words originate. In the origin of words there is the other, who "speaks" by presence (not as substance, *ousia*, but as self-revelation, *parousia*). Protosemiotics is an ineffable "saying''; it does not say something; it does not say anything! It exposes itself in proximity. It is the epiphany of sincerity. It is not truth but veracity, fidelity, the *veritas prima*: a stripping, a nakedness before the other, a silent responsibility before the one about whom nothing can be said because one is there entirely, next to the other.

4.2.2.2   So essential for semiotics (*semeion* in Greek means "sign," "mark," or "testimony") is originative proximity that without it the system of signs that are elaborated and produced as a bridge to cross distances in communication cannot emerge (4.2.5).

4.2.2.3   A person is, as it were, born too soon; prematurity is such that certain nerve centers produce up to 80 percent of their neurons after birth. Enrichment from maternal proximity—warmth, caress, nourishment—allows for a better structuring of the cranium as it grows after birth. Proximity, hence, enters into the physical constitution of the other. It is a proximity that will reactualize, on the sexual, political, or pedagogical level, in orgasm, joy, and enthusiasm, the first (and last) relationship that animates all human life and its semiotic process. What is semiotic poiesis if not the reestablishment of proximity in some manner?

4.2.3   Expression

4.2.3.1   Distance between one person and another demands the production of signs of communication, as when a shepherd on the mountain communicates with companions by whistling. To express ("press out," as when an orange is squeezed) is to impel toward the exterior something that is in the interior. Comprehending or perceiving has about it an aspect of passivity; expressing by exteriorizing semiotically is its correlative activity.

4.2.3.2   There is a certain semiotic in animals; they are capable of emitting sounds that indicate (the merely deictic character of the sign) certain stimuli. The dance of the bee signals the distance and direction of food. Innate or acquired (in the sphere of sensitive-motor animal intelligence) instincts are related to requirements of the species, but they are not signs as such nor are they interpreted in their meaning.

4.2.3.3   Only humankind has a semiotic function, is capable of symbolic poiesis: the sign (the signifying element) refers to the element signified (interpreted meaning) and, thereby, to a world (4.2.4). The human being is "the living being that has language" (*logos*), attains to self-expression, possesses apophantic capacity, says something about something. That which is said is the ontic fruit of the semiotic function.

4.2.3.4   Human expression follows a categorical code, a program of expressive principles. The code has an essential, genetic, constitutive, or hereditary level, a sort of "innate mental structure," as Chomsky would say, that acts initially as a "generative grammar," then matures its fruits progressively (Piaget), until it arrives at the adult level. This code is also cultural (socio-historical inheritance; Lévi-Strauss). This apriority of the expressive code has relevance to Aristotle's problem of categories (linked to the Greek language) or those of Kant (linked to judgments—that is, certain types of predication).

4.2.3.5   The child, because it is human, very soon discovers the sense of the sign—that is, the reference of a sign, a signifier, to a signified. The semantic dimension is the reverse of that of beings or things. The thing shows, manifests, uncovers itself. The discovery of the thing, of the being, is truth. Truth goes from the thing to interpretation; semantics goes from interpretation to sign.

4.2.4   Significative Totalities

4.2.4.1   The world is the quotidian existential totality (2.3). The world is expressed intentionally as an interpreted totality (2.2.5) or totality of sense. This is the level of the concept or mental sign (whose content is a real aspect of the thing, its meaning). For its part, the totality of sense is expressed through significative or significant totalities. They are of many levels (such as, for example, the system of highway signs in a given nation), but the fundamental one is language. By language I understand a totality of significant moments formed by elemental units that express phonetically (or in writing) the totality of sense in a moment of its history. The interpreted totality represents the world, and language expresses the interpretation.

4.2.4.2   Linguistic totality has a functional grammatical structure, a code constituted by categorical principles, which permits the expressed system (discourse as *continuum*, phrases, sentences) to have a strict internal logic among its elemental units that can be analyzed separately (lexemes, morphemes, phonemes, etc.). The respectivity of cosmic things or the phenomenality of the worldly meaning is reproduced syntactically in language. If a being is a worldly unit (or unit of meaning), the semantic linguistic unit is the word (as adequate semiotic structure).

4.2.4.3   The relationship of the signifier (for example, a word) to the signified (the sense that acts as intentional signifier with respect to the real signification: the thing itself in one of its aspects) is semantics. All signifiers have a denotation or immediate referent (the meaning), and a connotation or final reference to the world. All denotation of something is in the end connotative of the totality of the world. In the same manner, because of the semantic mutability of signification (which progressively changes meaning in a historical world), a signifier no longer totally, but only partially, signifies its signification. The mutability of signification is what constitutes the possibility of the history of languages (4.2.9.1).

4.2.4.4   Language, as expressive totality of the world, has as many modalities as the world itself. There is everyday language; there are languages of oligarchical cultures and languages of mass culture; there is the language of popular culture. There is sexual language (reproduced as language of desire, symbolically, in sleep; its semantics is interpretable), religious language (as Roland Barthes shows), political language (which is understood not by what it says but by what it glosses over, against whom it speaks, when, and why, etc.), and technical language.

4.2.5   Tautology

4.2.5.1   The one-dimensionality of everyday discourse, the impossibility of discovering a sense other than the one that has been imposed, the only sense accepted by all, the "everyone says," is converted into a gigantic tautology. What is said is said because everyone has always said it. The sense of meaning and of nonmeaning has been lost. Theories of communicaiton are frequently founded on such tautology with unspoken presuppositions as accomplices.

DIAGRAM 5

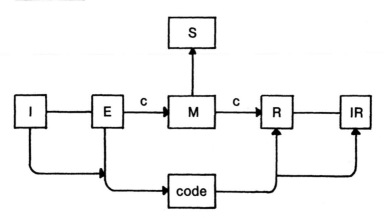

4.2.5.2   The factual sciences of communication present such communication as fact without obscurities or mystery, as sketched in diagram 5. The emitter (*E*) sends a message (*M*) to the receiver (*R*) by means of a channel (*c*), which can have impediments or resistance. The emitter transmits certain information (*I*) that has as referent a signification (*S*) that is tuned in by the receiver as information received (*IR*). The information has been encoded (between *I* and *⅓*) according to a certain code (*code*); it must be decoded when tuned in by the receiver (between *R* and *IR*).

4.2.5.3   The process of encoding is correlative to that of decoding. The information to be transmitted must be encoded semantically, syntactically, and phonetically in order to be decoded phonetically, syntactically, and semantically as information received from the emitter. All this can be projected into mathematical models and be given a high degree of technical sophistication.

4.2.5.4   What is overlooked is that these models presuppose an enormous systematic tautology. That is, it is naively accepted that information can be decoded, that there are no linguistic, social, political, or sexual conflicts. Communications experts, accepting as obvious what is the result of numerous abstractions, confuse abstract structures with real structures of communication. They forget that the system in force, frequently a dominative one, is one in which all are alleged to interpret what is said, although in reality they cannot give an account of the meaning of anything that is said.

4.2.6   Exposition

4.2.6.1   We now approach the antisemiotic moment par excellence or, more exactly, the point of departure, the source of origin, of new historical semiotic totalities. We have said that the proximity of the kiss or that of suckling without words (4.2.2) is replaced by the distance of semiotics (4.2.3–5). But suddenly, in the world of signs, gestures, marks, or words, springs forth the unforseeable, the unexpected, the ineffable that unsettles the semiotic totality. Someone lets out a howl of pain: "—Ooooh!" No words are spoken. Your hair stands on end; an eerie sensation crawls down your spinal chord; in expectant tension you attend to what it is that is happening to someone. Someone appears in a semiotic vacuum. Expression gives ground to exposition. Someone has been left exposed, as those who face a firing squad expose their flesh, their bare chests, to imminent assault. Others reveal themselves (*parousia*) apocalyptically; there is on their face, in their naked flesh, in their person, the same message beyond all coding. Exposition anticipates expression.

4.2.6.2   The other—the poor; the oppressed; the Latin American, African, or Asiatic; the violated woman; the alienated child—advances in defiance, pleading, provoking from beyond (*symbolon*) the world. The other in his or her bodiliness is the first word (*dabar* in Hebrew, meaning both "word" and "thing"), the significant identically signified, the historical and exterior content, the biographical metaphor, nakedness as self-revelation; the other is veracity more than truth. Truth is the discovery of the meaning of what a thing is in reality; veracity is a sincere revelation of what someone is as alterity (it always runs the risk of being taken for hypocrisy, merely apparent authenticity, falsity, or irony). The expression of the oppressed as exteriority always entails exposition, risk, valor.

4.2.7   Ideology

4.2.7.1   When exposition is repressed, a semiotic totality is imposed as ideological domination, as fratricidal, uxoricidal, filicidal tautology. The European alienated the word of the Amerindian by the conquest of the sixteenth century and the word of African and Asian cultures by the colonization of the nineteenth century. English, French, and Spanish semiotics destroyed the word of the Aztec and Inca, of Ghana, India, China, and Middle East caliphates.

4.2.7.2   Ideology (be it political, erotic-macho, or pedagogical) is a concrete discourse that justifies and conceals domination. The sign (it can be idea, word, form, image, sound, aroma) has as horizon of meaning only the oligarchical neocolonial (3.3.6.4) or imperialist culture (3.3.6.2). Popular culture is silenced (3.3.8); its expression is repressed, its exposition violated. The propaganda and indoctrination of the ideology of the empire and of the national oligarchy by all the means of communication bring about a conditioning of the masses as a market, as inculcated desires of the capitalist economic system of the center.

4.2.7.3   To discover the question of ideology is to open the chapter of conflictive semiotics (of the linguistics of conflict), which comes from the mandatory silence to which the peoples of the periphery, women, and youth have been reduced.

4.2.7.4   Science can be as ideological (5.7) as the conditioned mentality of the masses. The prevalent contemporary ideological mentality (that of the oligarchies of the empire or of dependent nations, as well as that of the masses insofar as they are oppressed, not insofar as they are popular exteriority) is the one that is founded on a dominative semiotic totality. A people, as an alienated mass, can have a naive ideological mentality that passively accepts the domination it undergoes. In this case the sign does not disclose the reality of oppression; it conceals oppression; it is false.

4.2.8   Semiotic Subversion

4.2.8.1   The ineffable, wordless "saying" (4.2.2.1) that springs from the exteriority of the oppressed questions the fetishist absolutization of a semiotic system (4.2.7.1). The wordless "saying," the provocative imperation of protest (4.2.6.1), is the revelation or deictic manifestation (*deiknynai* in Greek means "to indicate," "to show") of another significative space. The subversive word is *dabar* in Hebrew (which is not a mere comprehensive or expressive *logos*, but is operative, realizable, and subversive). Exposition (4.2.6) is linguistic subversion as revelation of the Absolute (3.4.8.1) in history through the epiphany of the poor.

4.2.8.2   The interjection as exposition of the pain of the oppressed (that is later articulated in the proclamations or manifestoes of liberation), the protest of women's liberation, the rebellion of the young man against his teachers, are messages, words, revelation, or metaphoric apocalypsis, for they take us beyond the spoken word toward the one who speaks as a distinct exteriority. It is impossible to decode that word (in its entirety) because its message remits me to a referent that is not a mere ontic meaning (something), but a metaphysical meaning (someone, the other). (It cannot be decoded entirely, but it can be decoded analogously, by approximation.) It situates this decoding not at the level of rational interpretation but at the level of acceptance of its meaning because the speaker says it (hence it is a historical act and one entailing the risk of faith; 2.4.8.4).

4.2.8.3   The only way to decode the meaning adequately is by carrying out a practical action of service (2.6.7.3) that allows the one who receives the message to approach the ambit of exteriority where the other person is. For those who find themselves in the prevailing semiotic totality, this means they must put themselves in an exterior critical situation without protection. That is why artistic geniuses in their bohemian lifestyle and political heroes in the persecution they endure and even in their death reach out to exteriority, a risk from which the new will come forth.

4.2.8.4   Semiotic, poietec, or poetic beauty finds exposition in the system of the *proyecto* of liberation of the oppressed; the future *proyecto* in the present system, the venture of the oppressed, the dawning today of what will be tomorrow. Artist and art expose to the system, as witnesses of what is to come, apocalyptically (if apocalypsis is the revelation of the word of the oppressed), the visage of the oppressed. That is why its exposition is ugly according to the rules and canons of beauty currently in force; but it is an innovation of the formal coherence of signs and is therefore procreation of the beauty of a new order.

The apparent ugliness of the countenance of the oppressed, the withered face of the farmer, the hardened hand of the laborer, the rough skin of the impoverished woman (who cannot buy cosmetics), is the point of departure of the esthetics of liberation. It is entreaty that reveals the popular beauty, the nondominating beauty, the liberator of future beauty. Estheticism is the dominating ideological imposition of the beauty admired by the cultures of the center and of the oligarchical classes (imposed by the mass media). It is the ideology of beauty.

4.2.8.5   The most oppressed classes do not always have the most acute critical awareness, but such awareness can be reached by classes that, although objectively not the most oppressed, are the ones upon whom ideological contradictions weigh the heaviest. That is why the philosopher (5.9.5.1–2 and 5.9.5.8), as an organic intellectual, as militant, can express the criticism of a people with the maximum of precision even if, by birth, culture, or work, the philosopher does not, from the beginning, belong to the oppressed classes.

4.2.9   Liberation of the Sign

4.2.9.1   A semiotics of liberation should describe the process of the passage of a given system of signs to a new order that surges forth when the old order is surpassed. Think, for example, of the coming into being of the romance languages from Latin by the invasion of exterior and oppressed Germanic peoples during the time of the Roman empire. In the same manner, the peripheral exteriority of Latin American, Arabic, black African, Indian, Southeast Asian, or Chinese semiotics will promote through their irruption into history (if a process of political liberation takes place; 3.1.7–8) a new global and future semiotics. The history of languages, for example, is the continuous fruit of such irruption and passage to new linguistic systems. The same can be said of the proposed semiotics of the oppressed classes (3.1.4), of liberated feminine culture, and of rebellious youth.

4.2.9.2   The praxis of semiotic liberation creates new words because it renews the sense of the world; it creates new cultural and historical codes. The expressive revelation of the people, which is welcomed only in silence, is the beginning of semiotic liberation. Its dynamism is the mobilization of the people itself, in whose exposition the provocative word is liberated.

4.2.9.3   Popular epic poetry of all peoples and of all historical moments is art par excellence. It is creative; it speaks of the ineffable, of what has never been told; it is the very narrative of popular liberation. The time will come when the poetry of Pablo Neruda or Ernesto Cardenal will become classic, that of a new order. In all events, popular art is the first art, the supreme expression of esthetics. It develops in daily life, in music, in dance, in painting, in the theatre. The murals of Orozco, Siqueiros, and Rivera in Mexico are there as the exposition of the people in a revolutionary stance. A popular esthetic must be formulated as a point of departure for the liberation of the sign and as expression of its real coherence.

4.3   POIETICS

4.3.1   *Status Questionis*

4.3.1.1   Poietics or philosophy of production really includes semiotics (4.2), but I have separated them for pedagogical reasons. In this section we turn to material production or the person-to-nature relationship (diagram 4), to physical nature, labor, and all its modalities (technology, design, art, etc.). Poietics concerns itself with a being as an artifact, as a product of the transformation of nature in culture (*D* in diagram 4). It concerns itself with productive labor in its most comprehensive sense, avoiding the not uncommon philosophical reduction that confuses poietics with esthetics or poetics, the "clean" part of human production.

4.3.1.2   I emphasize design because it includes as its integral moments technology and art—in its most genuine sense of operative, projective integration of science (4.3.2.5)—and the extension of art to daily life. The essential theme of design is that of endowing a product with formal coherence. It includes technology—and thus science in its poietic implementation insofar as this signifies functional coherence, use value. It includes esthetics because formal coherence, as such, is the beauty of a product.

4.3.1.3   In this way mechanical engineering, for example, and the inspired art of the artist are integrated into the objects used in the proxemic, in the person-to-artifact nearness of everyday life. Design is recent (it originated with the Industrial Revolution) but it is integrative because it constitutes the link with labor and culture.

4.3.2   From *Techne* to Design

4.3.2.1   The operative (practical) is not the same as the factive. The operable (*praktikos, agibile*) has to do with the realization of proximity with the other; the factible (*poietikos, factibile*) has to do with producing an artifact. In the same manner there are distinct methods or habits for the theoretical knowledge of science (5.1), for the practical exercise of prudence (5.4), and for poietic productivity (5.5). We must give this some historical clarification.

4.3.2.2   In effect, for Aristotle the methodical habit or knowledge behind the poietic act was *techne* ("art," "craft"). It was the skill used by the artisan and the artist (from the bricklayer of Athens to Phidias), in accordance with certain norms of production elaborated by reason (*orthos logos poietikos*). The *logos* of production is distinct from theory or praxis. The method of the theoretical *logos* is demonstrative; that of the practical *logos* is deliberative; that of the poietic *logos* is projective. The fruit of the theoretical *logos* is a demonstrated conclusion; of the practical *logos* a just and prudent decision; of the poietic *logos* an artifact with formal coherence (esthetic functionality).

4.3.2.3   Between the Renaissance and the seventeenth century, little by little, the classical *techne* (*ars* in Latin) began to diversify. On the one side appeared the artist, the man of the fine arts (the one who expressed the totality of the world in a work of art; 4.3.9.7–9); on the other side appeared the technician, the artisan, the one who knew how to manufacture artifacts (from a palace or a cathedral to a carriage, a cloak, or a good meal). The master or apprentice of the Middle Ages became the bohemian artist who lived under the patronage of a prince or a school of fine arts, or by the sale of his works, and the artisan was slowly transformed into the specialized laborer of the industrial world (since the English industrial revolution, approximately 1750).

4.3.2.4   The technician (who is not the nonspecialized laborer who works without method, skill, or craft), the empirical, expert artisan who includes in his work popular or vernacular art (not the art of the dominant classes performed by the artist of the reigning and dominating beauty of the museums) is displaced little by little by the technologist. That is, with the Industrial Revolution *techne* is transformed into technology. There appears a new *logos*. It is no longer, as for Aristotle, the artisan's *logos* of knowing how to manufacture thanks to long years of apprenticeship under a master. Now there is added to this *logos* (which is not discarded; the *logos* of the artisan should be present in the technologist) the scientific, theoretical, and practical *logos*.

Technology is the redefinition of *techne* from the scientific point of view. It is not merely applied science; on the contrary, it is the inclusion of science in technical activity, in the discourse of the poietic projectional *logos* (5.5.2). It is a maturation of technical discourse by means of the participation of science. The sugar in the sugar cane (let it represent science) changes in substantivity when ingested by an animal (let it represent technology). The sugar is not merely "applied to" the animal; it is incorporated into the animal's body. That is, technology is not applied science (concretized theory); it is scientific technique (poietics that includes in its own projectional productive process whatever it needs from science to achieve its own ends). Almost all scientists of the basic formal or theoretical sciences (especially mathematicians and physicists) find it difficult to comprehend that technology could be anything other than theoretical discourse.

4.3.2.5   In the twentieth century technology and art have been reintegrated. "Design" in English comes from the Latin (*designare*, to "mark out," "designate," "denote"); it means "to devise for a specific function," "to fashion (something malleable) according to plan." The twelve hundred designers who work for General Motors improve the styling of automobiles. The finished product is not only a functional (technological) artifact but one adapted to comfort (by beauty of its form, the feel of plush fabrics, etc.). Just as mechanical engineering (technology) determines the functionality of the transmission of an automobile, the designer decides the place for that transmission (subsystem), in relation to aspects of physical closeness and use (e.g., the position of the driver and the gearshift) within the total system— the field of ergonomics (biotechnology).

The responsibility of designers, inasmuch as they study the

direct person-to-artifact relationship, constitutes them as the technological-human moment par excellence. Technology is guided by the designer, who is not concerned only with the external appearance of a product, but with the formal esthetic-functional coherence of the totality of the artifact from its very beginning. Design is thus the contemporary synthesis of the ancient *techne*, the skill or methodology of poiesis as such. It is the projectional, integral, unificative synthesis of technology and art.

DIAGRAM 6

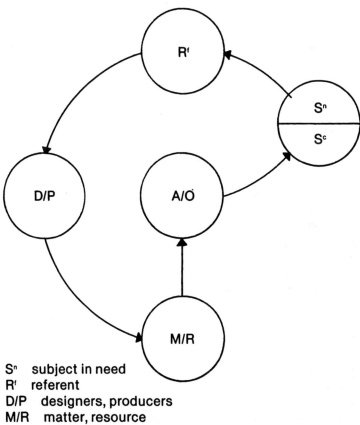

S^n subject in need
R^f referent
D/P   designers, producers
M/R   matter, resource
S^c subject of consumption
A/O   artifacts, objects

4.3.3   Negativity of Necessity

4.3.3.1   Human beings are finite, living beings. In order to live, they must replenish what their activity uses up. They are subjects with a lack of nourishment (the fruit of the earth, nature, agriculture, shepherding) to satiate their hunger, a lack of external covering to protect themselves from inclement weather, a lack of housing for the privacy of family living. "Lack of" is negativity. This negativity deepens with the appetite or desire for what will fill the lack. Necessity is the tension toward the object that satiates and of whose existence there is awareness. The object, the mediation, arises from the necessity of supplying what is lacking. The state of necessity produces a subject in need (S^n in diagram 6), origin of all productive acts and of all work.

4.3.3.2   One is, then, in a "state of necessity," conscious of something desired: the object that can satisfy necessity. In the capitalistic system there thrives a policy of the cultivation of desires. It is founded in the central thrust of the system itself and creates through publicity a collective desire or necessity—a market. The market produced not by a "natural" necessity but by propaganda is the fruit of an absolute criterion built into the economic system itself: to acquire the greatest possible profit from the smallest possible investment.

4.3.3.3   There are no primary (biological) or secondary (cultural) necessities as such: human needs are always biologico-cultural. There is no necessity that is fulfilled in a natural (precultural) manner. There is no cultural necessity that is not at the same time biologico-natural. The distinction between both types of necessity is so ideological as to absolutize the values of exchange and use.

4.3.4   Referent, Work, Matter

4.3.4.1   The productive act begins by conceiving positively what necessity demands negatively. Demands or requirements are formulated projectively as functional systems and subsystems of an artifact that does not yet exist; it is only possible, only imaginary. This I call referent (R^r in diagram 6) or *eidos,* the form to be given to a worked nature.

4.3.4.2 Once persons are schematically imaged in their functions (the "possible, tendential, ideative ground," Marx would say), they become designing or producing subjects (D/P in diagram 6). An *ego laboro* is immensely more valuable, more common, more unified, and more corporeal than an *ego cogito*. A person as a productive subject confronts nature (the noncultural or the nonworked; B in diagram 4) and constitutes it as matter. In poietic materialism the producing subject and work constitute nature as matter. The subject as history is the *a priori* of matter. Historical materialism judges the cosmological materialism of "everything is matter" as antidialectical and naive (3.4.8.2-3). In the producing act, matter ("that-with-which" something is done) is the resource (M/R in diagram 6).

4.3.4.3 The artifacts or objects (A/O in diagram 6) that surround us in our everyday world, in physical closeness, are products of human labor—tables, chairs, houses. But even trees in a garden and even natural parks left as a remembrance of pristine nature (4.1) anterior to the appearance of humankind are artistic products, natural museums, cultural moments (D in diagram 4). If some things are instruments, they were the object of human labor. Work on nature (poiesis, not praxis, as we shall see) is the full and integrated human action that effectuates or fulfills instruments, things-with-meaning, cultural objects, artifacts.

4.3.4.4 The theoretical act (in Greek, *theoria*) is contemplative, passive; it produces truth as discovery of whatever the being is. It is obtained through interpretation or previous demonstration. Its plenitude is ontology and science. The practical act (in Greek, *praxis*) is operative and active; it produces proximity with the other as justice; it is reached by decision, by imperation, by previous deliberation. Its plenitude is politics.

4.3.4.5 The poietic act (in Greek, *poiesis*) is factive, fabricative; it produces the artifact (that which is made by art: art-fact) as transformation of a cosmic thing into a sense-thing, an instrument. That is to say, the poietic act or work (intellectual or manual) changes the form of the matter (that which is worked upon) in order to give a real thing a structure (*morphe* in Greek) that serves a purpose: it is functional. The laborer has in mind a model (*eidos*) of the form that is to be given to cosmic matter, and by means of work (*ergon*), in a space that is no longer play-space (as for the child) but ergonomic, molds, with formal coherence (4.3.5), a cultural product.

4.3.4.6   Use value is what labor objectifies in natural matter and makes into an artifact, an instrument. It has value because it serves a purpose. Its functionality elevates the artifact above the mere real thing. The stone (real thing) of the Neolithic period is worth less than the carved flint that serves as the point of an arrow (artifact). The function of being able to pierce the hide of a hunted animal, of penetrating and resisting, is what makes the flint useful; it is the use value of such an artifact. The use value is not intrinsically a matter of economics; it has to do with poiesis, technology, design. Adam Smith clearly saw that work is the source of use value, but he did not see that it is not only part of the economy but also of ergonomics—the designing that includes technology, as we shall see.

4.3.4.7   Insofar as a product satisfies a need (consumption makes someone be a subject of consumption, S^c of the diagram 6), it has a functional value, a use value; but, and at the same time, it can be exchanged for something else. This is its exchange value. Exchange value—a thing as merchandise—is not absolute but relative to the sign value of a product, its disclosure of status ("I am different from the *hoi polloi*; therefore, I buy this!") or of fashion (accelerated obsolescence of a product in order to gain greater profits) in the capitalistic system of consumption and destruction. The sign value of a product refers to a whole semiotic or cultural system, which in reality fixes the sense of merchandise, commodities.

4.3.5   Formal Coherence

4.3.5.1   The formal coherence of an artifact is, in relation to the functional system where it is found, like a denotation with respect to a connotation (4.2.4.3). I am speaking here of the cohesion or unity of the artifact itself (relationships that are established in the totality of the being between the functional parts of its own structure), and not as it is a part of a larger system in which it is defined.

4.3.5.2   Organs are coherent, complicated, coordinated, supported intrinsically by their own constitution, essential parts of a living organism. In the human body they are the stomach, heart, brain, and the like. Each functional part is an organ that, although it performs its own function (the stomach digests, the heart propels the blood, etc.), coimplicates the other parts in the coherent structure of the whole. The stomach digests for the heart, which propels the blood to the stomach. The real substantivity of the living coherence, coimplication of its essential notes, is absolutely unique and inimitable (4.1.4–5). The formal coherence of an artifact is always minor; it is only mechanical, not living.

4.3.5.3   It should be understood that formal coherence is not like clothing or the outer form (styling) of a thing. The skin, the organs, and the form of a living organism are not independent. The technological act of design begins analogically at the very origin of a project, just as the form of an organism begins in the unicellular fertilized egg. The skin and the outer form are only the manifestations of functional subsystems.

4.3.5.4   Formal coherence, then, has a twofold aspect. On the one hand it is the adequate resolution of the functional problematics of the artifact, from the major subsystems to the ultimate subsystems or elementary moments (the functional form). On the other hand the final form of the product—visible, tactile—is the one that is appraised as being beautiful (esthetic value, always difficult to determine). The confluence of functional form (use value of the artifact) and esthetic form constitutes the best and adequate formal coherence of the artifact, objective of the poietic act or design. A good technological solution can be an unsatisfactory ergonomic resolution, inasmuch as it can propose an artifact that is excellent from the mechanical point of view but uncomfortable from the ergonomic point of view. And vice versa: a beautiful but useless artifact can be marketed because it has the appearance of usefulness (4.3.8).

4.3.6   Instrumental Totality and Undesigned Exteriority

4.3.6.1   Each artifact forms part of a cultural, functional, symbolico-significative totality. Its intrinsic formal coherence presupposes functional coherence with the cultural totality. Its incoherence, be it intrinsic or intrasystemic, determines its incompetence or dysfunctionality. The instrumental totality is what is called the material sphere of culture, but the expression is equivocal. In reality it is the artifactual level or the level of sense-things that are not only material but are signs (because they bear a form implanted by transformative, technologico-design work, esthetic ergonomics); they are things that have a function, which they fulfill within a totality of culture, semiotics, economics.

4.3.6.2   There will be as many functional totalities as there are worlds; more precisely, as many artifactual functionalities as there are practical systems. Just as the artifact is a mediation that is utilized at a distance from the other (2.2), the other is the one who defines the types of artifacts. There are systems of artifacts at the political level (from the highways of a nation to its factories), the sexual or domestic (from the house to the teaspoon), the pedagogical (from schools to hospitals), or the religious (such as a temple or an ornament). Each one of these structured totalities of artifacts predefines in certain ways the formal coherence of each product. The system precedes each subsystem or element.

4.3.6.3   In order to be able to evaluate any product, one has to know how to situate it in the instrumental totality in which it is to perform a determinate function. An automobile should be analyzed within the advanced industrial technological system that plays the role of subsystem within the economic system of imperialist consumption in its present stage. This system, on the other hand, is a subsystem of the political totality presently in force (which includes other subsystems, such as the governmental, military, etc.). Passage from the part to the whole, from the partial whole to the total whole, is proper to dialectics (5.2). Without dialectical discourse there cannot be scientific discourse or real technology.

4.3.6.4   A real thing (a branch on a tree, for example) is defined from its constitutive substantivity (4.1.4), independent of human intervention; an artifact (the branch as part of an arrow) is defined from human substantivity (4.1.5). Instrumental totality is nothing more than an internal unfolding of the world, which is a real moment of human substantivity. Therefore, the essence of the arrow, and not of the wood of the tree, is the worldly or cultural totality within which it fulfills a determinate function (in hunting, for example); the instrument is a moment of human essence.

4.3.6.5   The artifact, because it forms part of a system in which it receives its definition, cannot escape from frontiers that are fixed, for example, by the political sphere. The culture of the center is an instrumental system, as is also oligarchical neocolonial culture. In fact, the design of a peripheral nation or of a macho, authoritarian system functionally organizes artifacts so that they can be manipulated by and in favor of dominators. Design appears as its system of domination.

4.3.6.6   Outside the system presently in force and its dominant design is found a whole ambit that is judged by the oppressive totality as uncivilized, abject, undesigned. In the international order it is, metaphysically, what is considered by imperialist culture as barbarism; in the national order it is what is considered by oligarchical culture as vulgar and popular. The ambit that is undesigned—according to the measurement of the dominant design, according to its technology and criteria of beauty—is, in reality, designed in another manner. Latin American, African, and Asian cultures are, for the United States, at best, folkloric. For national oligarchies the culture and design of indigenous cultures (Amerindian, tribal, traditional) are backward, rude, behind the times.

4.3.6.7   Nevertheless, if there is to be any promising innovation in technology and design in the twenty-first century, it will depend on whether those ambits of exteriority, not designed for the prevailing system but of another design, will manage to articulate themselves in such a way that their traditional technology can be enriched by assimilating (from science) elements deemed necessary without losing its sense of history. If so, a vernacular, native, innovative technology and design will flourish.

4.3.7   Poietic Exteriority

4.3.7.1   What is needed is passage from an abstract exteriority—even if it seems to have a face—to a concrete exteriority by means of labor. The concept of exteriority must be complemented by that of "internal transcendentality" (2.4.8) to the same system as a totality. Exteriority is a transcendentality that cannot be defined entirely from and by totality. One of the forms it takes is that of "surplus work" that the system not only cannot absorb but that it denies, alienates, represses.

4.3.7.2   Untapped work potential—"surplus work"—a productive force unemployed by a system that does not know what to do with it (in contrast to the beginning of a system, when productive forces must double their efforts in order to achieve increased production)—leads to the conscious apparition of a historical subject exercising poietic or productive praxis.

4.3.7.3   Subjectivity concretely constituted by the structure of a system manifests itself as historical subjectivity—as an emergent class aware of its exteriority, by both anteriority and posteriority (the historical anteriority of the oppressed, the utopian posteriority of the struggle that begins for ushering in a new system). It takes shape in the space left vacant by the noncoincidence of labor and production, in the form of the unemployed time of the underemployed—that is, as marginality, lost time. But lost time can be subversive time, time in which awareness matures, in an emergent class, of the need for a new system.

4.3.7.4   It is precisely in the crisis of a productive system that historical subjects emerge. Poietic exteriority comes in the emergence of the internal transcendentality of historical subjectivity with awareness that it is capable of doing something more ("surplus work"). Unemployment leads to deeper awareness of the human condition; a face emerges and demands a new system.

4.3.7.5   The pure negativity of contradiction is neither the source nor the resolution of dialectics. Dialectical change is passage to a new totality. It takes place by the overcoming of a contradiction. Contradiction appears in the emergence of a historical subject—an unemployed class, with untapped productive potential. When the other one in the system emerges—as other with both exteriority and internal transcendentality (deeper consciousness of a class as capable of greater productivity, and consciousness of a longer history anterior to the dominating system), contradiction crystalizes. Opposition is real when, in view of a dominant class, there emerges a dominated class as a rebellious class, a nonconforming class, an *other* class. Neither passive negativity or contradiction (one class is not another class) nor active negativity (one class struggles against another class) originates and resolves itself in pure negativity. Negativity, passive as well as active, originates in the exteriority of internal transcendentality, in the analectical affirmation of the alterity of an emergent class, emerging as distinct. It is inevitable, dreadful, new. Its positive irruption founds opposition and struggle. The system enters into crisis.

4.3.7.6   The dialectical process as passage to a new totality cannot support itself only in the negative thrust of negation. It must also promote the affirmation of the alterity of the new system that arises from the manifestation of the exteriority of the other in the internal transcendentality of "surplus work," unemployed, unproductive.

4.3.7.7   It is because of this that the analectical moment of dialectical movement is the origin and resolution of that same dialectics and its negativity. The historical subject, as unused poietic or productive potential, is the origin of the affirmation of alterity, the internal manifestation of the exteriority or transcendental anticipation of the new system. It will be necessary to show how the essence of the subjectivity in power is the origin of "surplus work," beyond the totality.

4.3.8   Productive Alienation

4.3.8.1   Dependent and exploited nations behold with dismay the contradiction of an alien design on their own soil. They deplore the haphazard imitation of diverse technologies exported by powers of the center with conflicting poietic criteria. The main street in a rural village is coursed by a donkey and an oversize Chevrolet. Alongside the *campesino* dressed in clothing spun by his wife walks another dressed in the latest Western fashion. Cultural, economic, and political dependence is an internal contradiction affecting all instrumental constituents. The negation of popular culture also negates its technology and the possibility of a technology and design that would harmoniously plan the ecology of the nation, of the continent—the rightful goods of dependent groups.

4.3.8.2   An alienated design is an ideological design. It is not only the ideological concept of formulation that conceals domination (4.2.7). A form that deceives or exploits the dominated is likewise ideological; it is a form that hides domination to the benefit of a dominator. In design, the styling (stylization of a product so that its appearance fascinates buyers and escalates sales) fulfills the function of an ideological sign. A particular automobile has the appearance of enormous power, with fins to deflect or capture a possible current of air; in reality it is a car of reduced velocity, duration, and stability. The cleavage between the use value (functionality) and the sheer value of exchange and of status symbol (4.3.4.7) leads to the discovery of a profound sense of alienation, its ideologico-semiotic and technological meaning. Esthetics puts technology at the service of profit for capital investment.

4.3.8.3   In the dependent nations such ideologically embellished products can be acquired only by minority groups, oligarchical and dominative, to the detriment of the national balance of imports and exports.

4.3.9   Productive Liberation

4.3.9.1   Liberation on the level of technological design and production implies a self-determination that only politically and economically free peoples can have. These two freedoms are secured in an authentic, ideological, cultural revolution that knows how to appraise adequate national production. "Adequate technology" is not that of the folkloric production of alternative artifacts on a small scale, in the small-minded, reformist manner encouraged by the dominant capitalist system. It is a question of beginning with a technology and design that have other criteria, native to the underdeveloped countries.

4.3.9.2   The first criterion of all technology or design of liberation in the peripheral countries is the guarantee of the right to work. The need for manual labor, much greater than in the developed countries, highlights the imperative of full employment. The right to life is fulfilled not by guaranteeing the necessities of survival such as nourishment and health, but by fostering human dignity. It is by work that a person earns the right to life.

4.3.9.3   Other criteria are minimal use of capital, use of middle technology (though superior technology may sometimes be necessary), and use of national resources whenever possible (e.g., the use of natural, not enriched, uranium, so as not to depend on developed nations). Liberation of technology and design is an essential objective, though it may be a long-term one. China itself has abandoned in part the creation of its own national technology and has opened itself to the influence of foreign technology, which will bring with it a whole world of destruction and unnecessary consumption.

4.3.9.4   If the economic and technological labor that goes into products that bear the value of exchange, of sign, and of use would become imbued with the significance of being at the same time labor that goes into products that bear the esthetic value of art, when the laborer would work on matter to manufacture a useful product as the artist works on the same matter to create a work of beauty—at that moment economy and esthetics would become identical. If at the same time justice would reign in politics and sexuality (and therefore in pedagogy) and before the Absolute, then immediate proximity (2.1) would no longer leave room for antagonistic mediations (2.3)—that is, there would be no more alienation (2.5). This utopia, impossible in history, nevertheless can guide our reflection even though it be only to see the alienation in which we live and realize the need for liberation at diverse levels. The eschatological utopia is a source of clearsightedness, of praxis, and of poiesis.

4.3.9.5   But as long as the utopia is not realized, and it seems that by definition it is unrealizable, the truth is that the majority of nations (the peripheral, dependent, and oppressed ones) and the majority of their inhabitants (the farmers, laborers, and marginals), the everyday economic-poietic laborers, live in a vulgar selling of their being, their reality, and their lives for wages that do not even replenish the energy expended in their labor. The wretched of the earth live in a monstrous chasm between economy and esthetics. They work like animals to produce artifacts that others will use; they eat less than do animals, they cannot express their own culture; the fruit of their labor is alienated from them. It is hell on earth, the land that Europe founded when it sent the Amerindians to work in the gold and silver mines, when it enslaved Africans, when it colonized Asians.

4.3.9.6   In the liberating act the other recovers human appearance. The apparent ugliness (for the white and blond Occidental) of the copper Amerindian, of the black African, of the yellow Asiatic, the degradation of the sexual object, the prostituted woman, the passive attitude of sheer memory of the child who imitates the paternal culture. Such "ugliness" will soon appear as the most radiant and fascinating (but not fetishist) beauty.

The expression and exposition of such beauty—the countenance of an oppressed people, of its culture, its reality—this is the supreme esthetics, popular esthetics. It is the coincidence in the product or artifact of functional-esthetic coherence, of mediation as creation, of the useful as service or gift—the wedding gift of sexuality, the merited and worked gift of a new country in justice. It is the beautiful, fresh, warm, fragrant, and flavorful bread that renourishes life for love, for the embrace, the celebration, the kiss . . . in the freedom of the free persons who have liberated themselves from a prison.

4.4   ECONOMICS

4.4.1   *Status Questionis*

4.4.1.1   Economics is the part of philosophy that thinks out the practical-productive person-to-other relationship mediated by the product of the person-to-nature relationship. The economic relationship is concrete and real; in comparison with it merely practical or poietic-productive relationships (4.2–3) are abstract or lacking in historical and institutional reality. Practical relationships, even when they are totalized, are abstract with respect to economics. The practical face-to-face relationship, as a metaphysical moment in justice, is the ultimate instance of the reality of economics. All production, distribution, or interchange is done for someone (and this is the practico-metaphysical moment of economics, always, in all systems or conceptions of economics).

4.4.1.2   Economics, then, is the relationship of the practical level (political, sexual, pedagogic, and antifetishist) to the productive level (semiotics, technology, design, etc.). Without work (productive level) there is no concrete proximity (practical), but there is no poietics without practical reference. The unity of both is economics; someone makes a gift or sells to someone, or buys or steals from someone. The first "someone" is the point of departure of economics; the "something" is the product of a work; the "other" is the frontier of the practical, now economic, relationship.

4.4.1.3   Economics studies the mechanisms of concrete production, of interchange, distribution, and consumption of a given social structure, and the interdependencies among those mechanisms and structures. It questions present-day systems with regard to alienation of the other at the productive-practical level and liberation of the other.

DIAGRAM 7

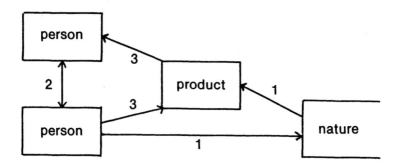

1 poietic-productive relationship
2 practical relationship
3 practical-productive or economic relationship

4.4.1.4   Scholars have frequently succumbed to economism (forgetfulness of practical or poietic moments) or to ideological positions that deny the consistency of economics (idealisms that justify economic oppression, as in the case of Scheler: he so over-rates spiritual values that he weakens material ones such as eating, clothing oneself, or dwelling). Both extremes will be surpassed by an economics with a metaphysical sense, where the practical-productive has its own unity, which derives from the human essence of the same relationship.

4.4.2   Primitive Economics

4.4.2.1   Human beings gather or produce from nature what is necessary to fill their needs (poietic), but always in a group, in a family, clan, tribe, or society (practical). The origination of the practico-poietic relationship makes of economics a primary human experience: we barter for the necessary things in life. Even the innocent suckling of the child is already, as we have said

(2.1.3.2), a utopian economics: it is nourishment exchange without work (on the part of the newborn).

4.4.2.2   The utopian economics of giving nourishment to the infant had an undifferentiated prolongation in primitive economies within which humanity for hundreds of millennia fulfilled in the individual all the functions of the group: hunting, gathering, fishing, maintaining a household. There were simple products and a primary community. This was the practico-productive mediation of the nomads, lost in an inhospitable and infinite nature. Humankind produced and reproduced the life of the group. Some products (that had use value) were already exchanged by barter with other members of the group (thus exchange value appeared in the world of economic relationships). Little by little one group would exchange with another group. Human intelligence had no trouble distinguishing between the use value (the "what-for") of a product and its exchange value (its value "for another").

4.4.3   Economic Systems

4.4.3.1   Human exchanges (in productive and practical systems) gradually increased across the millennia; they became systematized, reproducing and sometimes destroying themselves, some imposing their dominion over others. The practico-productive totality guaranteed survival (modes of production of human life). The distinct manner in which their terms related, the distinct content of the relationship itself, kept on generating in history diverse modes of practico-productive totality; in some cases they retained their primitive simplicity (nomadic clans or tribes of hunters, fishers, gatherers), and others began to be planters until, some eight millennia before Christ, some groups developed agriculture as such; others subsisted on shepherding; others improved hunting techniques and transformed them into war methods. Thus began the era of complex practico-productive totalities or Neolithic modes of production.

4.4.3.2   Because they excelled in the techniques of warfare (for example, in the domestication of the horse and the use of steel), the Indo-Europeans dominated politically (practically) the agricultural peoples of the valley of the Indus, of Mesopotamia, of what is today Turkey, Greece, Italy, and Europe in general.

Some persons dominated others (practical domination) and appropriated for themselves the product of the other's work. They did this in two ways: because they defined themselves as proprietor of the very being of the other (slavery) and thus possessed the other's life, work, and the fruit of that work; or because they demanded that part of the product of the other's work be given to them (tributary system). All the group economies practico-productive totalities or modes of production up to the fifteenth century can be reduced to these two.

4.4.3.3 On account of the crisis of the fourteenth century, Europe underwent the collapse of feudalism (recessive tributary system); this nearly coincided with the founding of overseas colonies. Thanks to revenue from rural areas and from the colonies, Europe witnessed the birth of a new practico-productive system, capitalism. During the eighteenth century, mercantilism became industrialized. Product as merchandise began to predominate.

4.4.3.4 The being of the capitalist economy is merchandise, the product that bears an exchange value. Merchandise or exchange value are not an absolute moment; they are relative to a totality that explains and sustains them: capitalist social formation. An economic system always tends toward a projected goal (within capitalism, "to-be-in-wealth"), toward the foundation whence come the possibilities or mediations that are like bridges that permit their realization. In economics such mediations are the products or fruits of human labor (4.3.4.5); they have been produced as mediations for a *proyecto*. The simplest is nourishment (by cultivation of the soil) in order to satiate hunger. In capitalism, however, products are produced not primarily to fulfill necessities but to be a mediation of profit; merchandise, not need. Merchandise, then, as mediation, lets us view the economic system as a totality. All economic reality takes place in a concrete system, be it microeconomic (e.g., the level of erotic economy or the industrial enterprise), or national, regional, or global macroeconomics. Small systems are only subsystems of the global economic system, which today is dominated by imperialist management of capital and the planetary dimensions of the transnational corporations. The controlling system is the capitalist, central mode of production, whose history Emmanuel Wallerstein records.

4.4.3.5 If all economy takes place in a system, the discovery of the basis of that system permits us to explain the parts from the viewpoint of the whole. It is necessary to know how to ascend from the abstract (the part: the company, for example, or the nation) to the concrete (the historical whole: a national or international economy). The ultimate foundation, the Being of all economic systems, is human labor not yet differentiated; *laboriousness*, work as work (indeterminate, unconditional, unsevered from the person-to-nature relationship). In each concrete historical system or social formation composed by one or many modes of production, work as work is the foundation of being, of the crystalized or objectified work—product as product.

4.4.3.6   A mode of production is always an internal moment or subsystem of a historical social formation. The mode of production includes person-to-nature relationship (4.3.2 and 4.3.4) and a person-to-person relationship (politics; 4.1). The mode of production is not only political (e.g., the master-slave relationship) or technological (the metallurgy of the Iron Age), but properly economic (5.9.3.5) insofar as it is the unity between politics and technology, and vice versa. Against economism it must be said that the mode of production does not determine absolutely the political or technological, but that it is the necessary condition that is conditioned (by politics and technology) and conditioning (of both).

4.4.3.7   Social formations are the concrete structures that are organized in reality, in history, by one or several modes of production, one being dominant and the others subordinate to it. Contemporary social formations are dominated by the capitalist imperialist social formation, as global and central system. Peripheral social formations—in Latin America, the Arab world, black Africa, India, or Southeast Asia (but not China, for it has a socialist social formation)—have diverse and even contradictory modes of production. There are modes of communal primitive production, tributary in some places; there are even some that perpetuate feudalism and slavery; and there is the mode of production of the simple small trader who is slowly absorbed into the dependent, capitalist, peripheral mode of production. Therefore, in analyzing peripheral social formations one must keep in mind precapitalist structures and the form of aggression taken by capitalism (whether mercantile, industrial, or imperialist.)

4.4.3.8   The historical concrete content of its foundation defines a system or social formation. In this manner the capitalist system is adequately defined by the fact that division of labor crystalizes in capital that absorbs the surplus value achieved by the productive work of the industrial laborer, whether of the center or the periphery. Dialectical and ontological description forms the beginning of the elucidation of economics as apodictic science.

4.4.3.9   Every economic product, merchandise, or being is always found in an economic system or totality that can be described dialectically (5.2), from the parts to the whole, and scientifically, from the foundation to its constitutive elements. This is true from the systems of the distant Paleolithic or Neolithic ages to industrial or subsequent society.

4.4.4   Economic Exteriority

4.4.4.1   As in all the anterior moments of our discourse—because reality itself imposes it—there always arises a moment that is not comprised within the system. It is an asystematic, asymmetric, anarchic moment, a kind of ana-economy (as there is ana-oedipus or ana-lectics). Something is beyond the present-day system of economics. Without doubt, that which is ana-economic—the exteriority of the system—cannot be anything else but that which has not been included in the totality. It retains autonomy and independence. It will be given a derogatory name because it does not adhere to the values of the system; it is not included within the *proyecto* of the system and cannot be manipulated by its mediations: the economics of poverty, of the poor, of the oppressed classes, of dependent, underdeveloped, "uncivilized" nations that have not been absorbed by the system.

4.4.4.2   It is easy to understand that the Neolithic systems that European colonial powers confronted, beginning in the sixteenth century, in Latin America, Africa, and Asia were exterior economic totalities to what a little later would be the center. What is more difficult is to rediscover such exteriority in the periphery after the impact of conquest, colonization, and imperialism. The preexistent economic systems were transformed into subsystems assumed within the system in force, into dominated or secondary modes of production in peripheral social formations. Nevertheless, there is always some economic exteriority if there are distinct structures (in indigenous minorities, in African and Asian popular classes), distinct procedures for exchange, distinct signification (exchange value is a cultural symbol or a status symbol [4.3.4.7] of a product because, simply, there is cultural exteriority [3.3.3.3–4]). In the capitalist mode of production, there is a marked distinction between hourly employees (the subjects of work) and salaried employees. National culture (3.3.8.2) and popular culture (3.3.8.3), the human productive subject as exteriority, set up an economy of exteriority.

4.4.4.3   In the economic (and therefore cultural) experience of China or Nicaragua (simultaneous national and popular exteriority with respect to the center) one could expect some novelty for the global economic system. Otherwise, that system will continue the policy of reformist modifications of a totality that is heading for the ruin of both humanity and nature.

4.4.5   The Alienation of Erotic-Pedagogical Economic Systems

4.4.5.1   All of what has been said so far can be situated on the level of sexual economics (topics suggested by Engels in *The Origin of the Family* or Freud when he talks about work as the postponement of desire) or on the level of pedagogy (issues treated, e.g., by Illich in his deschooling hypothesis or that of the death of medicine). Both levels are not mere subsystems of the political economy; they retain a relative exteriority.

4.4.5.2   In the totality of the family, the house (*oikos*, whence *oikonomia*), there can be found an economic-erotic system. The father goes out the door and comes back with his wages. The wife, alienated in the macho system, works as a "housewife" (married to a house) doing domestic chores, an unpaid servant of the male. Within the dominant classes her work consists in augmenting comfort and consumption (she is the principal target of advertising). Through the economic alienation of the wife, family alienation is maintained.

4.4.5.3   In the same manner there are economic-pedagogic subsystems or services (schools, social services, clinics, etc.). They all become autonomized and instead of serving the user, they systematically exploit users. The medical system through its chemical therapy produces new sickness; it demands unnecessary analysis; it eliminates popular, less expensive medicine; it increases the cost of medications and therapy. The school that shuns the traditional methods of educative communication makes itself the only means of education. In this way a people is left definitively illiterate and uncultured (because the school does not start from popular culture). The costly service systems in the periphery do not do their job. Bureaucracies dominate.

4.4.6   National and International Economic Alienation

4.4.6.1   We return here to a fundamental thesis of philosophy of liberation (see diagram 1). European expansion, beginning with the sixteenth century (1.2.2), and later American expansion (1.2.5), have alienated the economies of the peoples that are now their neocolonies (in Latin America, the Arab world, black Africa, India, Southeast Asia, with the exception of China, Vietnam, and a few other countries). Peripheral social formations (dependent nations) are dominated by the imperialist system. Its domination results in enormous profits from manipulation of the low price of raw materials and the high price of manufactured goods. Samir Amin has demonstrated that 80 percent of the benefits that the center realizes in its commercial interchanges come from the periphery. The work of the laborer and farmer and even the capital of dominated nations are continuously exploited. Part of the labor of the periphery is paid to the center in the form of licenses, insurance, exorbitant interest rates on loans, technology (inadequate), false sales reports of the products of transnational corporations in peripheral countries, and so forth. The theft of the surplus value achieved in the periphery accounts for the structured dissymmetry in the world of today. Philosophy of liberation takes this fact as the origin of a radical theoretico-epistemological rupture. It is on this level that the most devastating human alienation in our time takes place, the alienation of alienations, the one that conditions all the others.

4.4.6.2   Even though in an abstract, but precise, manner, the question of the dependence of peripheral countries—at the level of both invested and circulating capital—can be sketched as in diagram 8. A more developed country (*A*) gains "extra profit" (*ep*) in the sale of its products, whereas a less developed country "transfers" (surrenders) its surplus value (*sv*) in the sale of its products.

In terms of the "organic composition of capital," a more developed country (*A*) can produce merchandise at a lower market value (*mv*) than that of a less developed country (*mv¹*) because the peripheral country has a lower productivity due to less advanced technology. In the sale of its products to a less developed country, a more developed country can offer a sale price (*sp*) equal to what it sells for domestically ($sp = mv + \quad ep$). On the contrary, the peripheral country must sell its products at a lower price ($sp^{1} = mv^{1} - sv$) than if sold domestically, in order to compete. It thus transfers its surplus value to the more developed country ($a\ b =$ surplus value robbed from peripheral labor). This type of profit and transfer constitutes the *life* of the poor of the Third World, who feed the economy of the more developed countries.

DIAGRAM 8

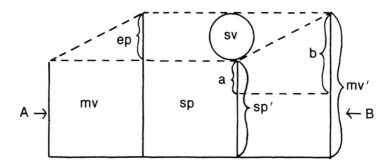

4.4.6.3   The alienation that reigns at the global level (discovered by the "theory of dependence") is doubled on the national peripheral level by internal geopolitical domination and dependence. Spatially, certain regions (populous capital cities: São Paulo, Buenos Aires, Mexico City, Cairo, Bombay, etc.; or more affluent regions because of industry, mining, etc.) wield power over others, achieving a fictitious appearance of high development (e.g., the bureaucracies of neocolonial African states), which contrasts with the level of extreme poverty of the majority of the population. External dissymmetry (imperialist center vs.

neocolonies) is reproduced internally (neocolonial center vs. urban and rural poverty). It is evident that privileged regions are geopolitical mediations of the center.

4.4.6.4   Developmentalist models of economy are intended to make the world believe that the origin of underdevelopment is the fact that backward countries do not imitate the models of the developed countries. The solution would be to bring capital and technology to the poor countries (substitution of imports). This developmentalist ideology does not understand or admit that the origin of underdevelopment is theft—international structural injustice that dates back five centuries: the exploitation of the periphery because of the low prices paid for its exports. There will not be any true development without cessation of dependence, without liberation of national economies, without transforming the capitalist imperialist social formation of the center, its very mode of production.

4.4.7   Peripheral Capital-Labor Alienation

4.4.7.1   Another mediation of center-periphery alienation or transnational-dependent national market alienation is the one that is carried out by means of dependent national capital (dependent capitalism). The theft of capital-labor surplus value (that is, the profit that capital extracts from what should be paid to workers) produces intranational distortion in the periphery that not only consolidates class differences but also impedes national liberation and entrenches the hegemony of imperialism.

4.4.7.2   All neocolonial national enterprises depend, for their technology at least, on the large transnational enterprises. Moreover, they live parasitically off their propaganda, organization, and expansion. Managerial dependent microeconomy is nothing else but a secondary mediation of the imperialist international macroeconomy.

4.4.7.3   The dependent neofascist models of economy (such as the Brazilian, or Chilean, Argentinian in 1976, with social repression and dependent capitalism) and populist models (a coalition of classes under the hegemony of the national bourgeoisie, with collaboration of the proletariat—Haya de la Torre, Vargas, Cárdenas, Perón, or Nasser) appear to be unacquainted with the fact that, in their essence, such models accept the transnationals and therefore permit capital-labor surplus value to leave the country in the form of center-periphery surplus value. If there is not a restructuration of the neocolonial system, there will not be economic liberation of the periphery. A new mode of production is necessary in dependent nations.

4.4.8   Economic Liberation of the Periphery and Its Laboring Classes

4.4.8.1   We are dealing, then, with an anti-economics, an economy that bears the ideological significance of micro-economics or of developmentalist or imperialist economics. Because economic alienation is the fulfillment of all alienations (inasmuch as it enslaves persons to work nature for the benefit of a dominator, emptying their very Being; 2.5), economic liberation is the concrete realization of human liberation, the process by which the oppressed hurl themselves into a new projection of a system of economics through the affirmation of their cultural exteriority.

4.4.8.2   Economic liberation of the dependent nation is the first objective. The *proyecto* of economic liberation should be realized in view of an operative model. Such models are essentially three in number: those that formulate development by the intervention of transnational corporations (dependent capitalism), by means of the managerial leadership of the national bourgeoisie (independent capitalism), or by the leadership of the popular classes (socialism). Populism is a version of the second formula, with claims of affinity with the third. In the end, it would turn to either the first or the third version.

4.4.8.3   In the periphery the largest national enterprises are those of the state. And because the bourgeoisies of the periphery "were born too late" (they cannot obtain surplus value from colonies, as the English and French bourgeoisies did, or as much surplus value from the proletariat as the exploitation of labor in the eighteenth and nineteenth centuries did), it is predictable that the exchange pattern of the periphery will tend either toward dependent capitalism (with fascist politics) or toward a socialism of transition (with popular or national politics)—the transition from one mode of production to another.

4.4.8.4 Bourgeois humanism, which was based on manual labor in its struggle against the hereditary nobility from the ninth century to the English and French revolutions, established private property and its inheritance as human and divine rights. It was thus able to accumulate and increase over the years a given capital possessed by the same hands, the same families, the same classes. Capitalism rests on this fixation, this institutional crystalization—exclusive possession perpetuated by inheritance.

4.4.8.5 Once some possess everything and the others nothing, freedom of economic production, of sales, of purchases, of advertising, is decreed: competition. It is evident that the big wolf will eat the little one, according to Hobbes's definition (1.1.7.3). Therefore, the liberation of the people or oppressed classes implies first the reestablishment of justice so that authentic economic freedom can be exercised—not the freedom by which the powerful destroy the weak, but the freedom in which equals can choose what is just. This will demand the dismantling of the structures that anchor the distortion and dissymmetry of the present economic order, which permits and promotes the system whereby some derive benefits through the purchase of the labor of others, sold to the highest bidder.

4.4.8.6 The system of capitalist enterprise, with hereditary capital on the part of some and the sale of their labor on the part of others (which originated during the Middle Ages with the guilds of masters and apprentices, went through a fundamental change due to the accumulation of colonial capital, was again redefined during the Industrial Revolution, and yet again with the coming of national and international monopolies), can no longer be imitated in the periphery. The liberation of the rural and working classes calls for a total economic revolution. Philosophy of economics must clarify this problematic, the one of transition to another global system, this time without a periphery, beyond the capitalist mode of production.

4.4.9 Economics of Liberation

4.4.9.1 Economics or service (*habodah*) to the other as other, to the oppressed, the poor, women, and youth is the economics of liberation; it is the act par excellence in which metaphysics is historically realized (2.6.7). It is worship offered to the Absolute (3.4.7), because praxis (the pedagogical suckling, the erotic kiss, the political embrace, the religious prayer) is equivocal until it is tested by factual, real, effective mediation. It is not a matter of becoming informed that the oppressed are hungry; it is necessary to give good bread to the hungry. Bread implies preparing the ground, sowing the seed, cultivating the field, taking in the harvest, grinding the seed, kneading the dough, baking the bread, storing it, transporting it, and putting in on the plate of the hungry person. It implies work, suffering, skill, technology, design, and art. It implies poiesis, justice, structures, equality, freedom, and *habodah*; it implies service, culture, and worship.

4.4.9.2   Liberative economy is service in justice, mediation that ministers to the other, technical innovation and technology for the other—for the other's growth, development, happiness. Without economy everything is an illusion, anarchy, or utopia (in the sense of flightiness: proclaiming the impossible because the mediations necessary for its realization are not worked on). Liberation does not imply only one *proyecto* and one enthusiasm, but planned, effectuated, viable mediations that are technologically efficient. Without economic liberation—which implies inspiration from popular, traditional, national institutions—there is no real liberation. If it is true that political revolution produces an opening in the previous system, only with the mediation of technological design and labor can a new system be organized in justice today. Without work, efficacious work with scientific mediation, there is no bread. Without bread a people is not liberated. It dreams of the fleshpots of Egypt, where at least there was bread. But without just distribution, bread is kept in the granary by the oppressor; the poor have no access to it.

4.4.9.3   Economy as service to the other, to the oppressed, builds the house—the home of the liberated family—the factory, and the assembly of the community where all forge their own destiny in political economy. It provides schooling, radio, and television. It constructs the cultural world and history—in justice!

5

FROM SCIENCE TO
PHILOSOPHY OF LIBERATION

In this chapter I shall develop a discourse that has as its theme the discourses of the preceding four chapters: a meta-discourse. It treats the question of methods, of knowing how to advance by way (*meta-hodos*) of theory, of practice, of poiesis, until the determination of the method of philosophy of liberation is arrived at and a model of the process of its critical discourse is proposed (5.9.4).

5.1 SCIENCE

5.1.1

Everyday comprehension and interpretation of the world is naive, not critical; it always gives beings their obvious sense. Nevertheless, it is critical, at least relatively, with regard to interpretations of peoples called primitive. Thus, for the Aztecs the sun is the god Huitzilopochtli; for the present-day average person the sun is a star around which the earth revolves constantly. For its part, scientific interpretation is critical with respect to the everyday interpretation of the average person because it can describe the sun in a much fuller and more precise manner. It can explain that the heat we receive from the sun is due to the combustion of 800,000 tons of hydrogen per second. Having a critical view of everyday beings presupposes digression from everyday ingenuousness and access to the level where the scientist functions as scientist.

5.1.2

The scientific method, traditionally, was defined as an explicative and demonstrative process. In his *Analytics* Aristotle explains the demonstrative process (apodictical: etymologically, a "showing from") starting from principles. Kant divides the

DIAGRAM 9

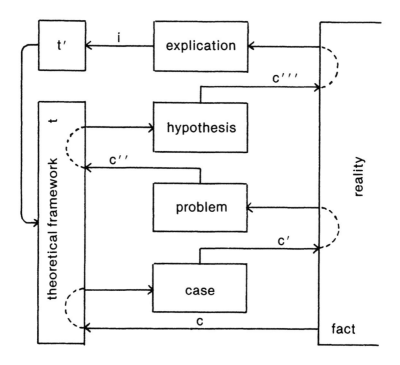

sciences into analytical, tautological, properly demonstrative (formal sciences such as logic and mathematics), and those that proceed by synthetic *a priori* judgments. These last-named sciences are determined by their principles, which define the conditions for the possibility of *a priori* scientific knowledge, with regard to both the categories of understanding and the materiality of experience. Today facts are interpreted by theories that lead to explications or conclusions with varying degrees of probability or falsifiability.*

5.1.3

The factual sciences have as their sphere of activity the ontic level of what are semantically referred to as natural beings (4.1.2.2). Their point of departure is facts. A fact is the real constitutive note of a thing by which it is actualized or appears in the world. A datum, on the other hand, is the enunciation of that note or the real phenomenal aspect of a thing insofar as it is real; it is the enunciation of a real moment. Thus the factual sciences (fact in Latin is *factum*) take into account as an essential category of their discourse real substantivity, be it physical (4.1.3), living (4.1.4), or even human (4.1.5)—insofar as the human is natural, not cultural or historical (5.3).

5.1.4

The scientific process starts from the fact as a phenomenon. The fact is, then, an object of experience through perception or through direct or indirect proof. Science does not concern itself with the fact as a fact but with the explication, the *why*, of the fact.

5.1.5

The science model proposed in diagram 9 is a purely pedagogical simplification of the scientific process. It begins with a *fact* that must be confronted (*c*) with an *a priori* theoretical framework or body of existent theories (*t*). Interpreted at first in its everyday sense, the fact, as representative of similar facts (a *case* to be studied), is then confronted (*c'*) with reality in order to gather data to be able to interpret the fact precisely, scientifically. One discovers or does not discover a *problem*. If there is a problem, it is defined clearly and precisely in an appropriate scientific

*Falsifiability is a concept developed by Karl R. Popper (*The Logic of Scientific Discovery* [Harper & Row, 1970]; *Objective Knowledge: An Evolutionary Approach* [Oxford University Press, 1972]).

code. The problem is then confronted (c^{11}) with a theory, with its laws, and with the totality of its systematic structures. From this confrontation a *hypothesis* for scientific investigation may or may not be worked out. If it is, the hypothesis is then confronted (c^{111})—by means of appropriate techniques, which implement in this decisive phase the specific scientific case method—with the fact, with other facts, and with their concrete and real system. From the techniques of explication, confrontation, and proof— the experimental method—a conclusion of explication must follow. If the hypothesis is verified, within varying degrees of probability, it is integrated (i) into the theory, which by this very integration is somewhat modified (t^1), either because it has been corroborated and thus has more force, or because it has been complemented, or because it has been negated (shown to be false). In all instances t^1 gives feedback to the theoretical framework and becomes the new theoretical framework for the next scientific investigation.

5.1.6

The principle of scientific, factual logic is no longer the principle of causality, at least not in its naive classic sense. It could be said that real substantivity, by its very constitutive structure, demands as principle the *real* coimplication of data and facts of experience. Coimplication as a principle and substantivity as a category differentiate factual sciences from purely formal sciences, whose proper sphere is abstract: they are concerned with logical beings or abstract quantity, having as their own category pure systematization and as their principle *formal* coimplication (not to be confused with real coimplication). Inasmuch as they are tautologous or analytical, the formal sciences cannot truly be called sciences of the real but only demonstrative or apodictic *a priori* methods. They are instrumental meta-discourses, scientific mediations.

5.2   DIALECTIC

5.2.1

If science is explication of the data of experience by theories, there is another methodical sphere that is not apodictic or scien-

tific (epistemic), but "monstrative" or deictic, a sphere that—
because it is the origin itself—cannot depart from (*apo-*) anything
anterior, as science does. In this strict sense, dialectic goes
through (*dia-*) various ontic horizons from totality (2.5) to totality until it arrives at the fundamental one. Aristotle in his *Topics*
showed that dialectic was a method beyond the scientific because
it could question the very principles of science derived from everyday opinions (*ta endoxa*). For his part Marx, in the few pages on
the method of political economy in the *Grundrisse*, describes the
dialectical method as the movement that ascends "from the abstract to the concrete" (*vom Abstrakten zum Konkreten anzus-
teigen*), until it reaches the simplest category (*die einfache
Kategorie*), which is nothing less than the foundation of totality.

5.2.2

The proper sphere of dialectic is the ontological—that is, the
passage from one horizon of beings to another until it reaches its
foundation. On the semantic level dialectic refers to concrete systems having as a point of departure (or of arrival, if one prefers)
the everyday world on its acritical level. The category proper to
the dialectical method is totality. Its principle is that of identity
and difference—that is, the dialectical method starts from the
very principle of science. It can think about the presuppositions
of all scientific theory and it does so from the world, from the
political, sexual, pedagogical, economic levels. It can think of
nature itself as a moment in the history of the world; it can question the totality of science. The ultimate presuppositions are the
theme of dialectic.

5.2.3

The scientific process begins with theory and explains its results; it is explicative. The dialectical process, with regard to
sciences, begins with theories or with science as a totality and
raises itself to their historical, social, or economic presuppositions. It raises itself from the abstract (science) to the concrete
(practical or poietic totalities; 3.1–4.4). It does not demonstrate
the foundation; but it shows it as first, through a *reductio ad
absurdum*, its corollaries, its final coherence in the identity of the

system as totality in which all differences (beings, parts, functions) recover their ultimate meaning.

5.2.4

The dialectical method can be used in all types of discourse, be it political, sexual, pedagogical, or antifetishist, or in the elucidation of the sciences of nature, semiotics, economics, or technologico-esthetics. It is, moreover, the ontological method of philosophy. Every horizon is the being that grounds everything included in its sphere. It is a critical method with respect to which the scientific method is often as ingenuous as the average person is with respect to the scientist. We have reached a fourth level of discourse: after the one of the more primitive culture, the one of the contemporary average person, and the one of the scientist, there is the one of the dialectician. Each is naive with respect to the one that follows it and critical with respect to the one that precedes it.

5.3   THE ANALECTICAL MOMENT

5.3.1

As we have seen in 2.4, exteriority is the sphere located beyond the foundation of totality. The sphere of exteriority is real only because of the existence of human freedom (2.4.6). The merely natural substantivity of a person (4.1.5) acquires here all its uniqueness, its proper indetermination, its essence of bearing a history, a culture; it is a being that freely and responsibly determines itself; it is person, face, mystery. The analectical* refers to the real human fact by which every person, every group or people (3.4.6), is always situated "beyond" (*ano-*) the horizon of totality. Negative dialectic is no longer enough. The analectical moment is the support of new unfoldings. The analectical moment opens us to the metaphysical sphere (which is not the ontic one of

---

*Through derived from the Greek particle *ano-*, I prefer the spelling "analectic," parallel with ana-economic, ana-Oedipus, etc. See Gilles Deleuze and Felix Guattari, *Anti-Oedipus* (Viking, 1977) and *Anti-Oedipus: Capitalism and Schizophrenia* (University of Minnesota Press, 1983).

the factual sciences or the ontological one of negative dialectic), referring us to the other. Its proper category is exteriority. The point of departure for its methodical discourse (a method that is more than scientific or dialectic) is the exteriority of the other. Its principle is not that of identity but of separation, distinction.

5.3.2

The analectical moment of the metaphysical dialectical method whose exercise and concrete development is practical, poietic, and scientifically critical on the level of the human sciences (but not on the level of factual natural sciences where there is no metaphysical exteriority but only physical substantivity) follows a certain sequence, already described somewhat in the process of revelation and communication in proximity (4.2.5.2). In the first place, totality is laid open to question by the provocative (apocalyptic) appeal of the other. To know how to listen to the word of the other (2.4.5) is to have an ethical conscience (2.6.2); if one cannot interpret adequately that word, because it bursts in from beyond the foundation, one can simply accept it out of respect for the person (2.4.8). To know how to risk one's life in order to fulfill the demands of the protest of the oppressed and throw oneself into praxis for them (2.6.7) is part of the process of the analectical moment. Theory is not sufficient in analectics. Speculation is the essential constitution in science and dialectic. Inasmuch as the ethical acceptance of the entreaty of the oppressed and the mediation of praxis is necessary in the analectical moment, that praxis is its first, primordial constitution, the precondition for the possibility of comprehension and clarification, which is the fruit of having effectively and really reached out to exteriority (the only adequate sphere for the exercise of a critical consciousness).

5.3.3

The analectical moment is thus a criticism and a surmounting of the merely negative dialectical method. It does not deny it, just as dialectic does not deny science but simply assumes it, completes it, and gives it its just and real value. The negative dialectical method of Marcuse, Adorno, or even Bloch is naive with respect to the positive criticism of the utopia of the political exteriority offered by the peripheral peoples, the working-class woman, the oppressed youth, and the dependent societies. All the methods to be described subsequently are defined by the analectical moment, without which all method is only scientific. The scientific is reduced to what is natural fact; natural fact is reduced in turn to the logical or the mathematical; and this, finally, becomes debased in scientism (5.7.3)—extremely naive and extremely dangerous.

5.3.4

The analectical moment is the *affirmation* of exteriority; it is not only the denial of the denial of the system from the affirmation of the totality. It is the overcoming of totality but not only as the actuality of what is in potency in the system. It is the overcoming of totality from internal transcendentality (2.4.8)—from exteriority that has never been within. To affirm exteriority is to realize what is impossible for the system (there being no potency for it); it is to realize the *new*, what has not been foreseen by the totality, that which arises from freedom that is unconditioned, revolutionary, innovative.

5.4   PRACTICE

5.4.1

Dialectic in its positive sense or "ana-dialectic" permits us to open ourselves to methods that not only are not scientific but are not even theoretical (because analectic is a method whose point of departure is an ethical choice and a concrete historical praxis). This is of great importance because without it one would not be able to describe the epistemological level of the human sciences (which retain analogies with the factual sciences but are distinct because natural beings are not human beings—beings with history, culture, and freedom). The practical method to which I refer is that of politics, not as political science (5.6.1), but as knowledge of *how* to operate practically on the level of public, social, governmental, trade union, or military decision-making. It is the practical method of politics as responsibility, as the responsibility of the citizen or the professional politician. The habit of knowing how to decide politically was called by the Greeks *fronesis* (*prudentia* in Latin). We have already distinguished between practical and poietical; here we are dealing with the methodical rationality of decisions that one must know how to make (*orthos logos praktikos*, said Aristotle).

5.4.2

Practical decisions are taken not only in the area of politics but also in sexuality, pedagogy, and on the level of antifetishism. Their point of departure is, passively, the appeal of the other (the oppressed as exteriority); operatively, it is the denial of denial (negation of oppression), and affirmation of exteriority. The essential category of this method is, negatively (metaphysically), that of exteriority; affirmatively and operatively it is that of liberation (and not now the mere freedom of Kant). The principle of the practical method is the principle of analogy (which includes the principle of distinction, passively, and the principle of innovation, creatively). It concerns an operative logic that semantically refers to political, sexual, pedagogical, and other decisions.

5.4.3

The model of a process of practical decision differs, evidently, from scientific (5.1) or poietic (5.5) method. The principles or fundamental criteria of that model express either the prevailing existential *proyecto* (the *telos* of classical thinkers) or the entreaty of exteriority; in any case, they concern the strategic goals of practical action, whether or not one has explicit consciousness of them. The strategic level is the light that clarifies (or beclouds, as in the case of Machiavellianism) the entire process that follows. Those goals determine the *case* as a *problem* to solve.

It is here, as also in posterior phases of the model, that a matter of great importance must be well understood. The practical, political person of action must turn to the sciences (factual, formal, and human) to resolve more adequately the question of one's consciousness of one's principles, unequivocal ways to define one's problems, maneuver with alternative hypotheses, and so forth. In all these moments it can be very useful for that person to know and make use of systems theory, the mathematics of sets, computer science, or cybernetics, but keeping in mind that this model is not an application of pure science to praxis but a utilization that realizes the praxis of that which serves it from science. This discourse is essentially practical, not a concrete level of science.

5.4.4

The essential moment of the process of practical decision is found in the moment of *deliberation*. Classical thinkers spoke of a practical argument or syllogism in which the principle was applied (*applicatio* or *Anwendung*) to the concrete case. That is why the Greeks and Latins took pains to detail the ethical makeup of this essential moment of praxis. In the first place, it was necessary to have a good view, a good *coup d'oeil* ("clinical eye"), of the real situation (*aisthesis*); a careful use of memory (history, analogous past experiences, human sciences); intuition of allied or enemy forces (*ratio particularis* proper to the cogitative faculty); discipline in knowing how to submit with docility to the real; serendipity (*sollertia*); realistic or practical sense (*ratio*); perspicuity or aptitude for foreseeing resources that will be necessary in the future; circumspection or a looking around that does not neglect details; and caution or precaution in knowing how to suspect and distrust. Given these conditions, one can choose the tactical means of execution. Decision is thus a desired practical judgment, a judged desire.

5.4.5

Contemporary sciences have developed a whole methodological implementation based on certain techniques that can help one learn to manage an immense number of variables, construct models that permit the evaluation of a great number of hypothetical alternatives, and consider their results by means of very precise approximations. Nevertheless, one must be clearly aware that the best computer cannot replace the fourteen thousand million neurons (with up to two hundred thousand connections of each one with the rest) situated in the human cerebral cortex alone. The method for the best practical decision is practical. It can use scientific means, but they must be integrated into a practical discourse that turns to science when it is considered useful, as it is considered useful, and insofar as it is considered useful. The practitioners of mathematical scientism are known to be the worst politicians. To manipulate beings of reason is not the same thing as to respect persons who conceal themselves in the mystery of their exteriority.

5.4.6

After making decisions, it is necessary to plan their implementation, with all the means that science and technology offer today to the practical person. Finally, the decision is executed and evaluated. The effected practical work is made a reality either to corroborate the system in force or to inaugurate a new order. In the latter case, the work is revolutionary and liberating. For its part, the correct evaluation of the executed decision modifies the fundamental practical criterion to which one resorts in future decision-making.

5.5 POIETICS

5.5.1

We have now seen in a very general sense what work, production, technology, and design are. In fact, poiesis or productive work or manufacture of artifacts has a projective method of production. It is projective because it deals with foresight or future realization of an artifact that does not yet have reality. Theory discovers what beings "already" are; poiesis produces beings that are "not yet." Thus the proper sphere of poiesis is the natural or material ontic, as a point of departure; but it refers semantically to artifacts or the cultural world. Its proper category is that of the formal coherence of the artifacts; its operative principle is that of poietic projectionality.

DIAGRAM 10

Alternative 1. Technology: Applied Science

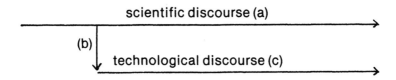

Alternative 2. Technology: technical Mediation of Science

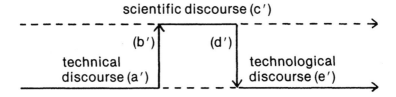

5.5.2

It is erroneous to think that pure science (a in diagram 10), beginning with its own exigencies and by an unknown principle of expansion, itself applies its own conclusions, and technology is its concrete creation. In this hypothesis c would be created by a by means of an applied movement b. On the contrary, it is the technical or technological discourse (a^i) that, in the face of a difficulty, limitation, or ambiguity, seizes upon (b^i), for technical reasons, to use scientific conclusions or theories (c^i). The process of the technological utilization of science (d^i) does not start from a scientific intention but, on the contrary, from a technical decision. We shall see to what extent alternative 1 is ideological. In reality, techniques or concrete technologies have impelled sciences in modern times to look for new technical solutions, starting from new theories. And inasmuch as practical principles are included in those of poietics, politics will not be absent from the very origin of sciences, even of those that claim to be "pure," at least in the choice of their themes.

5.5.3

The model of the technological process is assumed under that of design, which by including all the difficulties of the technological and esthetic model will permit us to discover the projectional productive sense of the poietic method (*recta ratio factibilium*, as it is said in Latin). As before, I summarize the process very briefly. The model of design has a double framework of reference: (1) projective criteria (which include as implied elements certain theoretical and practical moments) and (2) requirements of the present system—prevailing criteria—and requirements coming from exteriority—critical criteria.

5.5.4

From everydayness a work is proposed for design and it is interpreted as a possible *case* and defined as such with precision. The case is confronted with reality, whence are obtained data that permit a *problem* to be defined. When it is confronted with projective criteria, there begins the phase of the study of various alternative *hypotheses*. When one of them is chosen, it is specifically formalized as a *proyecto* to be undertaken. The production of what was projected and its evaluation close the process, whose conclusions are now integrated into the projective criteria and whose functioning comes to modify reality. If it has been an answer to appeals from exteriority, it is constituted as a new culture invented in the service of the oppressed—a revolution in technology, art, or design.

5.6   HUMAN SCIENCES

5.6.1

Methodical passage between the factual and human (not just social) sciences is effected through the analectical moment, which permits an integrative analysis of the *sui generis* variable of exteriority or freedom in its metaphysical sense such as we have described it above. The freedom of the other is not an additional variable; it is a variable of distinct substantivity, constitution, and significance. From exteriority arises the whole practical (political, sexual, pedagogical, fetishist) and poietical (technological, esthetic, design) ambit, the cultural historical world. In this manner the natural fact now has as a counterpart the cultural historical fact. These facts do not depend on human nature (taken in its merely vegetative, animal, precultural substantivity—though, in a certain sense, that is a mere abstraction because everything in the human person is cultural and historical). These facts depend on a cultural history; they are objects of sciences whose methods must incorporate essential moments of distinction. They are not natural factual sciences but human factual sciences.

5.6.2

Unlike practical or poietical methods, in the human sciences it is a question of theoretical methods, thus of sciences, but of sciences whose objects are not natural beings but human beings. Their ambit is not only ontic but also metaphysical; their semantic reference is the human being in whom freedom is a reality; their point of departure is a fact, but an ambiguous fact. The essential categories are those of totality or social structure, exteriority (passively), and liberation (as an operative category). Their principle is that of structural coimplication but equally that of analogy in the description of new historical practico-poietic orders. Neither the political sciences (whether sociology, law, political science, etc.), the psychological sciences (from individual to social psychology, psychiatry, etc.), the pedagogical sciences (didactic, etc.), history, communication sciences, nor economics can use the model appropriate for factual sciences (diagram 9). One must introduce the dialectical moment (5.2) to know how to situate each fact in its context or conditioning totality, and the analectical moment (5.3) to know how to detect the dysfunctional appeals that the oppressed continually launch from the exteriority of the established system.

5.6.3

For this reason, the model of the human sciences, and even more that of the social sciences, has as its proper component an ethico-political option. When the factual and human sciences are identified without more ado, this means that the only horizon of study is the horizon of the totality in force. Functionalism is a clear example of this identification. By eliminating the dialectical and analectical moments, human science, with the pretense of scientific authenticity, has fallen into ideological scientism.

5.7   IDEOLOGICAL METHODS

5.7.1

The culture of the center has accustomed us to opposition between ideology and science. Where there is science, there cannot be ideology. This exclusion is itself an ideology; the totality of a methodical, theoretical, scientific discourse can be ideological not only because of its intrinsic development but also because of what it attempts, its point of departure, its *proyecto*, or the fact of serving as mediation for a context that explains it and gives it significance. Thus even factual science and dialectical method, human sciences and practical or poietic methods—all can be ideological. We shall see in what situation every human act (theoretical, practical, poietical, and their respective methods) and their products (be they ideas, words, signs, forms, decisions, artifacts, etc.) can be ideological.

5.7.2

All meaningful mediation—semiotics—is ideology when it conceals and thereby justifies the practical domination of one person over another (on the political, erotic, pedagogical, or fetishist levels). That is, all theory or theoretical meaning, all practice or practical meaning, all poiesis or poietical meaning, that serves as concealment for domination is ideological. Thus science, practice, technology, art, design, and so forth, can be ideological. So we need neologisms—scientism, technologism, estheticism, politicism, eroticism, pedagogicism—to express the ideological position of the issues and methods that are our present concern.

5.7.3

Ideology is the ensemble of semiotic expressions that justify or conceal domination; when they are methodical, they justify it more completely. The ideological function in its essence is the relationship of the sign or signifier as justification of a dominating praxis. When it is scientific, it is more ideological than ever. For example, when a science prescinds from its social, economic, political (dialectical) conditioning, when it forgets that its mathematical formulas can help the soldier hit the target in Vietnam with incendiary bombs (i.e., when it does not listen to the analectical demands of the poor), that science becomes scientism. It is a science that believes that, just as it is, it has absolute autonomy; it is valid everywhere; its themes have originated from the internal exigencies of scientific discourse, which can be imitated by all the countries of the world as pure, uncontaminated, neutral mediations. Oscar Varsavsky and Orlando Fals Borda have exposed the dangers of scientism. Althusser falls into error by not discovering the concrete ideological sense of the science of the center.

5.7.4

Science and technology are necessary for the process of liberation of peripheral nations and peripheral, popular classes. But the worst enemies of intelligence and development are the pseudoscientists who import supposedly uncontaminated science. Their scientism rests on that supposition, and on the disequilibrium it introduces rests the incapacity for viable solutions. Also implicated are technologists who preach the necessity of importing technology (with which they introduce foreign techniques, as well as practico-political, economic, and poietic criteria that foster and consolidate neocolonialism in the underdeveloped world periphery). What is needed is redesign and innovation with criteria that are practical and poietic, national, congruent, and popular.

Methodical ideologies are the most ideological because they scientifically ground the praxis of domination. Scientists who do not succeed in really joining their science to the effective and dialectical conditioning of politics to discover its relative autonomy and who do not know how to hear clearly the demands that the oppressed launch continually against the system are pseudoscientists. They practice science, it is true, but only to conceal and justify the domination that the center and oppressive classes exercise over peripheral nations and oppressed peoples.

5.8   CRITICAL METHODS

5.8.1

With regard to the factual sciences, and in their proper exercise, one can have a critical consciousness of themes, analyses, and the use that can be made of results. All this permits scientists who have a politico-ethical consciousness to give a responsible account of their actions. This critical consciousness allows them to avoid being pseudoscientists, but it does not constitute their science an intrinsically critical science: by having as object of its method natural beings, not human beings as such, its critique is dialectical (because of its assumptions, as we have said) and not intrinsic. On the contrary, in practical (political, etc.) and poietical (technological, etc.) methods in the human sciences and, as we shall see shortly, in philosophy itself, critique is intrinsic to the specific object of the method because it deals with human beings. If only the dialectical totality is taken as ultimate horizon, critique can only and at most affirm the *proyecto* of the system. If, on the contrary, one begins with the demand for justice from exteriority, the same functional totality is placed in question by the exigencies implicit in the construction of a new, future, utopian order, one that is already an incipient *proyecto* of the people.

5.8.2

Political Machiavellianism or fascism, erotic "Don Juanism," pedagogy that dominates educational systems, imitative technologism, the pseudoscience of sociological functionalism—that is, establishing the system itself as alone, sufficient, fundamental, and absolute—constitute method in ideology, in alienation of intelligence and the mediation of domination. Opposed to this is a socio-economics that begins with a theory of dependence such as that of Samir Amin. It includes a sociology of liberation such as that proposed by Fals Borda, a psychology such as that of Frantz Fanon, which applies diverse principles so as to study the pathologies of dominated counties or of oppressed and popular classes, a history that describes the process in which the poor are the protagonists. It includes a political science that unmasks the imperial state (vis-à-vis the powerful National Security Council, the Pentagon, the Department of State, the transnational corporations, and the CIA, the Congress of the United States is as helpless as was the Roman Senate before the Emperor Augustus). And it includes a technology and design that formulate criteria of national industrial liberation against the pretentious "universal" technology and styling of the transnationals (which seek maximum profit for the producer as well as maximum capital and technology so as to diminish to a minimum the use of labor, as they squander and aggressively destroy nonrenewable resources).

A critical science is authentically science because it can give an account of totality with the most critical consciousness possible in this social formation in which we live. Only those who can interpret the phenomena of the system in the light of exteriority can discover reality with greater lucidity, acuity, and profundity. Only critical methods, those which are constituted in an ana-dialectical process (from exteriority, *ano-*, is produced the unfolding, *dia-* of the comprehension of a new horizon, *logos*), are today qualified to undertake substantive investigations in favor of peripheral nations, popular classes.

5.9   PHILOSOPHY OF LIBERATION

5.9.1   *Status Questionis*

5.9.1.1   The method of philosophy is analectically theoretical; intrinsically it is neither practical nor poietic although it is conditioned by both. The negative ontological or dialectical method is not sufficient. Besides, when it is taken to be that of first philosophy (philosophy of the praxis of liberation; 6.3.1), it justifies the system in force and grounds all ideology. The method of philosophy of liberation knows that politics—the politics of the exploited—is the first philosophy because politics is the center of ethics as metaphysics (ethico-metaphysical exteriority [2.4 and 5.3] is concretized in a privileged way in politics; 3.1), thus surpassing mere ontology (2.4.9). Between ideological science or scientism (pseudoscience) and critical science there exists an analogical difference similar to the one between philosophy of domination, of the system—ontology—and philosophy of liberation.

5.9.1.2 In the periphery, especially in Latin America, besides ontological philosophies (such as phenomenology, existentialism, etc.), there are philosophies that, absolutizing one of the possible accesses to reality, remain in an ideological position. In the first place, an analytical philosophy that claims that by studying logic, philosophy of language, epistemology, or philosophy of science, it has already accounted for all that philosophy can think of, reduces the capacity of philosophical reflection to thinking beings of reason. It prevents the clarification of practical and poietical reality; it castrates philosophy by depriving it of the possibility of political and historical criticism. It is necessary to put analytical philosophy into a political and dialectical setting that will open it to the wide world of the reality of oppressed nations, classes, and persons.

5.9.1.3 In the second place, Marxism, by its theory of dependence allows one to discover the theft by the center of the surplus value (of products) earned by the periphery, and to distinguish the social formations of the center from those of the periphery. But it is also necessary to locate the theory of dependence in a real, concrete, historical setting. Specificity or national peripheral exteriority (3.1.3) is explained not only by the fact of undergoing imperialist domination but by a national history. Without this enrichment, Marxism degenerates into a new ideology, especially if it is not historically joined with the popular classes.

5.9.1.4 In the third place, numerous historical philosophical analyses of the periphery, with immense positive material, need a theoretical setting or a strong structure of hermeneutic categories. Historical interpretation without a precise categorical framework can fall into an historicism without a guiding hypothesis and, above all, without conclusions that elucidate a national and popular praxis of liberation. The pseudoscience of an analytical philosophy without political framework, a Marxism without historical background and without real links with the people at their level of consciousness, and history without a theoretical framework are the three deviations into which today philosophy in the periphery can fall and does fall.

5.9.1.5 Philosophy of liberation claims to take up the positions considered essential above. It does so by an overcoming, but not eclectic, posture. It claims to pursue a discourse that organically includes the discourses detailed above, without destroying their nature but rather giving them their authentic sense. It further claims to overcome, historico-philosophically, Greek physiologism, medieval theologism, and the modern scientific mentality of the center as it works on an anthropology, a philosophy that has as its central pivot the person as free, as exteriority, as person, as oppressed. For this reason, politics in its ethico-metaphysical sense is its very heart. Of course I mean the popular politics of the exploited classes.

5.9.2   Problems and Hypothesis of Philosophy of Liberation

5.9.2.1   Of all the facts of daily experience in the world, philosophy of liberation has interpreted one as the fact that can gestate a new discourse. Since about 1965, there have been some Latin American philosophers who have asked themselves whether it was possible to do philosophy in underdeveloped countries. A little later the question was put another way: Is it possible to philosophize authentically in a dependent and dominated culture? That is, the facts of underdevelopment and then of dependence and the fact of philosophy appeared to be mutually exclusive or inclusive only with difficulty. Those facts reshaped themselves into a problem, into the central problem of philosophy of liberation: Is a Latin American philosophy possible? With time it grew into: Is a Latin American, African, or Asian philosophy of the peripheral world possible?

5.9.2.2   Peruvian Augusto Salazar Bondy, now deceased, answered courageously: No! No, because a dominated culture is one in which the ideology of the dominator has been adopted by the dominated—by the colonized, Memmi would say. The problem evanesces with a flat denial. Nevertheless, there is another possibility, an affirmative possibility. It has been put forward as a working hypothesis.

5.9.2.3   This hypothesis, under the thematic of a "philosophy of liberation," was launched by a group of thinkers from Argentina. The hypothesis is as follows: It appears possible to philosophize in the periphery—in underdeveloped and dependent nations, in dominated and colonial cultures, in a peripheral social formation—only if the discourse of the philosophy of the center is not imitated, only if another discourse is discovered. To be different, this discourse must have another point of departure, must think other themes, must come to distinctive conclusions by a different method. This is the hypothesis.

The present work claims to be an outline of what would have to be the first theoretical, *provisional* philosophical framework of such a discourse. That is, it is necessary not only not to hide but actually to start from the center/periphery, dominator/dominated, totality/exteriority dissymmetry, and from there to rethink everything that has been thought until now. And, what is more, it is necessary to think what has never been thought: the process of the liberation of dependent and peripheral countries. Its theme is the praxis of liberation. The option for that praxis is the beginning of a philosophical protodiscourse. Politics introduces ethics, which introduces philosophy.

5.9.3 Theoretical Philosophical Framework

5.9.3.1 This book is a first, a *remote* and *provisional,* attempt to describe briefly some *possible* theses of what a theoretical philosophical framework of philosophy of liberation must be. That theoretical framework must include the essential categories and the necessary moments of the discourse that is established with those categories, never taking leave of reality (of the world and of the cosmos, as nature or culture). This framework is a point of departure of interpretation as interpretation, not of the interpreted.

5.9.3.2 This theoretical framework is itself a discourse, though abstract. We begin its unfolding with history (chap. 1), with description of a fact, philosophy itself in this case, its development in human history. All the other themes of the theoretical framework must be taken into account in this historical description. What is unique in a historical description of philosophy of liberation is the use of categories such as center/periphery, oppressing classes/popular classes. All description will have to follow a historical method that pursues an ideological/anti-ideological standard of criticism. It is impossible today, for example, to avoid the problem of the imperialist ideology of national security, which justifies the exercise of worldwide geopolitical power.

5.9.3.3   In the second place, the discourse penetrates what may be called metaphysics if it is ethics, or ethics if it is metaphysics (chap. 2), where categories are described—as few as possible but enough—that will permit the continuing discourse to give a structural account of *omnitudo realitatis* (reality in its full sense). Among those categories some have priority. The fundamental one is totality (ontological; 2.2). Of primary importance is exteriority (metaphysical or ethical; 2.4). Proximity (2.1) is explained by exteriority. Mediation (2.3) is on the ontic level (which is not that of substantivity [4.1.3–5], which is cosmic or real). Alienation (2.5) is purely negative, passive. Liberation (2.6) is the operative anadialectical category that needs all the previous ones for its explanation (and we need it to describe the praxis of real historical liberation, which is the central theme of our reflection).

5.9.3.4   In the third place, the discourse accounts for the level that could be called practice (chap. 3). In it there are privileged moments such as politics (3.1) and sexuality (3.2), with pedagogy mediating between them (3.3). Antifetishism (3.4) is a kind of summation, summing up the three previous moments as absolutization or critique of political, erotic, or pedagogical systems. They maintain diverse relationships coimplicated by exteriority.

5.9.3.5   In the fourth place, poietics (chap. 4) or philosophy of production continues the discourse within (or conditioned by) praxis as the person-to-nature relationship, starting from nature (4.1) and the category of substantivity, so as to open itself to the first sphere of poietics: the functioning of signifiers or signs—semiotics (4.2). Just as pedagogy is mediation between politics and erotics, so economics (4.4) is primordial mediation between practice and poietics or technology (4.3). Politics gives practical criteria to economics; economics gives fundamental criteria to technology or design. Technology (e.g., the Industrial Revolution) conditions economics, which conditions politics. All naive simplification is ideological (4.4.3.6).

DIAGRAM 11

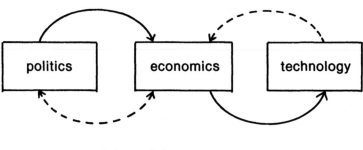

‐ ‐ ‐ ‐→ material conditionings
————→ practical conditionings

5.9.3.6 The theoretical philosophical framework is completed by reflection on discourse itself, in a methodological meta-discourse. Methods are diverse, depending on the activities that complete them or the objects with which they are concerned. We thus review the factual and formal sciences (5.1), the dialectical or ontological method of totality (5.2), the analectical moment or that of exteriority (5.3), and the practical (5.4) and poietical methods (5.5), which we use to categorize the human sciences (5.6). Methodical alienation is ideology, at its different levels (5.7); its counterpart is critical methodology (5.8).

Among the critical methods that of philosophy of liberation is found. Its method is not operative or productive but theoretical, speculative. In contrast to factual or formal sciences, it concerns itself not only with the ontic ambit but also with the ontological, in contrast to negative dialectical method, it also concerns itself with the metaphysical ambit or that of exteriority. Thus its theme is *omnitudo realitatis:* everything. Its point of departure is an ethico-political option in favor of the oppressed of the periphery: respect for the exteriority of the other; geopolitically and socially speaking, listening to the word of the other. The essential categories it uses in its discourse are described in chapter 2 and 4.1. Its principle is that of analogy (and not only that of identity and difference). The logic of liberation is still to be explicated and published; it becomes more necessary with every passing day.

5.9.4   A Model for Philosophical Reflection

5.9.4.1   In the Preface of this work it is stated that this theoretical philosophical framework is directed to the beginner in philosophy of liberation. In effect, its purpose is to be of service to anyone who wants to learn to think according to the progressive stages of philosophy of liberation. For the beginner, then, I propose a model of the phases of its logical development according to the implicit logic of liberation, of thinking about a theme. The philosopher must be able to think of all themes. Nevertheless, in the course of one lifetime the philosopher will be able to think about only a certain number of themes precisely, deeply, and originally. Because themes are infinite and time is short, it is necessary to know how to use time wisely to choose the fundamental themes of the epoch we live in. It is necessary to know how to use time wisely to commit oneself to the struggles of peripheral peoples and oppressed classes. It is necessary to know how to use time wisely in listening to their voices: their proposals, demands, customs, poetry; their successes and failures. It is necessary to know how to use time wisely and put aside secondary themes, those that are fashionable but superficial and unnecessary, those that have nothing to do with the liberation of the oppressed.

5.9.4.2   Something must be said about the criteria for selecting the themes to be thought about. In the first place, the absolute criterion is: to think about a real theme, and among real themes the most essential ones, and among essential themes the most urgent ones, and among urgent themes those that are more transcendent, and among the more transcendent themes those that refer to the peoples who are the most numerous, the most oppressed, the ones on the point of death, a death of hunger, of despair. The political, economic, technological theme is a cycle of themes with which philosophy must occupy itself today. But at the same time it is as important to know how to disqualify false problems as it is to select a viable theme.

Philosophy of the center gives us a wide gamut of false problems with its diversionary tactics and subtleties. Its philosophers sometimes appear to be the court jesters of the system that they entertain and amaze by their witticisms and games of logical sleight of hand. These are the themes of *homo ludens*—while others are dying! They are the themes of philosophies of language, of word juggling, which reduce to silence the cry of the oppressed. Even the pain of the oppressed they cannot interpret.

Ideological themes must not be treated except to show how and why they are ideological. Phenomenological ontology, a good part of analytical philosophy, and certain dogmatic Marxisms are luxuries or fireworks displays. They are not themes of philosophy of liberation.

Once a theme, a fact, is chosen, one can begin to unfold a precise discourse, at times explanatory, at times demonstrative, and always critical. Its purpose is to let light fall upon an access road to—or, if possible—the highway itself of liberating praxis.

5.9.4.3 The model of the discourse of philosophy of liberation, even though it is a method for theoretical thinking, is analogous to practical or poietical knowledge because it is analectical. The human critical sciences come ever closer in method to philosophy, but philosophy will keep its distance because of the different techniques it uses to explain hypotheses. In our case the *theme* to be thought comes from reality, be it the everydayness of the everyday world or a demand from exteriority. Reality for philosophy of liberation is always—directly, not indirectly—the praxis of liberation and all that impedes or promotes it. Inasmuch as what is most real in reality is praxis, the praxis of the philosopher determines the way of stating the *problem*. If it is interpreted from the ontological exigencies of the system in force, all its thought will be ideological camouflage. If the problem is defined from exigencies of exteriority, it will be a real, critical problem fertile with speculative, operative possibilities. When the problem is defined critically, it is confronted at the same time with the theoretical philosophical framework, in the history of the theme and in the history of philosophy (chap.1), and confronted with reality through experience and the sciences, from which will arise the hypothesis of philosophical reflection.

5.9.4.4 Once the *hypothesis* is determined, the essential moment of the philosophical method unfolds. First the theme is situated in totality (2.2). Then it is thought through as mediation (2.3). Then it is questioned from exteriority (2.4). Then, negatively, it is or is not judged as alienation (2.5). Finally, the real conditions of possibility of liberation of what is thought (2.6) are described. The conclusion or explication is the clear discernment of a theme as real (or abstract) fact in all its structure and context.

5.9.4.5   The conclusion, the discerned theme, breaks into reality as illumination of the praxis or poiesis of liberation. The philosophical conclusion fecundates and modifies reality, a transformation that goes toward constituting the history of the world. On the other hand, integrating new criteria into the theoretical philosophical framework also modifies it. The commitment of philosophers to the praxis of liberation and their work in defining a more precise philosophical framework will permit them to take on a new theme with greater resources, clarity, realism, and criticism. Discourse will engender new enthusiasm when its fruits are verified.

5.9.5   Description, Validity, and Relevance of Philosophy of Liberation

5.9.5.1   It is difficult to describe what philosophy of liberation is. Even to try to give some reasons for its validity may seem to be a naive, impossible task. Hence I shall propose only a few suggestive, approximative reflections. Philosophy of liberation is a pedagogical activity stemming from a praxis that roots itself in the proximity of teacher-pupil, thinker-people (the organic intellectual, Gramsci would say, "the intellectual in the people"). Although pedagogical, it is a praxis conditioned by political (and also erotic) praxis. Nevertheless, as pedagogical, its essence is theoretical or speculative. Theoretical action, the poietic intellectual illuminative activity of the philosopher, sets out to discover and expose (in the exposition and risk of the life of the philosopher), in the presence of an entrenched system, all moments of negation and all exteriority lacking justice. For this reason it is an analectical pedagogy (2.4 and 5.3) of liberation. That is, it is the magisterium that functions in the name of the poor, the oppressed, the other (2.4.6), the one who like a hostage within the system testifies to the fetishism of its totalization and predicts its death in the liberating action of the dominated. *To think of everything in the light of the provocative word of the people*—the poor, the castrated woman, the child, the culturally dominated youth, the aged person discarded by the consumer society—shouldering infinite responsibility and in the presence of the Infinite is philosophy of liberation. Philosophy of liberation must be the expression of the most thorough-going critical consciousness possible.

5.9.5.2 If the dialectical method allows one to be able to approach the foundation of scientific knowledge itself, the fact of approaching the exteriority of the system as totality allows one to be able to reach the maximum possible critical consciousness. If philosophy of liberation is the thinking of the praxis of liberation, in militancy, as an organic intellectual with the people, philosophy is transformed into the critique of all critiques, a radical, metaphysical critique beyond its own dialectical critique. Thus philosophy is death—death to everydayness, to the secure naivety of the system. It is risk—the risk of death, for this philosophy emerges, within the system, as a hostage and a witness to a new future order. It clearly formulates provocation—the provocation of the oppressed, but now enhanced by the theoretical comprehension of the structuring of the dominative system.

5.9.5.3 What pertinence does this methodical thinking have? I shall only repeat what I said to a student in Bogotá who asked me in 1975, "What guarantee can I have of the pertinence of this philosophy?" The absolute certitude of $2 + 2 = 4$ no philosophy will ever possess, not because it is not methodical but because the theme it ponders is humankind, its history, the reality of freedom. Nevertheless, there are many factors that bring out its pertinence. Let us look at a few of them.

5.9.5.4 The pertinence of a philosophy can be shown by its negative critical destructive capacity. It would seem that philosophy of liberation has a tremendous destructive potential because it can not only assume critical methods (such as those of analytical philosophy, Marxism, critical theory, etc.) but it can in addition criticize those critical methods, at least from a new angle, from geopolitical world exteriority, from the periphery, from the oppressed.

5.9.5.5 Positively, a philosophy must possess an efficacious theoretical constructive capacity. It would seem that philosophy of liberation achieves the formulation of a minimal theoretical philosophical framework, *though provisory*, that permits it to think the themes that are most urgent for the oppressed periphery, oppressed classes, women, and youth.

5.9.5.6 It would seem that the themes treated by philosophy of liberation are realistic: they clarify the praxis of militants in the process of liberation of the periphery. Given an explanation of the themes of philosophy of liberation, militants, even the most simple and least educated, better understand their situation, their problems. Enlightenment leads to mobilization. Metaphysically—that is, ethically and psychologically—this is easily understandable.

5.9.5.7   It would seem that the discourse of philosophy of liberation does not contradict itself; it has its own systematization, a logic of coimplication, which is the manifestation of coherence.

5.9.5.8   From a historical, empirical viewpoint, if this philosophy is critical, if it criticizes the system, then this system must criticize it, must persecute it. Philosophers who practice it have been targeted for bombings; they have been dismissed from their universities, expelled from their homelands; they have been condemned to death by the agents of imperialism, facism, and the extreme right.

5.9.5.9   In any case, no philosophy has ever had to justify itself to its own times. Its justification was its clear-sightedness; its clear-sightedness was its operability; its operability was its realism; its realism was the origin of its viability; its viability was the fruit of praxis. The praxis of liberation has been the cause of its unwelcome, its nonacceptance by the system. Exteriority is the unfathomable spring of wisdom, that of the commonplace, dominated, poor peoples. They are the teachers of the wise, and philosophy is wisdom. With Pedro Mir, the Caribbean poet, in his "Countersong to Walt Whitman," we want to sing:

> And now,
> the hour of countersong has arrived.
> We the railroad workers,
> we the students,
> we the miners,
> we the farm laborers,
> we the poor of the earth,
> the populous of the world,
> we are the heroes of daily work,
> with our love and our valor,
> enamored by hope.

APPENDIX:
PHILOSOPHY AND PRAXIS*

Upon presenting a thought in English that originated in Spanish, I have to say with Kant that "despite the great wealth of our languages, the thinker often finds himself at a loss for the expression which exactly fits his concept."[1] But the difficulty in my presentation is not due only to language; it is much more due to the different points of view of the philosophical thinking of North Americans and Latin Americans, the daily realities of the two being so far apart.

A. PHILOSOPHY AND IDEOLOGY

Philosophy is not only thinking demonstratively or scientifically.[2] It is also thinking critically and dialectically,[3] for it can think about its own principles. On the one hand, philosophy is not only to know (*Kennen*) objects or to have ontic knowledge (*Erkenntnis*) of the understanding (*Verstand*), but it is also an ontological or metaphysical knowledge (*Wissen*).[4] Inasmuch as it is a metaphysical knowledge (*Wissen*), it always has reference to praxis; because of its origin and destiny, it is also wisdom.

The inevitable reference to praxis, as we shall see—praxis understood in its fundamental meaning (as *Lebenswelt*, *ta endoxa*, as the total structure of the actions of an epoch)[5]—places philosophy on an ideological level, if by ideology is understood the systematic whole of ideas that explain, justify, and camouflage an entrenched praxis. All theoretical exercise has its own autonomy, but only a *relative* autonomy.[6] The relative autonomy

*An address given to the American Catholic Philosophical Association, Philadelphia, April 1980 (not included in the original Spanish edition of this book).

of philosophy, in this instance, has reference to the concrete historical totality from which it emerges and to which it returns— everyday praxis. I shall take two classic examples, easily comprehended, to demonstrate that even in the case of the greatest philosophers, it is impossible to avoid a significant share of ideological "contamination."

A.1   Aristotle and Pro-Slavery Contamination

In his *Politics*, I, 1, the founder of logic tells us:

Nature (*physis*) would like to distinguish between the bodies of freemen and slaves, making the one strong for servile labor, the other upright and altogether useless for such service. . . . It is manifest, then, that some men are by nature (*physei*) free, and others slaves, and that for these latter slavery is both expedient and right [1254b27–1255a2].

Noteworthy is the term "clear," "manifest" (*phaneron*), "evident," or "self-evident" (in German, *selbstverständlich*). Equally noteworthy is the certainty with which Aristotle attributes to nature the origin of the historico-political difference between the free man and the slave. The philosophical argument is totally contaminated by the ideological "daily evidence" of Hellenic slavery.

A.2   Thomas Aquinas and Macho Contamination

The example I shall give is essentially theological, but the argumentation is anthropological; we could say it belongs to philosophical anthropology. Talking about the transmission of original sin, Thomas Aquinas explains:

Now it is manifest (*manifestum*) that in the opinion of philosophers the active principle of generation is from the father, while the mother provides the matter. Therefore, original sin is contracted, not from the mother, but from the father: so that, accordingly, if Eve, and not Adam, had sinned, their children would not contract original sin

[*Summa Theologiae*, I-II, q. 81, ad 5c]. Accordingly we must assert that if we consider the conditions attaching to these persons, the man's sin is the more grievous, because he was more perfect than the woman [ibid., II-II, q. 163, ad 4c].

Again something is "manifest," evident, obvious. It does not matter that the argument is from authority; what matters is that it is accepted by all that the male gives Being to the child; the woman gives only the matter (ibid., III, q. 32, ad 4c). Man is superior to woman. The masculine (macho) ideology is the totality of ideas that justify the domination of the male over the female (sexually, economically, politically, and pedagogically), and it contaminates all the reasoning of Thomistic moral philosophy.

To say that ideological moments contaminate philosophical reasoning does not mean that such reasoning is invalidated. It only indicates that it is a human, fallible, finite, perfectible discourse. That is to say, it is not an absolute knowledge (*Wissen*). This is so because its reference to praxis is to concrete historical action, unfinished and ambiguous.

B.   DIALECTIC BETWEEN PHILOSOPHY AND PRAXIS

Philosophy finds itself relatively determined by praxis. There is neither an absolute determination nor an absolute autonomy. These types of determination touch all the instances of theoretical exercise.

B.1   Determination on the Part of the Subject: Interests and Goals

The philosopher or subject of philosophical thinking (*PS* in diagram 12) is not an "absolute I" as Fichte claimed,[7] but a finite subject, conditioned, relatively determined by the everyday world to everyday praxis, joined necessarily to a historical subject, to a social class, to a people, to a subject of basic practices.

Philosophical subjectivity (*PS*) clings to and depends upon (arrow *a*) the historical subjectivity (*HS*) that carries it. The *ego co-*

gito (I think) is first of all an *ego laboro* (I work), *ego opero* (I do), or *ego desidero* (I desire) of a group, of a people. It is true that one can make an abstraction and consider only the subject-object re-

DIAGRAM 12

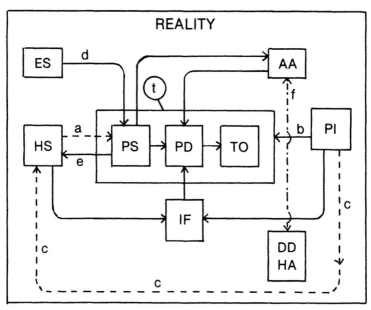

- - - - - - ➤ determination

—·—·—·—·➤ practical opposition

————————➤ other types of relationship

AA	academic apparatus
DD	dominant discourse
ES	empirical subject
HA	hegemonic apparatus
HS	historical subject
IF	ideological formation
PD	philosophical discourse
PI	practical interest
PS	philosophical subject
TO	thematic object

lationship (indicated by *t*), but it is only an abstraction—that is, taking the part for the whole (the philosophical subjectivity for the practical overall reality).

In the same manner, as proposed by classical thinking, the human end (*beatitudo, telos*) is the object of tendency (*bonum*) or appetite, which is identified with Being (*esse*). Today we would call such an end a practical interest (*PI*) of a projected undertaking of a social class (to which the philosopher belongs). The "interest" situates the theory in a practical manner in two ways: because it establishes (arrow *b*) the relevance or pertinence of the thematic object (*TO*) to be thought philosophically, or because it also grounds (arrows *c* and *a*), as a project, the practical totality of the class, nation, or group that constitutes the historical subject situated "under" the philosophical subject.

Because Being (*esse*) is identical to "interest" (*bonum*), it is the foundation of the intelligibility and pertinence of the thematic object, which, moreover, must be thought about because of practical exigencies of praxis itself. Throughout history, the themes of philosophy have sprung forth primarily because of the practical exigencies of the age in which the philosophers lived. If Hegel began his ethics or philosophy of right in the following manner, it was because the prevailing capitalist praxis clearly determined it—not absolutely, but sufficiently:

> Right is in the first place the immediate exterior being (*Dasein*), which freedom gives itself in an immediate way, i.e., possession (*Besitz*), which is property ownership [*Philosophy of Right*, §40].

That is, the thematic object that was imposed on Hegel as first in his practical philosophical discourse and as the first determination of "free will" is private property, the bedrock of the capitalism that is mirrored in his philosophy.

B.2   Methodical and Categorical Exigencies

Praxis determines philosophy, although not absolutely, in a much more intimate manner in the constitution of philosophical discourse, be it because of the method chosen, or be it because of

the necessity of constructing categories that adequately corre-
spond to the practical *a priori* totality. In effect, if one chooses a
reformist praxis or one that basically reaffirms the system in
force, one will discard critical, holistic, or dialectical methods—
and one will claim to discard them because they are naive, nonscientific, invalid. Karl Popper, with his methodical proposal of
"falsifiability" of great precision,[8] falls into superficialities in his
work *The Open Society and Its Enemies*, where he confuses
dialectics with the predictability of future events.[9]

In the same manner, from the point of view of a practical option, the world (*Welt*) for Wittgenstein, comes to be identified
with "the sum total of reality" (*Die gesamte Wirklichkeit*)[10] so
that he says later on that the "feeling (*Gefühl*) [of] the world as a
limited whole—it is this that is mystical."[11] For this reason *beyond* the world "it is impossible to speak about the will insofar as
it is the subject of ethical attributes."[12] With this idea philosophical ethics is impossible: if "the *sense* of the world must lie outside
the world" as that about which nothing can be said, one has to
keep quiet on these topics.[13]

All these antidialectical, antiholistic thoughts are perfectly coherent to a praxis that reproduces the system. They are the philosophy of domination or of justification of oppression because they
are anti-utopian—utopia here understood as the projected undertaking of liberation of the oppressed in the present system. It is a
perfectly ideological scientific objectivity.[14]

The adoption of a dialectical method is demanded by a praxis
of radical commitment to the oppressed.[15] Radical criticism is not
exercised over the parts of the system; it confronts the totality in
its entirety as a totality. If one "cannot speak about this" (*man
nicht sprechen kann*), one would have to silence, by assassination,
the millions and millions who cry out "I am hungry!" Does this
"proposition" make sense? Those who believe that it does not
have meaning should stop eating so that they can feel in their
corporality the wound of hunger that has no reality because it is
found beyond the system.

In the same manner, certain categories—"substance," for
example—do not permit critical philosophical analysis of certain
concrete historical situations of praxis. But the category of "to-

tality," the fundamental category of dialectics, and that of exteriority[16] allow for a more adequate discourse because of a radicalization of meaning in the most material sense.[17]

The philosopher will not give in to the fear of losing a professorship, of being expelled from a country, or of being discriminated against because of a praxis that intrinsically challenges the dominant philosophical discourse. Affective-erotic subjectivity always articulates itself within social structures. The conduct of the petit bourgeois philosopher in systems of violence has been studied by Rozitchner.[18]

B.3   Philosophical Hegemony and Relative Autonomy

One fundamental aspect in the relationship between philosophy and praxis is almost always overlooked. There is no philosophical practice without an academic "apparatus" for instruction and learning. This has been true from the Academy and the Lyceum to the universities, periodicals, and conferences of today.[19] Needing to create a consensus, the dominant classes organize a hegemonic ideologico-academic apparatus. Philosophy plays a central role in the dominant ideological formation and within the hegemonic apparatus.[20]

From what has been said, we can conclude that all philosophy is determined by its dialectical relationship with praxis. It is clear that philosophy has its own autonomous theoretical status: no one denies the specificity of theoretical philosophical discourse. This autonomy, however, is not absolute (*simpliciter*) but relative (*secundum quid*). Within concrete, historical, integral reality, philosophy is relative to praxis because of its historical subjects (that is to say, the philosophical movement, apparatus, class, nation, epoch, etc.) and their interests. Philosophy is also relative to praxis because of the thematic objects, the method, and the categories it uses. Not to keep in mind these conditions of possibility, these relative determinations, is to make of philosophy a complete abstraction (*totum abstractum*), an ideological fetish that will be enshrined at the center of the hegemonic academic apparatus of the dominant classes in the developed countries. Thus a national and worldwide consensus will be created that will justify the capitalistic exploitation perpetrated by the so-called free or "Western and Christian" civilization.

C.   EXIGENCIES FOR A PHILOSOPHY OF LIBERATION

I call philosophy of liberation the strictly philosophical discourse, the scientific-dialectical knowledge (*Wissen*), that gives thematic priority to the praxis of liberation *of the oppressed*. The oppressed are considered historically and socially as a class, geopolitically as a nation, sexually as repressed by macho ideology and practices, pedagogically as alienated and completely enclosed by an idolatrous fetishism. *Philosophy* of liberation also gives priority of origin and foundation to the liberation of philosophy from the naivety of its allegedly absolute autonomy as a theory. Philosophy *of liberation* is a theoretical knowledge (*Wissen*) articulated historically and concretely by the praxis of liberation of the oppressed—the first preconditioned for the possibility of such thinking. Far from agreeing that "all philosophy is a criticism of language,"[21] it affirms that philosophy is a criticism of oppression and a clarification of the praxis of liberation.[22]

C.1   Exigencies for a Philosophical Theory of the Praxis of Liberation of the Oppressed

The oppressed as "origin" and "space" that gives rise to critico-liberating philosophical discourse indicates that it is a practical, ethical discourse. The point of departure of this discourse is the human situation produced by the praxis of domination. That is, the practical precondition for the possibility of beginning a true discourse makes philosophy of praxis the first philosophy (*prima philosophia*). It is not a philosophy of any praxis whatsoever but of the praxis of *liberation*, the criterion or absolute tribunal of the truth of its discourse. Liberative orthopraxis permits a pertinent philosophical discourse that penetrates reality here and now.

The oppressed are the *poor* in political terms (person, class, nation), the *woman* in the macho sexual system, the child, youth, the *people* in the pedagogy of cultural domination. All the problems and topics of logic, philosophy of language, anthropology, and metaphysics acquire new light and new meaning when viewed from the absolute and nevertheless concrete (the opposite of universal) criterion that philosophy is the weapon of the liberation of the oppressed.

Sub lumine oppressionis, from the viewpoint of the oppressed, all ideology or philosophy of domination allows a glimpse into what it conceals—domination. Surpassing the horizon of Being of the system, philosophy of liberation reaches out to the exteriority of the other (the oppressed as other than the system), to the fount from which proceeds the light of being (the *Erkenntnissquelle* of Schelling).[23] Schelling, who was, in effect, Hegel's teacher, had indicated that beyond the Being (of all system) one can find the Other: "the originating cause is free." "The Lord of Being (*Herr des Seins*) is a much higher and more appropriate notion than the one that says that God is Being itself."[24] In the totality of the system (contrary to Wittgenstein, who thinks that "God does not reveal *in* the world"),[25] *in the world*, the self-revelation of the absolute Other takes place through the oppressed.[26] The very body, the corporality, the flesh of the oppressed (their hungry, tortured, violated bodies), when exposed (as the hero is "exposed" before the firing squad) within the system, is a subversion of the law and order that alienates them. It is the revelation of the Absolute in history as an epiphany, not only a phenomenon, an epiphany through the poor. The face (*pnín* in Hebrew, *prosopon* in Greek), the person, the corporality, the flesh (*basar*) of the poor is itself the originating word (*dabar*) from which arises the philosophy of liberation. Philosophy of liberation does not think about words; it thinks about reality.

Thus when the oppressed who struggle against the death that the system allots to them begin, through the praxis of liberation, the struggle for life, novelty irrupts in history beyond the Being of the system. A new philosophy, a positive one, necessarily makes its appearance. The novelty is not originally and primarily philosophical; it is originally and primarily historical and real; it is the liberation of the oppressed. It is secondarily a philosophical theory as a strategic instrument or weapon of liberation itself.

C.2   Exigencies on the Part of Historical Subjects, Their Interests, and the Thematic Object

In the philosophy of liberation the coherent, organic articulation of the philosopher in union with a historical subject (class, women's liberation movement, culturally oppressed people; *HS* in diagram 12) is a decisive question. Concrete articulation from within a people is a *conditio sine qua non* for the philosophizing of liberation (arrow *e*). It is not some "experiment" that has to be conducted at a certain time. It is a permanent way of life, integrated into the everyday life of the philosopher under penalty of mere repetition, ideologization, loss of reference to the truth of reality—that is, to the actual, ever changing, historical manifestation of reality.[27]

The empirical subject (*ES* in diagram 12), who can be a member of the oppressed classes or a petit bourgeois by origin, is called to be an organic philosopher of liberation by a conversion to critical thinking (indicated by arrow *d*). The philosopher thus enters into a space of risk, anxiety, and danger, in a new lifestyle—that of philosophical subject (*PS*). To be a philosopher of liberation can mean losing one's freedom in prison, enduring the pain of torture, losing a professorship at a university, and perhaps being killed, given the situation in Latin America.

To be "organic" (arrow *e*) with the historical subject means to resolutely acquire a *class position* with an oppressed people; it means to become involved in and form part of the popular movement of the working class or of marginal groups, in movements for national liberation or that of women, or in groups organized for popular ideological, racial, or cultural struggle.

The philosopher elaborates the philosophical discourse (*PD*) of liberation on themes that must be grounded theoretically at the highest levels of abstraction in order to give to concrete political analysis all its practical effectivity.[28] Only thus will it respond, on the one hand, to the necessity of clarifying to the utmost degree the class consciousness of the oppressed and, on the other hand, to the explicit philosophical formulation of the ideological formation (*IF*) of these classes. Philosophy of liberation is, to be precise, a philosophy that responds to the implicit content of the ideological formation of the oppressed and, in the final analysis, to the interests of their class, nation, sex. Philosophy of liberation is, then, a "weapon" of the oppressed; it thinks through and clarifies the most urgent themes; it organizes its own rational resources; it explains its articulations; it transforms itself into a standard of the ideological struggle against the dominant discourse (*DD* in diagram 12) of the system in force and against its hegemonic apparatus (*HA*). Of course, the philosophical antidiscourse also needs to start promoting its own (antihegemonic) academic apparatus (*AA*)—schools of philosophy, publications (books, magazines), symposia, and movements.[29] The antihegemonic apparatus can be expected to be the object of the violence of persecution, the sadism of oppressors.

The struggle (arrow *f* in diagram 12) between philosophy of domination and philosophy of liberation manifests on the theoretical level the violent class struggles provoked by domination. On this level, as on others, the philosophers of poor countries will need the solidarity of philosophers of wealthy countries, who are responsible for what their transnational corporations, their political leaders, and their armies cause outside their country's boundaries.

C.3   Method and Categories

Some of the exigencies at this level were mentioned in B.2, above. I shall now touch on other aspects. In the first place, if the dialectical or ontological method is accepted as the appropriate one to discover the meaning of the functional parts of a given system—a problem avoided by logical neopositivism, sociological functionalism, and various other philosophical positions— philosophy of liberation gives particular importance to the analectic moments of the dialectical process. In its essence, the dialectics of the dialectical method consists in the rational movement that passes from the part to the whole, or from a whole to a more extensive whole that includes it.[30] But the possibility of such passage—not the "Holy Thursday of reason" as Hegel would say, but the "Easter of reason"—does not rest only on the negation of negation in totality (moment of negativity) and not even on the affirmation of totality (which would not "surpass" it with a radical metaphysical—not merely an ontological—surpassing

[*Aufhebung*]). It is possible because of the affirmation of exteriority, which is more essential than is negation for a philosophy of the oppressed as an originating and a liberating fulfillment.

For example, the liberation of Nicaragua, as a process in which a nation dependent on the United States passes to being a free country (from a first totality to a second totality), does not take place only because of the negation of the oppression produced by capitalism (negation of negation). Nor is the process liberating only because of the affirmation of the democratic bourgeois potentialities of prerevolutionary Nicaragua. The liberation occurs also, metaphysically speaking, because of the affirmation of what Nicaragua is as *exteriority* (to capitalism), *as a totality* (what Nicaragua is, as an origination from the precapitalist, humane, heroic, and historic past; and what Nicaragua is today as a *proyecto*, a real utopia not contained even as a potentiality within bourgeois prerevolutionary Nicaragua).

The analectical moment of the dialectical method (anadialectical method) gives absolute priority to the *proyecto* of liberation of the other as new, as other, as distinct (and not only as different within the identity of the whole). In the final analysis, it can be affirmed that the analectic moment of dialectics is founded on the absolute anteriority of exteriority over totality, even to affirming the priority of the Absolute Other as creative origin over creation as a work, as a finite and therefore perfectible totality. The metaphysics of creation is the ultimate foundation (*Grund*) of political historical liberation (social revolutions), the erotic liberation of women, and the pedagogical liberation of the child and of the people. Beyond Being (if *Sein* is understood as the horizon of totality) *there is* reality; there one can find reality in its most consistent, future, and utopian horizon: anthropological exteriority (the other, the needy, the poor) or absolute exteriority (the absolute other, the Creator who appeals to the system through the epiphany of the poor when the system becomes lulled into a fetishistic, antidialectical "normalization").

In the same manner, a category such as face-to-face, which measures all practical human relationship as the origin and the end of history, gives sufficient light to interpret the injustice or alienation of the other as a mediation of the *proyecto* of the whole, from the immediacy where one lets the other be other than oneself in that other's real, metaphysical exteriority. From the experience of respect for and service to the other as other is judged every human political, pedagogical, or erotic relationship that is a "reifying instrumentalization" of the other as a mediation for one's own *proyecto*. The relevance or pertinency of both, and the method and categories used, depend on the articulation that the philosopher carries out with the praxis of liberation.

C.4   Political Space, Repression, and Antihegemonic Apparatus

Latin America today finds itself in an exceedingly complex situation. It is suffering the agonizing pains of giving birth to a new historical era. Philosophy of liberation is a theoretical and strategic product of a profound revolution that encompasses South and Central America and the Caribbean.

Philosophical thinking must have at least a certain modicum of freedom. When it lacks minimum freedom, philosophy emigrates; it exiles itself; it dies, and the body of the philosopher goes to jail, from Boethius to Gramsci (imprisonment is a form of dying), or to the cemetery (as my colleague from Mendoza, the philosopher Mauricio Lopez, and my philosophy student, Susana Bermejillo, a young woman beaten to death by undercover police in 1975).

C.4.2   Critical philosophical discourse has a growing political "space" in Brazil, Peru, Ecuador, Santo Domingo, and Panama, given the crisis of military dictatorships and the opening up to certain types of social democracies. The road is difficult; a long history of oppression and a lack of critical thought make the way difficult. The temptation of many is populism, because radical revolutionary positions are not "acceptable."

C.4.1   Philosophy of liberation is repressed today in Argentina, Uruguay, Chile, Bolivia, Paraguay, Haiti, El Salvador, Guatemala, and Honduras. Political "space" for critical thought is nonexistent. The military ideology of national security—learned in great part in the schools of the United States, such as West Point or the School of the Americas in Panama—does not tolerate, not even physically, the philosophical subjects of liberation or their dialectic and popular counterdiscourse. Repression reaches even to the psycho-social level, and torture is used as a means to persuade "anarchists" to return to the Western and Christian "order."[31] To be a philosopher of liberation in this situation is to be in mortal danger. In any event, the danger of accepting self-censorship (*autocensura*), or of holding hands with reformism or developmentalism (*desarrollismo*), is always there.

Those of us who are in exile, in the more ample political "space," develop our discourse of liberation with a twofold purpose: on the one hand, to fashion a clear and radical criticism of theoretical errors (such as populism in political philosophy) and, on the other hand, to set ourselves to the task of clarifying the great strategic themes that are expected to be the most relevant in the coming decades.

C.4.3 It seems, on the contrary, that the political "space" for philosophical thinking is closing in Colombia, where the military makes its presence felt more and more in national life as farmer and worker movements emerge. The philosophy of liberation grows there, and it still has possibility in populist and Christian thought, even if it has to be camouflaged. The situation is disquieting. Renowned social scientists have been imprisoned and tortured.

C.4.4 The philosophical discourse of liberation can be exercised with relative freedom in Mexico, Venezuela, Costa Rica, and Puerto Rico. That is, they are "spaces" of philosophico-critical productivity that can be "exported" to countries submerged in the most horrible repression or countries where a philosophy of liberation has not yet come to life. Again, it is at this level that the philosophers of developed countries can help us form a double front in a true "alliance for critical philosophy": on the front of the repressed countries (publishing critical works and sending them to countries we cannot enter, not even by means of books), and on the First World front (creating a trend of opinion favorable to critico-liberating thought developing in the countries of the Third World).

C.4.5 In the socialist process in Cuba and Nicaragua, philosophy of liberation, in the near future, will have to treat topics different from those in other countries where revolution is still a future event. The central thought to be explored within the situation of present growth in Cuba is not so much the political but the technologico-productive and ideological. On the one hand, the increase of productivity, development of productive forces, is in need of a philosophy of production, which I would call a philosophy of poiesis. In this manner, philosophy of liberation would open a new chapter, affirming that technology is not universal, is not absolutely autonomous, but that it corresponds to needs and requirements determined by the degree of development of social formation and by participation in the scientific-technological revolution.

A second fundamental question in the socialist Latin American countries is that of being able to formulate a new theory of religion. This theory would from the Marxist discourse where atheism as antifetishism and materialism as a last instance of worship (to offer to another a product of work) permit religion to be constituted as praxis and infrastructural work, as a positive and liberating structure. This question is a strategic one for the Latin American revolution, and for every other Third World revolution, because it would allow a whole people to be impelled, with a profound religious consciousness, into the liberating process, not only not denying its ties to religious transcendence but also relying on it to furnish absolute motivation for revolutionary praxis.

D. TOWARD AN INTERNATIONAL DIVISION OF PHILOSOPHICAL LABOR

Philosophy of liberation, as philosophy of the oppressed and for the oppressed, is not a task only for thinkers of the countries of the Third World. Philosophy of liberation can be exercised in all places and situations where there is oppression of person by person, class by class, racial minority by racial majority. Depending on the "space" where the discourse arises, diverse topics will be relevant. The themes can be different, but not the type of discourse, or its method, or its essential categories. In the United States it is possible to work out a philosophy of liberation from the experience of the oppression of the people by a system of consumption where the rationality of profit-making is beginning to show its true irrationality; from the suffering of the black and Hispanic minorities; from the humiliation of women not yet liberated; and specially from the ideological manipulation that conceals from the public what "the empire" does outside its boundaries to poor peoples that it impoverishes even more.

In the countries of the center, philosophy sometimes turns in upon itself and reduces its task to justifying itself (philosophy of language, of logic, etc.), without thinking through the great issues relevant to the final years of the twentieth century. In Asia and Africa philosophy concerns itself with other topics of liberation (dialogue with ancient cultures, authenticity, the question of neocolonialism). In Latin America, with differences from country to country, I have already sketched some thematic spheres within diverse political "spaces."

In conclusion, an international division of the philosophical labor, assigning to diverse groups and countries distinct tasks, would permit us to begin a fruitful dialogue where uniformity of themes would not be demanded, nor would certain thematic objects be spurned because they are not relevant to one or another group. Respect for the other's situation begins with respect for the other's philosophical discourse.

NOTES

1. *Critique of Pure Reason*, A 312, B 368.

2. Edmund Husserl has already tried to show in his own way that it was necessary for philosophy to reach the level of science. See "Philosophy as a Rigorous Science" where he clarifies: "Philosophy, however, is essentially a science of true beginnings, or origins, of *rizōmata pantōn*" (*Phenomenology and the Crisis of Philosophy* [New York: Harper & Row, 1965], p. 146).

3. See my work *Método para una filosofía de la liberación* (Salamanca: Sígueme, 1974), pp. 17ff. For Aristotle, dialectic is useful "for the philosophic sciences. . . . Further, it is useful in connection with the ultimate (*ta prota*) bases (*archon*) of each science; for it is impossible to discuss them at all on the basis of the principles peculiar to the science in question, since the principles are primary in relation to everything else, and it is necessary to deal with them through the generally accepted opinions (*endoxon*) on each point. This process belongs peculiarly, or most appropriately, to dialectic; for being of the nature of an investigation (*exetastike*) it lies along the path to the principles of all methods of inquiry" (*Topics* I, 2, 101a, 26b [Cambridge: Harvard University Press, 1960], pp. 277–78).

4. Since Kant, "knowing" is of objects (*Erkenntnisse der Gegenstände, Critique of Pure Reason*, I, I, 3, A 139): knowing is of science; "rational faith" is of the Ideas. For Hegel, on the contrary, ontological knowledge (*Wissen*) is the intellectual act par excellence and is therefore philosophy. "This notion of philosophy is the self-thinking Idea, the truth aware of itself!" (*Encyclopedia*, 574; in Hegel's *Philosophy of Mind* [Oxford: Clarendon, 1971], p. 313). *Cognitio* or *cognoscere* is not *sapere* or *scire*, even in classical thought.

5. The later Husserl spoke more and more of the notion of "lived world" (*Lebenswelt*), which made ready for the concept of being-in-the-world (*in der Welt sein* of Heidegger) (*Die Krisis de europäischen Wissenschaften*, III; Husserliana VI [The Hague; Nijhoff, 1962], pp. 105ff.). For Aristotle *ta endoxa* indicated everyday existential comprehension. By all means one will have to surpass the passive position (intel-

lectual sight) of both notions to arrive at a notion of praxis in the sense of "structural totality of human actions" of a group, a social class, or a historical community. In this primary meaning, praxis *precedes theory*. It is *in* and *whence* theory arises. Praxis or the action decided on is *posterior* to the theoretical act and integrates itself as one moment in the totality of *a priori* praxis.

6. Theoretical exercise in its totality is suggested by classical thinkers: "There is a fourth order that reason in planning established in the external things which it causes" (Thomas Aquinas, *Commentary on the Nicomachean Ethics* [Chicago: Regnery, 1964], vol. 1, p. 6).

7. "The I posits itself . . . I as absolute Subject" (Fichte, *Grundlage der gessamten Wissenschaftslehre* [1794], vol. 1, 97).

8. *The Logic of Scientific Discovery* (New York: Harper & Row, 1968), pp. 78ff.

9. Princeton University Press, 1966, pp. 84ff.

10. Ludwig Wittgenstein, *Tractatus Logico-Philosophicus* (London: Routledge and Kegan Paul, 1961), 2.063, p. 8.

11. Ibid., 6.45, p. 13. This is precisely how the oppressed through practical totality feel the world (the system). But about this "feeling" of the oppressed, there is for Wittgenstein no philosophy.

12. Ibid., 6.423, p. 72.

13. Ibid., 6.41, p. 71. In this way it is impossible to pass complete judgment on the capitalist system as a whole, the task of dialectics. Popper and Wittgenstein will not make this critique that they discard or deny as holistic, foolish, or impossible. The reformist choice, justifying capitalism by claiming to demonstrate the impossibility of a way out (the critique of utopia and socialism limits itself by its own impossibility), becomes methodically antidialectical.

14. For a kind of journalistic example, see Noam Chomsky, "Objectivity and Liberal Scholarship," in *American Power and the New Mandarins* (New York: Vintage, 1969), pp. 23ff.

15. From the time of Aristotle, "our programme was, then, to discover some faculty of reasoning about any theme put before us from the most generally accepted premises that there are. For that is the essential task of the art of discussion (dialectic) and of examination (peirastic)" ("On Sophistical Refutations," in *Basic Works of Aristotle* [New York: Random House, 1941], 183a37-b1, p. 210).

16. See Michael Theunissen, *Der Andere* (Berlin: Gruyter, 1965) and Emmanuel Levinas, *Totality and Infinity, an Essay on Exteriority* (Pittsburgh: Duquesne University Press, 1969).

17. By "matter" or "materialism" I understand not the indemonstrable affirmation that all is eternally *cosmological* matter (see Engels, *Dialektik der Natur* [Berlin: Dietz, 1951]). This would be a *naive* mate-

rialism. I take "matter" and "materialism" in the practico-productive meaning: nature as *matter* (that with which) of human work. The "I work" is the *a priori* constituent of "matter" as a practico-productive (and not a cosmological) category. In this sense *material determination* (never absolute) is an instance that can never be left out of any historical anthropological consideration. On the other hand, "matter" refers to the Hebrew notion of "work-service-cult" (*habodah*); see G.W. Kittel, ed., *Theological Dictionary of the New Testament* (Grand Rapids: Eerdmans, 1971)—*diakonía, energemata*, etc. See my work, *Filosofía de la producción* (Mexico City: Universidad Metropolitana, 1984) and my preliminary study on Karl Marx, *Cuaderno tecnológico-histórico* (Universidad de Puebla, 1984).

18. Leon Rozitchner, in *Freud y los límites del individualismo burgués* (Buenos Aires: Siglo XXI, 1972), analyzes the subject as far as showing the determinations of the system in its most profound subjectivity. That is to say, "class struggle is included in human subjectivity as the nucleus of one's most individual existence," according to the Argentinian thinker.

19. See Christine Buci-Glucksmann, *Gramsci et l'Etat* (Paris: Fayard, 1975).

20. See Antonio Gramsci, *Quaderni del Carcere*, 19 (XXIII), II, no. 13 (Rome: Rinaudi, 1975), vol. I, p. 1250.

21. Wittgenstein, *Tractatus*, 4.0031, p. 19. That a philosophy of language is necessary and useful is not to be denied, but it is to be an "instrument" of philosophy and not its essense and ultimate finality. Aristotle already suggested that the art of rhetoric, which was the ultimate finality for the Sophists, was for the philosopher seeking truth only a means to avoid being confused by the Sophist: "As far as the choice of ground goes, the philosopher and the dialectician are making a similar inquiry, but the subsequent arrangement of material and the framing of questions are the peculiar province of the dialectician" (ibid., p. 675).

22. Besides the works cited in the talk by M. Christine Morkovsky, at the 1979 ACPA meeting, see my works, *Filosofía de la liberación* (Mexico City: Edicol, 1977), *Política* (Bogotá: Editorial Nueva América, 1979), *Filosofía de la religión* (Bogotá: Editorial Nueva América, 1979), and my talk at the Third National Colloquy of Philosophy (Puebla, Mexico), "Filosofía, aparatos hegemónicos y exilio."

23. *Einleitung in die Philosophie der Offenbarung oder Begründung der positiven Philosophie*, in *Werke*, VI, B, p. 398.

24. "Erlanger Vorträge," in *Werke*, V, pp. 305-6.

25. *Tractatus*, 6.432, p. 73.

26. See my work, *Religión* (Mexico City: Edicol, 1977).

27. Gramsci's notion of the "organic intellectual" is more or less the

issue here, though in Latin America it includes concrete characteristics that we cannot take up in this short exposition. See Jürgen Habermas, *Theorie und Praxis* (Berlin: Suhrkamp, 1963). Lukacs explains that "organization is the form of mediation (*Vermittlung*) between theory and praxis" (*Werke,* vol. 2 [Neuwied, 1968], p. 475).

28. For example, the work of Alberto Parisi, *Filosofía y dialéctica* (Mexico City: Edicol, 1979) (on dialectical logic).

29. Our *Revista de filosofía latinoamericana* (Buenos Aires) was stopped in its second issue in 1975 by the military repression in Argentina. Eighteen of the thirty-two professors of philosophy in the philosophy department of the School of Philosophy and Letters at the National University of Cuyo, in Mendoza, Argentina, were expelled. The same thing occurred in the national universities of Salta, Tacumán, Córdoba, Rio IV, Rosario, Buenos Aires, La Plata, Bahía Blanca, Comahue, etc. The books published by Siglo XXI (which had published my work. *Para una ética de la liberación latinoamerica*), by order of the government, were cut with a paper cutter, each into four parts (so they could not be sold even as waste paper). All these acts of vandalism were approved and justified by eminent rightist Catholic thinkers. Half of the students in the Department of Philosophy of Mendoza were expelled by the university, and they were not allowed to study in any university in the country. This is the policy that dependent capitalism advocates with regard to philosophy in Latin America. It is only one example.

30. Without any doubt the work of J.P. Sartre, *Critique de la raison dialectique* (Paris: Gallimard, 1960), aided in the rediscovery of "the matter of dialectic." I posed this problem in my work *Método para una filosofía de la liberación,* pp. 162ff.

31. See the work of General Golbery do Couto e Silva (a West Point graduate), *Geopolítica do Brasil* (Rio de Janeiro: Olympio, 1967), pp. 24–27.

GLOSSARY OF CONCEPTS

(Some terms cross-referenced in this glossary are to be found in the Glossary of Non-English Words).

Absolute 3.4 (→ antifetishism)
Absolutize 3.4.2.1
Acritical 2.3.4, 5.2.2
Alienation 2.5, 2.5.5
   —cultural 3.3.6
   —of design and technology 4.3.8
   —economic, worldwide 4.4.6; capital-work 4.4.7
   —pedagogical 3.3.5
   —political 3.1.5–6; international 3.1.5; national social 3.1.6
   —semiotic 4.2.7
   —of woman 3.2.5
Alterity 2.4.4.1, 4.1.5.2 (→ exteriority; metaphysics; the other; otherness)
Anadialectical 2.6.9.3, 5.3, 5.4.1, 5.8.2
   Analectical 5.3, 5.3.1, 5.3.4, 5.6.2
Analogy 2.6.9.3, 3.1.9.3–4, 4.1.6.1, 4.2.9.2, 5.3
Anarchy 2.1.2.2, 2.6.5.1 (→ alienation)
Annihilation 2.5.3 (→ alienation)
Anteriority 2.1.2.2, 2.2.2.1; metaphysics 3.3.3.2; passive 2.6.5.1 (→ responsibility)
Antifetishism 3.4, 3.4.1.2 (→ metaphysics)
Anti-Oedipus 3.3.7
Apocalypse 2.6.1.1, 4.2.6.1, 5.3.2 (→ revelation)
Apodictic 5.1.2, 5.2.1
Apophantic 4.2.3.3, 5.1.2, 5.2.1
Archeological 2.1.4.3, 2.1.6, 3.4.1.1 (→ *arche*)
Army 1.1.1, 1.1.5.1; imperial 3.1.6.3; national 3.1.6.3 (→ soldier)
Art 4.2.8.4, 4.3.6.6, 4.4.3.7 (→ esthetics)
   —popular 4.2.9.3, 4.3.2.4
Artifact 4.3.1.2, 4.3.4.5, 4.3.5.1, 4.3.6, 4.3.6.1., 4.3.6.5
Artisan 4.3.2.3
Atheism 4.3.2, 3.4.4, 2.6.2.3, 3.4.3.3, 3.4.4.3
Autoeroticism 2.5.8.2, 3.2.5.3
Barbarism 1.1.4.1, 4.3.6.6
Beauty 4.2.8.4, 4.3.1.2, 4.4.9.6
   —erotic 3.2.9.3; future 2.4.5.2; natural 4.1.6.4; popular 4.2.8.4

Obvious 5.1.1 (→ acritical; everyday; existential; naive)
Oedipus, oedipal situation, 3.2.5.2, 3.3.4.2, 3.3.5.4, 3.3.7, 3.4.2.3 (→ anti-Oedipus)
—African 3.2.6.2
—second Oedipus 3.3.1.1
Of itself 4.1.4.1 (→ essence; *ex se*; from itself; reality; substantivity; thing)
Ontic 4.2.1.1 (→ beings; mediation; nearness)
Ontic movement 2.2.8.2 (→ dialectical movement)
Ontological good 2.5.2.3
Ontological hero 2.5.3.1; liberator 2.6.8.3, 3.4.4.4
Ontological openness 2.4.7.4, 2.6.3.2
—clitoral-vaginal 3.2.7.2
—mammary-oral 3.2.7.2
—metaphysical 2.4.8.4, 2.6.3.2; to the other 4.1.5.2 (→ exposure)
—phallic 3.2.7.2
Ontology 1.1.4.3, 1.1.5.1, 2.2.1.1, 2.2.6.3, 2.3, 2.4.9, 2.5.2.1, 3.2.4.1, 4.4.3 (→ totality)
—classical 1.1.1, 1.1.2.1–2, 1.1.4
—erotic 3.2.3.2
—method 5.2.2 (→ dialectics)
—phallic 3.2.9.1
Openness (→ ontological)
Oppressed classes 3.1.4.1, 3.1.4.4–6. 3.1.6, 4.4.9
Oppressed as oppressed 2.6.4.1, 3.1.3.2 (→ alienation)
—as other, as exteriority 2.6.8.2 (→ metaphysical)
Order of manifestation 4.1.3.1 (→ manifestation)
—of constitution 4.1.3.1 (→ essence; reality; thing)
—new 2.6.4.1–2, 2.6.7.1, 4.2.8.4, 4.2.9.1
—of physical objects 4.1.3.1
—or revelation 4.1.3.1 (→ apocalypse; provocation)
Organic 4.1.4, 4.3.5.2 (→ coherence; substantivity)
Organic intellectual 3.3.8.1, 3.3.8.4, 3.3.9.2–5, 5.9.5; of the periphery 3.1.7.1
Origin 3.4 (→ *arche*)
Origination of essence 4.1.4.6 (→ evolution)
Orphan 3.3.5.3
Other, the 2.1.2, 2.4.4–5, 2.5.6, 4.1.5.5, 5.3.1
—absolute 3.4.4.3–5
—as other 2.4.7.3
—political 3.1.3.1; as a people 2.4.5
Otherness (→ alterity)
Pain 2.6.3.1, 2.6.8.2, 4.2.8.2 (→ cry)
Pantheism 3.4.5.2, 3.4.8.2
Parts 2.2.6; essential 4.3.5.2 (→ coherence; essence)
Passivity 2.6.2.3, 2.6.3.2
Paternity 3.3.3.1
Patriarchalism 3.2.7.1
Peace movements 4.1.8.6
Pedagogical contract 3.3.5.3
Pedagogism 5.8.2 (→ ideology)
Pedagogy 3.3
People 2.1.4.2, 3.1.3–4, 3.3.8, 3.4.1.2 (→ class; nation)
Percept 2.3.6.2

GLOSSARY OF NON-ENGLISH TERMS

Latin, L.
German, Ger.
Spanish, Sp.

Greek, Grk.
Hebrew, H.

A se, L.: by itself 4.1.4.1 (→ *ex se*)
Abgrund, Ger.: profound, without grounding, beyond the foundation 3.4.1.1
Absolutes Wissen, Ger.: absolute knowledge 1.1.7.2
Agibile, L.: what is to be done, acted on 4.3.2.1 (→ *praktikos*)
Aisthesis, Grk.: sensibility, sensation, intuition 5.4.4
Amauta, Sp.: sage of the Incan culture 3.3.2.3
Ananke, Grk.: necessary for opposition to the contingent 2.5.2.2
Anarchia, Grk.: beyond the origin, foundation 2.6.5
Ano-, Grk.: beyond, higher 5.3.1, 5.8.2
Apatheia, Grk.: impassivity, indifference 3.2.9.1
Apo-, Grk.: from 5.2.1
Applicatio, L.: applied ethical conscience 5.4.4
Arche, Grk.: origin, principle, cause 2.1.2.1, 3.4.1.1
Ars, L.: art 4.3.2.3 (→ *techne*)
Ataraxia, Grk.: serenity 3.2.9.1
Auto, to Grk.: the same, identical 3.2.2.2
Basar, H.: flesh, human being, 3.2.3.2
Begriff, Ger.: concept 2.3.7.2
Bios praktikos, Grk.: practical life 2.3.4.1
Bios theoretikos, Grk.: contemplative life 2.3.4.1
Boulesis, Grk.: desire, fundamental appetite 2.4.9.3
Cogitativa, L.: instinct by which the lamb, for example, flees from the wolf 5.4.4
Cogito, L.: I think, I am conscious 1.1.7.2, 2.1.1.1 (→ *ego*)
Conceptus, L.: concept 2.2.7.2
Continuum, L.: constant 4.2.4.2
Dabar, H.: word, thing, to reveal 4.2.6.2, 4.2.8.1
Dasein, Ger.: be-there, entity, existent 1.1.7.2
Deíktes, Grk.: the one who shows, indicates, signals 4.2.8.1
Desarrollismo, Sp.: developmentalism 4.4.6.3
Dia-, Grk.: through, throughout 2.3.8.1, 5.2.1, 5.8.2
Diakonia, Grk.: service, help, work 2.6.7.3
Dialectike, Grk.: dialectic 5.2.1, 5.8.2
Eidos, Grk.: idea, model, real essence 2.3.7.2, 4.3.4.5
Eigentlichkeit, Ger.: authenticity 2.5.2.1
Einklammerung, Ger.: enclose in parentheses 3.4.9.4
Endoxa, ta, Grk.: the believed, everyday 5.2.1

213

Ens, L.: being (pl., *entia*, beings) 2.3.8.2

Ergon, Grk.: work 4.3.4.5

Eros, Grk.: love, propulsion 3.2.2.2, 3.2.4, 3.2.7.1

Esse, L.: Being (no plural) 2.4.3

Ethos, Grk.: custom, habit, character 2.1.4.1, 2.3.4.3, 3.1.5.5, 3.1.9.5

Ex nihilo, L.: from nothing 3.4.5.2

Ex se, L.: from itself, 4.1.4.1

Existere, L.: to exist, to stand outside the origin (*ex-sistere*) 3.4.7.2

Facere, L.: to make, do, produce 3.4.2.1

Factibile, L.: the made, produced, done 4.3.2, (see *Poietikos*)

Factum, L.: fact 5.1

Gewissheit, Ger.: certitude 2.5.4.1

Gnosis, Grk.: initiate's knowledge, gnostic, 2.5.2.1

Gott ist mit uns, Ger.: God is with us 3.4.2.2

Grund, Ger.: foundation, reason (*ratio*), Being 3.4.1.1

Habodah, H.: work, service, cult 2.6.7.3, 3.4.8.5, 4.4.9.1

Homo, L.: human being, human species 2.2.3.2, 2.3.2.1, 4.1.5.1

Homo homini lupus, L.: the person who plays the part of a wolf vis-à-vis another person 1.1.7.4

Homo habilis, sapiens: anthropological names for the first and the actual human type 4.1.5.1, 4.1.5.4

Homo ludens: the one who plays, celebrates, rejoices 3.4.9.1, 5.9.4.2

Homo naturae lupus, L.: the person who plays the part of a wolf vis-à-vis nature 4.1.7.1

Hybris, Grk.: confusion, mixture, evil, barbarism 2.5.2.3

Imago patris, L.: father image 3.2.5.2

Logos, Grk.: speech, reason, comprehension, horizon 1.1.5.2, 4.2.3.3, 4.2.8.1, 5.8.2

Meta-hodos, Grk.: (to travel) along a road, method 5.1–9

Morphe, Grk.: form, structure 4.3.4.5

Natura, L.: (*Natur*, Ger.): nature 2.1.1, 4.1.2.3

Natura naturata, L.: created nature 4.1.2.3

Ob-audire, obedire, L.: hear what is ahead, obey 2.6.8.3

Offenheit, Ger.: openness 3.2.7.2

Oikia, Grk.: house, habitation 4.1.6.3

Oikonomia, Grk.: running a household, economics 4.4.5.2

Omnitudo realitatis, L.: reality in its totality 5.9.3.3

On, to, Grk.: being, what is 2.3.8.2 (→ *ens*); plural, *ta onta*, beings 1.1.5.1

Ordo cognoscendi, L.: order of existential comprehension, of interpretive knowing 4.1.2.1

Ordo operandi, L.: order of praxis, primarily political 4.1.2.1

Ordo realitatis, L.: order of cosmic anteriority or exteriority; constitutional, essential order 4.1.2.1

Orthos logos poietikos, Grk.: knowing how to make a product 4.3.2.2 (→ *factibile*)

Orthos logos praktikos, Grk.: knowing how to make a decision 5.4.1 (→ *agibile*)

Otium, L.: rest, time to think 3.4.9.1

Ousia, Grk.: substance, essence, being 4.1.3.5

Parousia, Grk.: make its appearance, appear, present itself 4.2.2.1, 4.2.6.1

Parthenos, Grk.: virgin 3.2.9.1

Pathos, Grk.: passion, passivity, suffering 2.4.5.2

Phos, Grk.: light 1.1.5.1

Phronesis, Grk.: practical wisdom, prudence 5.4.1
Physis, Grk.: nature, cosmos, being 2.1.1, 2.5.2.2, 4.1.2.3
Pním, H.: countenance, face, person 2.4.4.2 (→ *prosopon*)
Poietikos, Grk.: the workable, viable, producible 4.3.2.1
Polis, Grk.: city-state 3.1.8.3
Pragmata, ta, Grk.: useful things, sense-things 1.1.5.1
Praktikos, Grk.: the operable, having to do with praxis 4.3.2.1
Prinziphoffnung, Ger.: hope principle 2.2.4.2
Prosopon, Grk.: face, mask, countenance, person 2.4.4.2
Proyecto, Sp.: self-projection into the future 2.2.4 (→ *telos*)
Prudentia, L.: prudence 2.5.8.3, 5.4.1 (→ *phronesis*)
Pulchritudo prima, L.: first beauty 3.2.3.1
Ratio, L.: reason, ground 5.4.4
Rechtlos, Ger.: without any rights 1.1.4.2
Recta ratio agibilium, L.: right way to make a decision (→ *praktikos*)
Recta ratio factibilium, L.: right way to make a product 5.5.3 (→ *poietikos*)
Res, L.: thing 2.3.8.1
Res eventualis, "eventful thing," with a history (= human being) 3.4.7.4, 4.1.5.5
Schole, Grk.: retreat, solitude, 3.4.9.1
Semeion, Grk.: sign, signal 4.2.2.2
Sexualobjekt, Ger.: sexual object 3.2.3.1
Sollertia, L.: ingenuity, subtlety 5.4.4
Sorge, Ger.: care, help, move toward the ground 2.4.9.3
Speculum, L.: mirror 2.4.9.1
Substantia, L.: substance, essence 4.1.3.5
Symbolon, Grk.: symbol 4.2.6.2
Systema, Grk.: put a stop to, systematize, place with 2.3.1.1
Techne, Grk.: technique, craft, art 4.3.2.2
Telos, Grk.: end, goal, foundation, Being 2.5.9.1, 5.4.3
Terra mater, L.: mother earth 2.1.7.1, 2.3.2.2
Theoria, Grk.: theory, contemplation of the gods 4.3.4.4
Trieb, Ger.: instinct, impulsion, desire, appetite
Ursache, Ger.: cause, origin, principle 3.4.1.1
Veritas prima, L.: first truth 4.2.2.1
Wunsch, Ger.: desire, pulsion 3.2.2